GRAND THEFT
CHILDHOOD

THE SURPRISING TRUTH
ABOUT VIOLENT VIDEO GAMES
AND WHAT PARENTS CAN DO

Lawrence Kutner, Ph.D.
and Cheryl K. Olson, Sc.D.

Simon & Schuster

NEW YORK LONDON TORONTO SYDNEY

SIMON & SCHUSTER
1230 Avenue of the Americas
New York, NY 10020

Copyright © 2008 by Lawrence Kutner, Ph.D., and Cheryl K. Olson, Sc.D.

First Simon & Schuster hardcover edition April 2008

SIMON & SCHUSTER and colophon are registered trademarks of Simon & Schuster, Inc.

For information about special discounts for bulk purchases, please contact Simon & Schuster Special Sales at 1-800-456-6798 or business@simonandschuster.com

Designed by Paul Dippolito

Manufactured in the United States of America

10   9   8   7   6   5   4   3   2   1

Library of Congress Cataloging-in-Publication Data

Kutner, Lawrence.
    Grand theft childhood : the surprising truth about violent video games and what parents should know / by Lawrence Kutner and Cheryl K. Olson.
       p.   cm.
    Includes bibliographical references and index.
    1. Video games and teenagers. 2. Violence in mass media. 3. Youth and violence. I. Olson, Cheryl K. II. Title.
HQ784.V53K88 2008
302.23'1—dc22   2007037653

ISBN-13: 978-1-4516-3170-8

To our son Michael Sol Kutner, who introduced us to this topic and guided us in many ways; and to Sol and Roz Kutner, for their unwavering support of our family.

Contents

Preface

We never expected to write a book on violent video games and teenagers. It began as an academic research project at the Harvard Medical School Center for Mental Health and Media, a division of the department of psychiatry at Massachusetts General Hospital (MGH). We quickly discovered two things: everyone had strong opinions, and very few people had strong data on which to base those opinions. That was true for us as well.

So, with the help of funding from the U.S. Department of Justice, we put together a multidisciplinary, multigenerational research team and set about gathering data in a way that had been rarely done in the past by video game researchers: we actually talked to children and their parents. When we'd mention our research to others, they'd immediately start asking questions. Were video games "as bad as they say"? Were they benign entertainment? Did they help children become smarter or more physically coordinated? Were they the root cause of obesity? We didn't know, but we were looking for clues.

The results of our research have been published in a series of papers in academic journals. Many of those papers contain detailed statistical analyses that would be inappropriate for a book like this, although we offer some of the basics in chapter 4. If you'd like to learn more about the research results, we encourage you to look at those articles.

We also want to emphasize that our research should be viewed as a step toward understanding and gaining perspective, not as an ultimate conclusion. One of the simultaneous joys and frustrations of conducting research in areas like this is that you end up with more questions than you had when you started.

For example, our focus groups on violent video games were limited to teenage boys and their parents. We assumed that girls were much less likely to play violent games than boys. Yet our surveys of more than 1,200 middle school students found that the M-rated *Grand Theft Auto* series was extremely popular among girls. We also found some preliminary evidence that girls play those games differently than boys do. Researchers will need to look into that to find out what's going on.

We expect our findings and our analyses to be controversial. They don't fall neatly into either side of the highly polarized discussions of the effects of video games on children. We expect our statements to be criticized and cherry-picked to support conflicting and impassioned claims.

Our hope, however, is that what we say will be taken as a whole and with its limitations kept in mind. We did not set out to prove anything about video games. We have no vested interests for or against them. We wanted to look at them and the children who play them from a different point of view, and then analyze what we discovered. So it should come as no surprise that our findings cannot be reduced to simple statements, pro or con.

In the course of our research, we ran across a lot of muddle-headed thinking, misuse of scientific data, and political posturing on the part of people from all points of view. We strove to shine a light on these without regard to individual agendas or politics.

While our names appear on the cover, we owe a tremendous amount to our research team and to others who provided guidance and support. Primus inter pares is our codirector at the center, Eugene V. Beresin, MD, professor of psychiatry at Harvard Medical School and MGH, and director of the combined child and adolescent psychiatry residency training program at MGH and McLean Hospital. His insights, support and hard work have been invaluable, as has his friendship.

Armand Nicholi, Jr., MD, clinical professor of psychiatry at Harvard Medical School and MGH, was instrumental in getting this project under way and continued as an adviser throughout the process.

Our research team included Jason Almerigi, PhD; Lee Baer, PhD; Molly Butterworth; Danielle DeLuca; Catherine Garth; Sarah Hertzog; Lionel Howard, PhD; Michael Kutner; Spencer Lynn, PhD; George Nitzburg; and Dorothy E. Warner, PhD. What an amazing group!

Jerrold F. Rosenbaum, MD, chairman of the department of psychiatry at MGH, provided intellectual and political support for our work, as did Michael Jellinek, MD, and Chester Pierce, MD. Richard M. Lerner, PhD, at Tufts University provided guidance, perspective and encouragement.

Congressman Frank Wolf, a long-standing advocate for children's well-being, helped connect us to the Department of Justice and made the research possible.

Many researchers from other institutions freely gave of their time to help. So did people from the video game industry and children's advocates. Our literary agent, Laurie Liss at Sterling Lord Literistic, and our editor, Sydny Miner at Simon & Schuster, helped make this book a reality.

We've interspersed comments from some of these people throughout the book. When there is no footnote attached to a comment, it came from a conversation with us rather than a published paper or Web site. The people quoted have confirmed that these comments are accurate. Finally, we would like to thank the nearly two thousand children and parents who let us know what they did and why they did it, and who shared their unvarnished opinions.

CHAPTER 1

The Big Fear

We've been seeing a whole rash of shootings throughout this country and in Europe that relate back to kids who obsessively play violent video games. The kids involved as shooters in Columbine were obsessively playing violent video games. We know after the Beltway sniper incident where the seventeen-year-old was a fairly good shot, but Mr. Muhammad, the police tell us, got him to practice on an ultra-violent video game in sniper mode to break down his hesitancy to kill.

—Washington State representative Mary Lou Dickerson on The NewsHour with Jim Lehrer *(PBS), July 7, 2003[1]*

THIRTEEN-YEAR-OLD DARREN AND A HALF DOZEN OF HIS video game–playing friends are sitting around a table at the Boys and Girls Club in a working-class section of Boston. We're talking about the games, especially the violent ones. They've all played them.

Darren had a tough time in school earlier this week. On Monday, a teacher said something that embarrassed him in front of his classmates. When he went home that afternoon, he plugged in his video game console, loaded *Grand Theft Auto 3*, blew up a few cars and shot a half-dozen people, including a young blonde woman. When asked, Darren admits that the woman he killed in the game looked a lot like his teacher.

■   ■   ■

If you listen to the politicians and the pundits, the relationship is blindingly clear: playing violent video games leads children to engage in real-world violence or, at the very least, to become more aggressive.

❖ In August 2005, the American Psychological Association issued a resolution on violence in video games and interactive media, stating that "perpetrators go unpunished in 73 percent of all violent scenes, and therefore teach that violence is an effective means of resolving conflict."[2]

❖ The attorney for Lee Malvo, the young "DC Sniper," claimed that the teen had taught himself to kill by playing *Halo* on his Xbox game console. "He's trained and desensitized with video games . . . to shoot human forms over and over."[3]

❖ Columbine High School shooters Eric Harris and Dylan Klebold were avid computer gamers. According to psychologists Craig Anderson and Karen Dill, "One possible contributing factor is violent video games. Harris and Klebold enjoyed playing the bloody shoot-'em-up video game *Doom*, a game licensed by the U.S. Army to train soldiers to effectively kill."[4]

We hear that youth violence, as reflected in violent crime and school shootings, is a growing problem, and that young game players are socially isolated and unable to form interpersonal relationships.

❖ The growth in violent video game sales is linked to the growth in youth violence—especially school violence—throughout the country.

❖ School shooters fit a profile that includes a fascination with violent media, especially violent video games.

❖ A British study by *Save the Children* was described in the press as finding that "children are struggling to make friends at school because they spend too long playing computer games."[5] A spokesperson for that organization added, "Children have always played alone, for example with dolls or train sets, but these activities required a certain level of imagination—they stimulated their brains. That is not the case with modern computer games, which do children's thinking for them and put them in their own little world."[6]

We're told that the game ratings and content descriptors provided by the Entertainment Software Ratings Board (ESRB) are all that's needed to help parents protect their children from violent and other inappropriate content.

❖ The ESRB employs child development specialists who play each game thoroughly before assigning it a rating that helps parents select which games are most appropriate for their children.

❖ Video games that are rated T ("may be suitable for ages 13 and older") are less likely to desensitize a child to real-world violence than video games that are rated M ("may be suitable for ages 17 and older").

❖ Checking the ratings on the games our children bring home—and not allowing M-rated games—is the best way to protect our children from video game violence.

All of these statements are wrong! Some are misunderstandings; others are outright lies. In fact, much of the information in the popular press about the effects of violent video games is wrong.

Torturing the Data?

Guy Cumberbatch, PhD, is a psychologist specializing in media research. He directs the Communications Research Group in Great Britain and has been studying the effects of mass media on violent behavior for several decades. He sums up that research succinctly:

> The real puzzle is that anyone looking at the research evidence in this field could draw any conclusions about the pattern, let alone argue with such confidence and even passion that it demonstrates the harm of violence on television, in film and in video games. While tests of statistical significance are a vital tool of the social sciences, they seem to have been more often used in this field as instruments of torture on the data until it confesses something which could justify publication in a scientific journal.
>
> If one conclusion is possible, it is that *the jury is not still out. It's never been in.* Media violence has been subjected to lynch mob mentality with almost any evidence used to prove guilt.[7]

The strong link between video game violence and real world violence, and the conclusion that video games lead to social isolation and poor interpersonal skills, are drawn from bad or irrelevant research, muddleheaded thinking and unfounded, simplistic news reports:

❖ The allegation that "perpetrators go unpunished in 73 percent of all violent scenes" is based on research from the mid-1990s that looked at selected television programs, not video games.[8]

❖ The video game *Halo* involves shooting an unrealistic gun at a giant alien bug. It is not an effective way to train as a real sniper. In court, Lee Malvo admitted that he trained by shooting a real gun at paper plates that represented human heads. Also, Malvo had a long history of antisocial and criminal behavior, including torturing small animals—one of the best predictors of future violent criminal behavior.[9]

❖ It's unlikely that Harris and Klebold's interest in violent video games or other violent media played any significant role in their actions. An FBI investigation concluded that Klebold was significantly depressed and suicidal, and Harris was a sociopath.[10]

Youth violence has decreased significantly over the past decade.[11] You are more likely to be struck and killed by lightning than to die in a school shooting.[12]

❖ Video game popularity and real-world youth violence have been moving in *opposite* directions. Violent juvenile crime in the United States reached a peak in 1993 and has been declining ever since. School violence has also gone down. Between 1994 and 2001, arrests for murder, forcible rape, robbery and aggravated assaults fell 44 percent, resulting in the lowest juvenile arrest rate for violent crimes since 1983. Murder arrests, which reached a high of 3,800 in 1993, plummeted to 1,400 by 2001.[13]

❖ The U.S. Secret Service intensely studied each of the thirty-seven non-gang and non-drug-related school shootings and stabbings that were considered "targeted attacks"* that took place nationally from 1974 through 2000. (Note how few premeditated school shootings there actually were during that twenty-seven-year time period, compared with the public perception of those shootings as relatively common events!) The incidents studied included the most notorious school shootings (e.g., Columbine, Santee, Paducah), in which the young perpetrators had been linked in the press to violent video games. The Secret Service found that there was no accurate profile. Only one in eight school shooters showed any interest in violent video games; only one in four liked violent movies.[14]

❖ On the other hand, reports of bullying are up.[15] While bullying may not make the headlines, it makes a big difference in the everyday lives of our children.[16] As you'll see in chapter 4, our research found that certain patterns of video game play were much more likely to be associated with these types of behavioral problems than with major violent crime such as school shootings.

For many children and adolescents, playing video games is an intensely social activity, not an isolating one.

❖ Many games involve multiperson play, with the players either in the same room or connected electronically. They often require that players communicate so that they can coordinate their efforts. Our research found that playing violent video games was associated with playing with friends.

❖ For younger children especially, games are a topic of conversation that allows them to build relationships with peers.

❖ Although it came from a reputable organization, the widely cited British study claiming that increased use of electronic media has led to

---

* The Secret Service defined a targeted attack as "any incident where (i) a current student or recent former student attacked someone at his or her school with lethal means (e.g., a gun or knife); and (ii) where the student attacker purposefully chose his or her school as the location of the attack. Consistent with this definition, incidents where the school was chosen simply as a site of opportunity, such as incidents that were solely related to gang or drug trade activity or to a violent interaction between individuals that just happened to occur at the school, were not included."

social isolation among children based its findings on the personal opinions of an unspecified group of primary school teachers who were asked to compare today's children (ages five to eleven) to what they remembered about children who were in their classrooms when they started teaching, not on scientific observations of children conducted over time. Blaming supposed deterioration of social skills among kindergartners and first graders on MP3 players and time spent surfing the Internet is a bit of a stretch, to say the least. Also, the "study" was part of a publicity campaign for Friendship Friday, an annual fund-raising event in Great Britain for Save the Children.[17]

The current ESRB rating system, while more effective and informative than other media rating systems, has significant flaws that need to be addressed.

❖ ESRB raters don't actually play the games at all. They watch videos of excerpts of the games that have been provided by the manufacturers.[*] Until 2007, the Entertainment Software Rating Board employed temporary workers with no background in child development to rate its games. Their previous online help-wanted ad for game raters stated:

> The ESRB is looking for adults with flexible hours that would be available to come to our office in midtown Manhattan on a freelance basis (1-4 times a month) during normal (9-5) business hours to rate video games. Experience with children is preferred. Prior experience playing games is not required and training will be provided.[18]

That approach has recently been revised. The ESRB now uses full-time employees to rate games, although training in child development (or even being a parent) is still not required. The new (2007) online help-wanted ad for game raters reads:

---

[*] The often-heard demand from politicians and others outside the industry that game raters play all possible parts of a game before assigning a rating is naïve and impractical. Making judgments based upon appropriate video excerpts makes much more sense, especially since publishers face significant costs, including fines, if the ESRB revises a rating upward after a game is released.

Prospective candidates should have:
- Experience with children
- Interest in and familiarity with video games
- Strong communications skills (verbal, written)

Parents and those with video game playing abilities are preferred, though these are not requirements. Salary is commensurate with qualifications and experience. Training will be provided.

❖ According to research on the effects of violent media, the ESRB may have parts of its ratings system backward! One of the predictors of which violent media are likely to result in violent real-world behavior is material that does not show the realistic negative consequences of violence, such as pain, suffering and blood.[19] Violent video games that are rated M are more likely to show those negative consequences. Those that are rated T or E achieve such lower ratings in part by not showing those negative consequences: dead bodies just disappear; blood is animated rather than realistic.[20] Also, those games in which the player is rewarded with extra points for avoiding a violent confrontation (e.g., the *SWAT* series) are given the same M rating as those games in which the player is given extra points for piling up virtual corpses.

❖ Our interviews with adolescents and their parents found that while parents thought they knew which games their children were playing, for the most part they did not. Also, a growing number of games—some of them extremely violent, sexist and racist—are available for play online and are not rated by the ESRB. Neither of these is the ESRB's fault, of course, but they point out some of the limits of any game rating system.

As Darren tells his story about feeling angry, then playing the violent video game in which he blew up cars and shot several people, including one who looked a lot like his teacher, the other kids sitting around the table nod their heads. It's clear that at one time or another, they have each done something similar. "I guess I got my anger out," Darren says. "Then I sat down and did my homework."

The Game Made Him a Zombie

The United States is by no means alone in its common assumption that video game violence leads to real-world violence. On January 11, 2006, an allegedly drunk twenty-year-old man entered a synagogue in Moscow, brandished a knife, and injured eight people, six of whom required hospitalization. The Russian newspaper *Pravda* reported the story:

> Alexander Koptsev was a quiet and unsociable young man. He had no criminal record and was leading a decent lifestyle. Alexander suffered a severe psychological trauma a year ago, when his sister died, the *Kommersant* newspaper wrote. Being unable to handle his grief, the man became a secluded individual, started spending most of his time indoors and developed an addiction to computer games.
>
> Alexander Koptsev was playing a game called *Postal-2* before he left home and went to the synagogue in Moscow center. The game models a situation, in which the character is supposed to kill as many people as possible in the streets of the city. . . .
>
> The game which the young man was playing made him a zombie. The man was programmed to demolish and kill. It was believed not so long ago that the descriptions of such mental disorders could be found in fictitious novels and stories. However, those addicted to computer games often suffer from the so-called video game epilepsy syndrome. Ardent gamers suffer from headaches, facial muscular spasms and eyesight disorder. The syndrome does not lead to aggravation of mental abilities of a human being. However, it develops certain peculiarities typical of epilepsy: a person may become highly suspicious, aggressive and hostile about everything and everyone. A person who suffers from the video game epilepsy syndrome can easily grab a kitchen knife, leave the virtual world and look for victims in reality.
>
> The incident in the Moscow synagogue is an alarming signal indeed. However, this signal warns about the growing influence of virtual reality on the human mind.[21]

This is utter nonsense, of course. In his confession to the Moscow police, Koptsev said absolutely nothing about video games; he stated that he was envious of the Jews' standard of living and spoke of his "desire to die."[22] Clearly, this was a very troubled young man.

While there have been some reports in medical journals of an increase in the number of seizures among children over the past century, especially among children watching television or playing video games who are already diagnosed with epilepsy,[23] these are extremely rare events when compared with the number of children and the amount of time spent playing video games. In some of those children, flickering lights (such as those on a television or computer monitor) can trigger seizures. These seizures are not associated with the types of dramatic paranoid or violent behaviors described in the *Pravda* article.

Our Journey as Parents

The prolific scientist and author Isaac Asimov famously stated, "The most exciting phrase to hear in science, the one that heralds new discoveries, is not 'Eureka!', but 'That's funny . . .' " So it shouldn't be surprising that our first step into what would become several years of full-time research was our casual observations of our son, who liked to play video games.

One of us (Cheryl) is a public health researcher specializing in media influences on health-related behaviors. The other (Larry) is a clinical psychologist and journalist specializing in child development and parent-child communication. We're old enough to have been teenagers at a time when the few video games available had titles like *Pong* and *Space Invaders*. But we're young enough to feel very comfortable working and playing with computers and other technology.

Neither of us were "gamers" a few years ago; one of us is today. (The other can take it or leave it—a sure sign of a generation gap.) Our teenage son, Michael, had first played simple computer games in childcare when he was about three years old. Those games had crude graphics and agonizingly repetitive (to an adult) music. They involved completing simple tasks, such as lining up an animated fire truck with a mark on the screen so that the cartoon firefighters could rescue a cat in distress.

He played the games a few times and loved them. Like other children that age, he was completely fearless when it came to interacting with computers. While his teachers hesitated over the new and complicated devices, he and his classmates saw computers as friendly toys and plunged ahead.

This is a pattern seen in the introduction of all new technologies. Our own parents were initially uncomfortable around microwave ovens, color televisions and electric typewriters. Our grandparents were unsure about commercial aviation. Although they would surely deny it now, our children will one day balk at some of the future technologies that their own children will readily embrace.

Since we had personal computers in our offices at home, we decided to look into video games when Michael was about five years old. A few stood out as developmentally appropriate and nonviolent, including a series that featured an animated purple car named Putt-Putt.

In one particularly endearing game, *Putt-Putt Saves the Zoo*, the child, acting as Putt-Putt, is asked to solve a series of simple one-step and two-step problems in the rich environment of an animated zoo. With each successful solution, one of the six lost baby animals at the zoo would be reunited with its parents. The child could also take time out to play ice hockey with polar bears, dance with penguins and interact with magical flowers. It was utterly charming, nonviolent and both emotionally and cognitively spot-on for a preschooler.

The graphics in these games were much more complex and sophisticated than those of earlier generations of computer games. In fact, when our son played them, the video was a bit choppy and the audio was occasionally out of sync. The computer he used simply couldn't do all the mathematical calculations quickly enough to run the game smoothly. Interestingly, this was the same computer that Cheryl had recently used to do all of the statistical calculations for her doctoral dissertation in public health at Harvard. Her computer was good enough for graduate school, but not powerful enough for our five-year-old's games of *Putt-Putt*. This was a harbinger of things to come in the world of video games.

When Michael was in kindergarten, he asked the teacher whether they could play video games as part of their class work. She said no. We heard about this when we received a phone call from the school principal. Our son, at age five, had apparently decided to go over his teacher's head with the request and had set up a one-on-one meeting with the principal to discuss making video games a part of the curriculum. Clearly, he was captivated by the technology. She was not.

The games he played over the next few years were similar in tone to the *Putt-Putt* games, although they became much more sophisticated. The technology changed as well. By the time our son was in fourth grade, he insisted that we buy him a Game Boy. We had recently moved to Switzerland, which meant that he was attending a new school. Pokémon was an international craze among kids, and our son wanted to take part. We bought the Game Boy and the Pokémon cartridges.

As we watched and listened to him, it became apparent that the primary attraction for him wasn't the Pokémon games themselves, but the social interactions they triggered with peers. It gave the boys—as with many video games at that time, it was mostly boys who played—a nonthreatening common experience to talk about. This let them build relationships and explore new social roles.

Our son and his friends reveled in their mastery of the games' arcane rules and in their knowledge of the characters' names and special skills. These were things that the adults around them did not comprehend or appreciate, which gave the children a highly valued sense of power and importance. Michael would electronically trade Pokémon characters with his friends the way his father had traded baseball cards a generation earlier.

The game characters were mostly cute, mythical animals with a variety of strengths, weaknesses and special powers. The focus of the Pokémon plots, however, was an ongoing series of battles between the mythical animals in which the loser is knocked out or faints. While the characters were cute and the actions were highly stylized, the games focused on violence.

This is not necessarily bad. A game of chess, after all, is a simplified portrayal of warfare in which pawns (commoners) are readily sacrificed to protect more valuable pieces. Yet few people express concerns about children playing chess, and many people actively encourage it as a form of intellectual exercise.

But looking at the plotlines of Pokémon piqued our interest in why these games were so attractive. Was it the children's identification with the characters? Was it the opportunity to "collect" characters? (Children this age—especially boys—tend to be avid collectors of all types of things.) Was it the social interaction?

Over the next few years, violence became a more prominent feature of bestselling video games, including some of the ones our son played. The media routinely offered stories on the dangers of playing some of these games, both in the news and in the plots of entertainment programs. These days, an episode of a television show in which a young video game designer or an avid gamer kills someone has reached the level of cliché.

Other parents spoke to us of their concerns. These ranged from fears of children becoming living time bombs ready to reenact the violent plots of the games in the real world, to concerns about whether the games prevented kids from getting enough exercise, thereby leading to an epidemic of obesity. In other words, would they become serial killers, couch potatoes or something in between?

Perhaps there was an emotional component to why video games in general and violent games in particular were so popular. We had noticed that our son, like many children, would sometimes isolate himself and play games on his Game Boy, game console or computer when he was feeling frustrated, angry or depressed. As adults, we could recall doing similar things, such as "vegging out" in front of a television during times of stress or curling up with a book when we felt overwhelmed. Was this any different? Did the violence in the game matter?

This led to a fundamental question: Should we, as parents, be worried about our children playing violent video games? The research literature, which we'll examine in chapter 3, was of little help. Too many of the studies were poorly designed, or bore little relevance to the real world. Perhaps most important, almost nobody had bothered talking directly to children to see what they had to say about why, when, where and how they played video games. We thought we'd try.

The Study

In 2004, we began a two-year, $1.5 million multifaceted study of violent video games and children at the Harvard Medical School Center for Mental Health and Media, which is a division of the Department of Psychiatry at Massachusetts General Hospital. The U.S. Department of Justice funded the research.[24]

Our researchers came from a variety of fields: child and adolescent psychiatry, adult psychiatry, public health, clinical psychology, developmental psychology, educational psychology, public policy—we even had an evolutionary biologist working with us. This allowed us to look at the issue from a broad set of perspectives. (Our research assistants, who were recent college graduates preparing themselves for doctoral programs in psychology, relished telling their friends and parents that they had found a job that actually paid them to play video games!)

Two things separated our study from most of the research that came before us:

❖ We didn't have a political or social agenda, or other vested interests. We weren't out to prove a point or to defend an industry. Studying video game violence was only a small part of what we did professionally, so the outcomes of the research didn't affect our careers. We didn't own stock in the companies that developed the games or sold the hardware. Although we all had ideas about what we might find, we disagreed amongst ourselves. Some of us were gamers; others were not. Some of us were the parents of teenage children; others were not. As researchers, we simply went wherever the data took us.

❖ We interviewed and surveyed a large number of children and parents to find out what they actually did, why they did it, how they felt, what they thought and what they feared. Much of the earlier research on violent video games involved artificial situations, such as having college sophomores play a new game for a few minutes in a research laboratory, or measuring fraction-of-a-second differences in how long someone blasts an air horn or triggers white noise from a computer (a surrogate, the researchers claim, for aggression or for violent behavior) after playing a violent game. Instead, we studied real families in real situations.

Much of what we found surprised us. The data were both encouraging and, at times, disturbing. The more we analyzed our own data and looked at other research, the more we realized that we—parents, politicians, researchers and child advocates—probably worry too much about the wrong things and too little about more subtle issues and complex effects that are much more likely to affect our children.

It's clear that the "big fears" bandied about in the press—that violent video games make children significantly more violent in the real world; that children will engage in the illegal, immoral, sexist and violent acts they see in some of these games—are not supported by the current research, at least in such a simplistic form. That should make sense to anyone who thinks about it. After all, millions of children and adults play these games, yet the world has not been reduced to chaos and anarchy.

It's also clear that parents are both concerned and confused about violent video games. They are the first generation of parents to deal with children who use this technology. (Although, as we'll describe in chapter 2, their own parents and grandparents and great-grandparents had similar fears about the new media of their day.) We want to protect our children from potentially harmful consequences, but we don't know how to do that or what those consequences might be.

We may be asking the wrong questions and making the wrong assumptions. For example, instead of looking for a simple, direct relationship between video game violence and violent behavior in *all* children, we should be asking how we might identify those children who are at greatest risk for being influenced by these games. We should look at why children say they play both violent and nonviolent video games. (Some of the most popular games, even among teenage boys, are not violent. Our research also found that, contrary to popular belief, a few of the most popular games among teenage girls are extremely violent.) We should ask whether children who spend a lot of time playing video games are failing to learn important interpersonal and social skills, or whether they're using the games to *improve* their social relationships with peers.

Are some types of violent video games having more subtle, but potentially more destructive, effects on today's youth? Do they make sexist or racist behavior more acceptable? Do they reinforce the perception of women as sex objects? Do they lead to increases in "under the radar" problems such as bullying?

Those are the types of questions we began asking, both through our own research and through reviews of others' research. We also looked at whether the current game rating system makes sense and how it compares to other systems around the world.

To do this, we conducted written surveys of a diverse group of more than 1,200 middle school students about where, when and why they play games. We asked detailed questions about their favorite games and movies. We asked whom they played video games with. They answered questions about bullying and destructive behavior, depression, attention problems, attitudes and feelings. They told us about their after-school activities, family and peer relationships, and more. This allowed us to see how each of these issues is related to video game play.

We also surveyed over five hundred parents of these middle school students. We learned what they were doing to limit their children's access to violent video games and how their kids often told a different story. We looked at whether they played video games with their kids, and how they used game ratings.

We conducted group interviews with forty-two teen and preteen boys who routinely played violent video games. We asked about why they played those games, the influence of violent video games on their lives, what games they thought children should and should not play, and what they did that their parents don't know about.

At the same time, and in a separate room, we conducted group interviews with twenty-one parents of those boys. We found out how much (or how little) they knew about their children's game playing. We learned about their fears. We listened as they told us about their efforts to monitor and control what their children played and the information they wanted to protect their kids. We also talked about what they saw as the benefits of playing video games.

We conducted experimental research that measured critical aspects of the brain waves of college students as they played either violent or exciting nonviolent games. We also analyzed what's right and what's wrong with the designs and execution of earlier experimental research and the conclusions drawn from those studies.

We reviewed state, national and international efforts to regulate children's access to video games. We looked at what motivates these policies, who's promoting them, whom they affect and why most of them don't succeed.

We developed and tested a new game rating system for research that addresses more of parents' concerns in a simple, clear format. We compared this new rating system to the current ESRB system.

Finally, we conducted a survey of several hundred video game developers to find out what they think about the role of violence in games and its effects on our children.

These Are the Good Old Days

Harold Schechter, PhD, a professor of English at Queens College in New York City, has focused much of his career on studying the portrayal of violence in popular culture. He states, "I have little doubt that fifty years from now, parents will be raising a howl over virtual-reality shoot-'em-ups that allow their kids to actually *feel* the splatting blood from the blown-off head of a holographic zombie, and that they will pine for the idyllic days of 2004, when children enjoyed such harmlessly cartoonish pastimes as *Resident Evil* and *Grand Theft Auto*. From the vantage point of the present—when the latest state-of-the-art entertainments seem to offer unprecedented levels of stimulation and lifelike gore—yesterday's popular culture always seems innocent and quaint."[25]

The Ultimate Video Game

Our research team has gathered at the Boston offices of the Federal Bureau of Investigation to get a glimpse of the future. Special Agent Ed Kappler, the chief firearms instructor, is demonstrating what some people in law enforcement call the ultimate video game: FATS, the firearms training system.

The equipment looks more like a home theater than a gaming system. A video projector sits in the center of the room. Special Agent Kappler is in the back corner, typing instructions into a computer. He introduces us to another senior agent who will demonstrate the system by going through a simulated "incident." This agent has nearly fifteen years of field experience. He's been through a lot of advanced training in law enforcement. He's on the FBI's SWAT team. Clearly, he's a man who knows what he's doing. He's the levelheaded guy you'd want by your side during a crisis.

The agent picks up a specially modified standard-issue pistol that fires a laser beam instead of bullets. Compressed air simulates the "kick" of firing real ammunition. Special Agent Kappler dims the lights as a life-size video image is projected on the wall. We hear the premise behind the scenario: "You've been called to a government warehouse after closing time following a report of suspicious activity."

We see several stacks of corrugated boxes inside the warehouse and hear the creak of a metal door opening to the right. A man walks in carrying another box.

"FBI! Put down the box and show me some identification." The agent startles us with the intensity of his voice. It is practiced and forceful. He is taking control of the situation. He has drawn his gun but is keeping his trigger finger alongside the barrel, away from the trigger itself.

"Good evening!" says the man on the screen, who's wearing slightly scruffy work clothes. "I'm the shift supervisor. I just needed to finish a few things before leaving."

"Put down the box, and show me some identification *now*!" says the agent.

"OK, OK. Just give me a second." The man places the corrugated box on top of the others. He then jumps behind them, quickly pulls out a pistol and fires at the agent. (In another version of this scenario, the man with the box takes out an ID card that proves that he really is the shift supervisor, not a thief. The agent going through the simulation, as in real life, never knows what's going to happen.)

After diving for cover within our darkened room, the agent fires at his attacker with two sets of double-taps: pop-pop, pop-pop. Every one of us can feel our heart beating more quickly, even though we're just observers and know that this is only a simulation.

The projected image on the wall freezes as the lights come back on. The FBI agent holding the simulator's laser-firing gun is sweating. Special Agent Kappler asks him to recount what just happened, to tell step-by-step what led up to the incident and to his decision to fire back.

Surprisingly, to us at least, the FBI agent can't give a detailed or even a clear account of what transpired. He's a consummate professional. He's been through hundreds of these FATS scenarios. He's trained to observe and recall exactly this type of information at a crime scene. Yet his heart is beating so quickly and his nervous system is so aroused that he can barely get more than a few words out.

And it's only a game.

Special Agent Kappler replays the scene on the wall as we watch. The computer has calculated when the FBI agent's shots were fired and where they hit. The first entered a corner of a box; the second and third hit the perpetrator in the shoulder. The fourth hit the wall.

The FATS system we're using is not designed to test or improve marksmanship. Rather, it helps improve agents' judgment on when to use lethal force. Except for the ability to replay the incidents and to trace the path and timing of the agent's bullets, the system is fairly primitive. The on-screen characters don't respond in different ways based upon what the agent says or does. The instructor has no way of knowing whether the perpetrator's opening shots would have hit the agent. Future versions of the system are likely to incorporate such features.

Still, the nature and size of the projected images and the cold metal feeling of an actual pistol in your hand tell your body that this is quite different from seeing those same images on a small computer screen and responding by using a keyboard or a plastic joystick. The threat feels real, and your body responds at a cellular level.

Next, one of our researchers tries FATS. She's a developmental psychologist, not a trained police officer, although that's the role she will be playing in the simulation. Special Agent Kappler shows her how to cock the gun and move its safety switch so that it can fire the laser beam. She's nervous but excited.

The room lights go out as a video image appears on the wall. She's told that she is supposed to back up her partner, a young uniformed female officer who is questioning a suspect who's standing on the sidewalk. The muscle-bound man on the screen is easily twice the uniformed officer's weight. He's skittish and uncooperative. He reaches out to touch the officer's shoulder.

Special Agent Kappler coaches our researcher to say something that will help her regain control of the situation. "Don't do that!" she says to the man on the screen. Her voice is surprisingly dry and weak, as if her body is unsure of whether to be aggressive or to flee.

We watch as the man on the screen grabs the police officer, quickly takes her gun from its holster and holds it to her head. She is now a human shield, trapped between the violent armed perpetrator and the backup officer—the game player. "Get out of here, or she dies!" he yells. The police officer he's threatening looks terrified.

Our researcher has her gun drawn. Should she fire at the man holding the gun? If so, will she hit her partner? Will he kill her partner anyway? What about the children who are playing on the street behind him? What about her own safety?

Special Agent Kappler freezes the video and turns on the lights. Our researcher's hand is shaking. Her breathing is quick and labored. The pupils of her eyes are clearly dilated. Her mouth is dry.

We've been watching the clock. "How long do you think that incident took?" we ask her.

"Between five and seven minutes," she replies. "Maybe a little more."

"Actually, it was seventeen seconds."

We have glimpsed one path toward the future of video games.

Violence vs. relevance

One reason why the experienced FBI agent may have had so much difficulty recalling the details of the incident—indeed, he had more trouble than our researcher, who was simply pretending to be a police officer— is the relevance of the information. To our researcher, the incident in the game was very different than the daily events in her life. She knew that it was highly unlikely that she would ever be put into that situation with a real gun and real lives on the line. Her intense emotional experience was, at its roots, similar to what she would feel watching a well-produced adventure movie or reading an exciting novel.

For the FBI agent going through the warehouse theft simulation, the experience was different because the context was different. He knows fellow agents who've been shot at and, indeed, he may have been shot at himself. He understands that in the course of his work he will have to stop quite a few suspicious characters. Some of these people will be armed; a few may even try to kill him. To the FBI agent, it is not just a game. The situation, people, equipment and responses are all realistic and relevant to his daily life. His emotional and intellectual frames of reference are completely different than those of our researcher.

We saw hints at this important difference when we interviewed young teenagers and preteens who routinely played violent video games. While many of them enjoyed the ability to shoot people, drive tanks, blow up buildings, steal cars, evade the police, massacre aliens and stab zombies, they recognized that these actions were fantasies.

They knew this was play. They also knew that they were unlikely to be in the situations that form the pretexts of the violent games.

> James: "Really violent games, like in *Vice City* where you can just go around killing anybody, they're less realistic. The environment, the people are real, but not the actions."

> •   •   •

> Carlos: "But if you're like angry, angry at someone, and you really want to take out your fear on him, you just play a game. It's like that's taking out fearing all for you."

> Researcher: "It takes out your anger and your fear?"

> Carlos: "Yeah."

> •   •   •

> Josh: "When I play video games, it's like I have a power. I have a power to do anything. I can get away with it. If I wanted to kill, I could. So don't mess with me. . . .

> "I wouldn't be able to kill somebody [in real life]. But in video games I could. It's a video game!"

Indeed, when they did express violent urges based on video game situations or characters, those urges almost always were directly related to their day-to-day concerns and frustrations as children, as well as normal childhood fantasies.

Researcher: "Which character would you like to be?"

Vinnie: "Sub-Zero [a ninja-like character in *Mortal Kombat*]. Sometimes I have dreams of being him."

Researcher: "And what would you do?"

Vinnie: "Freeze people. Freeze time—then I could get out of school early. Nobody would see what time it is."

Carlos: "Freeze the teacher."

Vinnie: "Yup, can't get us! . . . I'd freeze the entire world and make my own kingdom."

Carlos: "I would be Scorpion [a "reincarnated specter" in *Mortal Kombat*]."

Researcher: "What would you do with your day as Scorpion?"

Carlos: "I can just tell the teacher to not give me homework. No, don't give me homework."

Researcher: "So you'd stop people from doing things you don't like."

Carlos: "Yeah."

Vinnie: "I love his costume, actually."

Carlos: "And I'd rule the world with my brother. We would make everyone wear cool costumes."

• • •

Josh: "I like Jin [a character in *Tekken Tag Tournament*] because he's the most powerful fighter out of all the fighters."

Researcher: "How would you be like Jin if you could be?"

Josh: "When somebody's getting bullied or something, and they can't defend themselves, I'd just go help them out."

When we asked these groups of preteens and young teenagers who routinely played violent, M-rated (age seventeen and older) games how old they thought someone should be before playing such games, they gave a predictable answer: twelve or thirteen years old—roughly a year younger than they were. At the same time, they were very concerned about younger children playing violent video games and often expressed the same logic and even used the same words that their own parents used when explaining why young children should not be allowed to play violent, M-rated games.

For the most part, however, it was not the violence that these children wanted to protect their younger brothers and sisters from. It was the language. In group after group, the children showed deep concern about what they called "swears."

That was, we came to realize, something that directly applied to their lives. They might not be able to blow up a car, fire a submachine gun, freeze an opponent, battle a zombie or engage in a samurai-style tournament in the real world. But they could swear. It was the use of language that most easily bridged the gulf between their fantasy game worlds and reality.

Justin: "Little kids, they don't know the basic meanings of life. So once they see that, they're going to think, 'Oh, that's how life goes. You can swear and go around hitting people.'"

·   ·   ·

Ivan: "I wouldn't let my little sister play *True Crime: Streets of LA* [a violent game in which the player takes on the role of a recently suspended Los Angeles police officer who fights street gangs, drug runners, corrupt cops and even zombies] because they say swears."

·   ·   ·

Matthew: "I don't like my little brother or sisters to watch me play *Grand Theft Auto: Vice City* because of the language. They might swear at other people 'cause of the attitude—how they do it in *Vice City*. They always give people attitude and swear at other people [in the game]. And that could make my family look bad, like my mom isn't raising us regular or anything."

The other issue that struck close to home with these young teenagers and preteens was sex—but quite differently from the way that many parents expected or feared. The children's normal adolescent awkwardness and concerns came out in the way they responded to the sexual content of some of the video games.

Researcher: "Are there any games that you think you shouldn't be allowed to play at age thirteen?"

Patrick: "Sort of like . . . *The Sims* [a nonviolent game in which the player creates computer-simulated people and their environment]."

Ramon: "Yeah, *The Sims*. 'Cause they go to people and, like . . ." [pause]

Patrick: "They go to, like, people and, like . . ." [pause]

Ramon: "Kiss."

Patrick: "Yeah."

Researcher: "So, because of the kissing, you don't think you should be able to play that game. How old should you have to be?"

Ramon: "Kissing. Like, fifteen."

Patrick: "Fifteen, yeah. Maybe fourteen."

Josh: "I agree with both of them."

Randy: "Also, *BMX XXX* [a game that combines a BMX bike competition with videos of naked women in a strip club; it was a public relations disaster for the publisher, which soon filed for bankruptcy.]"

Researcher: "How old would you have to be to play that game?"

Randy: "Twenty."

Josh: "I disagree. You could be like seventeen or eighteen. If you're eighteen and you still live with your mom, and your mom comes in the room and you just beat the level and she sees the girl pull up her shirt . . ."

[There's nervous laughter from the kids in the room.]

Researcher: "So, obviously you've played this."

Patrick: "See, he's played it!"

Josh: "No, I haven't!"

Researcher: "Well, how do you know what she did?"

Josh: "'Cause in a magazine . . ."

Researcher: "You read about it."

Josh: "Yeah."

Ramon: "There's this new game coming out called *Playboy: The Mansion* [a game in which the player takes on the role of Hugh Hefner in both his business and private lives.]"

[Some of the kids in the room gasp.]

Ramon: "That's not good for eight-year-olds."

Patrick: "That's for, like, twenty-year-olds."

Josh: "That's for, like, a hundred!"

CHAPTER 2

Déjà Vu All Over Again, and Again

The difference between the surreptitious pornographic literature for adults and children's comic books is this: in one it is a
question of attracting perverts, in the other of making them.

—*Fredric Wertham, MD*,
Seduction of the Innocent *(1954)*

THE LIBRARY OF CONGRESS IN WASHINGTON, DC, CALLS ITS
collection of nineteenth- and early-twentieth-century popular novels,
known as dime novels, "American Treasures." It has proudly accumu-
lated nearly forty thousand titles.[1]

Film scholars and social scientists have written hundreds of books on
the gangster films of the 1930s, starring the likes of Edward G. Robinson
and James Cagney. They are considered film classics and are required
study for aspiring filmmakers around the world.

Cultural historians consider the late 1930s through the 1950s to be
the golden age of comic books. Characters introduced in that era, such as
Superman, Batman, Wonder Woman and the Crypt Keeper, are still cultural icons and have been reinvented for other media and new generations of children.

By today's standards, the writing and plotlines of those popular nineteenth-century paperback novels about street life in the city and the tam-
ing of the western frontier seem quaint, charming and simplistic.
Scholars see the social and economic upheaval of Prohibition and the
Great Depression reflected in the celluloid images of fictitious mob

bosses and glamorous speakeasies. The early gangster films were like classic Greek dramas, with larger-than-life protagonists who suffered a predictable fall from power and a tragic ending. The one-dimensional characters and heavy-handed "crime does not pay" messages of the comic books are now overshadowed by an awareness of their artists' creative use of shading and perspective, and their writers' sly social and political commentary.

Today we view dime novels, gangster films and comic books as fanciful and harmless period pieces. Yet in the years following their introduction, they were each labeled by politicians, religious leaders, social activists and even some health professionals as bringing about the imminent destruction of moral values, culture, the rule of law—even of civilization itself. Among the claims: Reading adventure tales would lead children into lives of corruption and degradation. Watching films would cause children to abandon their moral values and to rob stores and dynamite trains. Comic books would teach and inspire readers to commit rape and burglary.

In retrospect, such charges seem preposterous and even laughable. History has shown that those horrific fears were completely unjustified. Yet, outrageous as they were, they bear a striking resemblance in both tone and content to today's concerns about the effects of violent media— especially violent video games—on youth. Indeed, an article on violence and horror in entertainment media published in the March 24, 2007, edition of *The New York Times* described a then-upcoming Federal Trade Commission report:

> It will examine the selling practices of a mainstream entertainment industry that . . . has become increasingly dependent on abductions, maimings, decapitations and other mayhem. . . .
>
> If the new study were to find that the industry has violated or has outgrown its voluntary standards, it might kick the issue back into the political arena ahead of a presidential election. There it could trigger fresh calls for regulation. . . .[2]

To gain perspective on the current fears, political posturing and industry responses, it's useful to look at the past, for that past truly is prologue.

He Thought We'd Wind Up with Brains Full of Mush . . .

"When I was growing up, my father thought that my brothers, my sister and I watched too much TV," says Jonathan Bloomberg. His father is a psychiatrist.

"He thought we'd wind up with brains full of mush because of what we were watching. He also thought, like a lot of people back then, that we might get cancer of the brain because we watched so much and we sat so close to the TV set. In fact, we even took out a tape measure to make sure that we sat at least six feet away."

These days Dr. Bloomberg, like his father, is a psychiatrist. He directs the Bloomberg Institute for Child and Adolescent Development in Northbrook, Illinois, and teaches at the University of Illinois College of Medicine.

"My happiest childhood memories are of my brothers and sister and me watching the Saturday night shows on television," he recalls. "It was two hours of bliss. I learned social skills by watching *The Mary Tyler Moore Show*. The Mary Richards character that she played was someone to look up to, not just for little girls, but for little boys, too."

Now that he's the father of five boys, Dr. Bloomberg admits that he's conflicted about how his own children use media. They play a lot of sports video games. He likes it that his younger children try to copy the skateboard moves they see on Tony Hawk games. He's impressed by how his sixteen-year-old, an avid basketball player himself, has taken notes on how the animated players in a basketball video game move when they dunk the ball. "He's studied it like a choreographer and then tries to replicate what they do on a real court. He's less than six feet tall, but because of that he can dunk the ball, too," Dr. Bloomberg said.

But he's disturbed by a few of the other games they play, adding, "Some of the games can be a bit much, especially when they involve things like holding prostitutes hostage in *Grand Theft Auto*. I also sometimes have second thoughts about some of the television shows they watch, like *South Park* and *The Simpsons*. But those shows are so funny, and they really enjoy them. In retrospect, watching television was good for me. And probably *South Park* is good for my kids. There's a lot of laughter at the dinner table."

The Perils of the Printed Word

It was the change in technology that triggered grave concerns about the influence of violent media on youth. Not today's youth, mind you, but the children of the mid-1800s.

There's no doubt that the popular media of that time were filled with violence and sex. Horace Walpole's book *The Castle of Otranto*, published in 1764 and generally considered to be the first gothic novel, set the tone for the popular literature of the day. (Within the first two pages, sickly Prince Conrad is crushed to death by a giant feathered marble helmet on his wedding day. Soon, his father declares his aim to have sex with Conrad's fiancée so that she can bear him another son as a replacement. The eighteenth-century novel's over-the-top plot is surprisingly similar to the story lines of some of today's fantasy video games!)

When Walpole's book was published, there were no worries about the detrimental effects that such violence, sex, graphic imagery and generally questionable behaviors might have on children. The reasons were simple: few people could read, and books were too expensive for most poor and working-class people.

All of that changed in the first half of the nineteenth century through a confluence of events. Shifts in the English educational system increased the number of children being taught to read. In 1810, Friedrich Koenig and Andreas Friedrich Bauer developed the steam-powered printing press, which could print tens of thousands of pages each day, many more than the old hand-powered Gutenberg presses that had remained largely unchanged for about 350 years. Koenig and Bauer sold one of their first working presses to the publishers of the London newspaper *The Times*, which spearheaded a dramatic growth in newspaper publication and readership. Paper itself was also becoming less expensive because of a combination of improved manufacturing at paper mills and the use of less expensive raw materials such as esparto grass.

As a result, printed publications of all types became much more affordable. People—ordinary people, including children and members of the working class—were now not only able to read, but could purchase reading materials of all types.

Some of these nineteenth-century publications drew upon and

adapted the literary techniques of the gothic novel authors and made them more attractive to hoi polloi. Serial publications—the precursors of today's magazines—flourished and were filled with violence, crime and adventure. *The Newgate Calendar* recounted the lives and deeds of famous criminals. *The Terrific Register* offered lurid and supposedly true tales of murders, torture, ghostly sightings, perilous escapes and bizarre customs. Charles Dickens is said to have avidly read *The Terrific Register* each week.

Edward Lloyd, a publishing entrepreneur, exploited the public's growing taste for violent stories through such financially successful serials as *Lives of the Most Notorious Highwaymen, Footpads,*[3] *etc.* (sixty issues) and *History of the Pirates of All Nations* (seventy-one issues). He also plagiarized Dickens with such thinly disguised titles as *Oliver Twiss* and *Nickelas Nicklebery*. Because his serials were both inexpensive and filled with scenes of gore, he referred to them as "penny bloods."

In 1866, Edward Brett decided that he could improve upon Lloyd's marketing techniques by publishing violent stories aimed specifically at children using a serial format known as a storypaper. Schoolboys were the protagonists and heroes of his tales, such as *The Wild Boys of London, or The Children of Night*. This 105-issue serial featured a gang of boys who lived in the sewers, robbed corpses and battled the police.

One critic at the time described this genre of children's literature as "penny dreadfuls." It was, perhaps, a misleading appellation. The stories were filled with adventure and fantasy. Almost all condemned vice and promoted virtue, although occasionally with a nod and a wink. Still, many of these stories were held up as moral lessons.

At the same time, an inexpensive form of theater known as the penny gaff was cropping up in the cities, offering similarly gory stories as diversions and entertainments to working-class adults and, especially, to children. One critic described the cultural shift and its implications:

> On another occasion it chanced to me to visit a penny gaff in that dark and dolorous region, the New Cut. There the company and the entertainment were of a much lower character. A great part of the proceedings were indecent and disgusting, yet very satisfactory to the half grown girls and boys present. In the time of the

earlier Georges we read much of the brutality of the lower orders. If we may believe contemporary writers on men and manners, never was the theatre so full—never was the audience so excited—never did the scum and refuse of the streets so liberally patronise the entertainment as when deeds of violence and blood were the order of the night. This old savage spirit is dying out, but in the New Cut I fear it has not given way to a better one.[4]

Victorian society blamed juvenile crime on these cheap publications as well as on the penny gaffs, and paid little attention to the contributions of poverty, urban migration and prostitution. In fact, crime was decreasing dramatically in England during the peak of these stories' popularity.[5]

American publishers caught on quickly to the demand for violent serialized fiction and produced their own versions, known as dime novels. Among the most successful early publishers were the brothers Erastus and Irwin Beadle, who created Beadle's Dime Novels in the mid-1800s. The brothers gave explicit instructions to their authors, including:

Authors who write for our consideration will bear in mind that
We prohibit all things offensive to good taste in
expression and incident—
We prohibit subjects or characters that carry an immoral taint—
We prohibit the repetition of any occurrence which, though
true, is yet better untold—
We prohibit what cannot be read with satisfaction by every right-
minded person—old and young alike[6]

It was a nice thought. While some publishers aspired to such standards, others catered to the growing demand for the kind of vivid writing that had appeared in the penny bloods and penny dreadfuls.

The early dime novels came wrapped in orange paper, with their soft covers nearly absent of illustration. A typical book cover from 1861 read: "Beadle's Dime Novels. The Choicest Works of the Most Popular Authors. *A Sea Tale of '76. The Privateer's Cruise and the Bride of Pomfret Hall.* By Harry Cavendish." The focus of the cover was the name of the publisher. The only illustration was a symbolic dime.

Over the next few decades, the appearance of these dime novel covers shifted dramatically. Detailed engravings illustrating a vivid scene from the book, initially in black-and-white and later in color, soon appeared. Many of these cover illustrations depicted violence, especially fights. Sometimes the people doing the fighting were young women.

Such images were often quite shocking and titillating to the readers of the time. For example, the black-and-white cover of DeWitt's Ten Cent Romances' *The Female Trapper* (1873) shows a young woman in a diaphanous dress firing a pistol at an unseen target. Log Cabin Library's *Jesse James the Outlaw* (1897) has a full-color illustration of a woman firing a pistol during a train robbery at one of the robbers who is threatening a male passenger. (Interestingly, all of the train robbers are dressed formally in jackets and ties!) Rough Rider Weekly's *King of the Wild West's Cattle War, or Stella's Bout with the Rival Ranchers* (1907) depicts Stella in a windblown skirt improbably standing atop a hog-tied steer and threatening two men with a hot branding iron.

Vice City

Enter Anthony Comstock, the chief special agent for the New York Society for the Suppression of Vice. Comstock was a media darling of the late nineteenth and early twentieth centuries. His crusades against pornography, alcohol, tobacco, birth control and abortion made headlines for more than thirty years.

In 1872, Comstock accompanied a police captain and a reporter for the *New York Tribune* on a raid of two stationery stores where he had purchased pictures and books that he declared obscene. Six people were arrested, and Comstock made headlines. Eager to build upon his success, he took a suitcase filled with the pornographic items he had collected to Washington, DC, where Congress was dealing with some much more serious scandals of its own involving bribes of its members by the construction company Crédit Mobilier and fraud involving congressional underwriting of the expansion of the Union Pacific Railroad.

The legislators seized this opportunity to divert the attention of the press and the public from these growing political scandals and crimes. They embraced Comstock's cause and passed legislation he had written (known today as the Comstock Act) that prohibited the possession, advertising, sale and interstate transport of "obscene" materials, as well as information on contraception and abortion.

Then, as now, politicians and other public officials recognized that they could gain tremendous political leverage by rallying to protect children from both real and imagined threats to their innocence and virtue. The press flocked to such stories, no matter how little data supported the sometimes outrageous fears and claims. Few people dared to point out the flaws, for doing so exposed them to the risk of being labeled "anti-child."

The Congress of 1872 took full advantage of this hysteria to deflect attention from its members' financial and ethical transgressions. They appointed Anthony Comstock a postal inspector, which gave him broad police powers that he exercised with great vigor and much press coverage. His motto was "Morals, not art or literature." By the year 1900, according to a report of the New York Society for the Suppression of Vice, he had arrested 2,385 people and destroyed 73,608 pounds of books, along with many other items.[7]

But Comstock's concerns were not limited to sex. He worried that the crimes depicted in dime novels—including those stories aimed specifically at girls—would lead to copycat murders, burglaries, abductions and counterfeiting. In his 1883 book *Traps for the Young*, Comstock referred to dime novels and storypapers as "evil reading [which] debases, degrades, perverts, and turns away from lofty aims to follow examples of corruption and criminality."[8] He added with typical melodramatic flair that such "vile books and papers are branding-irons heated in the fires of hell, and used by Satan to sear the highest life of the soul."[9]

Even Comstock and his colleagues would be quick to point out that not all dime novels focused on crime and sex. By the end of the nineteenth century, books by Horatio Alger, Jr., were a treasured staple in American homes. Alger is best known for his more than 130 dime novels, almost all of which embraced the same basic plotline: a young boy works hard to escape the clutches of poverty. It's not the work itself that helps the boy succeed, but rather an extraordinary act of bravery or selfless honesty that brings the child into contact with a rich and powerful older man who often takes him on as his ward, tutors him in the ways of accepted society and changes his life for the better.

The underlying messages in these books were held up as exemplars of the strict Victorian morality being promoted by Comstock and others—an image that was further reinforced by the fact that Alger had graduated from Harvard Divinity School and had worked as a minister while starting his writing career. Surely there could be no better leader of a moral cause and no more appropriate defender of children and supporter of the innocence of childhood. This, cried the pundits, is what children's media should be.

Home libraries proudly displayed his books as a sign that they shared the author's views on the importance of moral rectitude and selfless behavior. To this day, the Horatio Alger Association provides scholarships and other awards to people who have overcome great adversity to become successful. Indeed, the phrase "a Horatio Alger story" has entered the vernacular as a term for a morally enlightening tale about achieving success through a combination of hard work and righteous, unselfish behavior.

Yet Alger's own behavior and values shed quite a different light on his writings.[10] True, he was an ordained minister. He left his church in Brewster, Massachusetts, in 1866 for the life of a full-time writer after being confronted with evidence and admitting that he had sexually abused at least two boys in his congregation. The formal findings of the investigation that were submitted to the Unitarian Church stated it in more flowery terms:

> Horatio Alger, Jr., who has officiated as our minister for about 15 months past, has recently been charged with gross immorality and a most heinous crime, a crime of no less magnitude than the abominable and revolting crime of unnatural familiarity with boys, which is too revolting to think of in the most brutal of our race. . . .

Alger skipped town before anyone could press criminal charges. His father, also a Unitarian minister, helped quash the scandal and wrote a letter to the American Unitarian Association promising that young Horatio would resign from the ministry and never again seek another church.

Once he moved to New York City, Alger became involved with

orphaned and abandoned boys, some of whom are said to have inspired the characters in his books, such as *Ragged Dick; or Street Life in New York with the Boot-Blacks* (1868). He also "adopted" three teenage boys. The extent of his ongoing predatory sexual relationships with these and other children is unclear, since his sister followed his request and destroyed all of his personal writings upon his death in 1899.

Few of Alger's contemporaries were aware of the subtext of his boy-saved-by-kind-older-gentleman plots; they simply embraced the surface messages. Indeed, the North American Man/Boy Love Association (NAMBLA), an organization that promotes sexual relationships between men and young children, named its New York City chapter after Horatio Alger.

In retrospect, we can also see the stirrings of feminism in the plot-lines written by other Victorian-era popular writers. The independence and assertiveness that social critics of the time found scandalous and worrisome are now encouraged as a healthy part of girls' emotional and social development. It would not be the last time such changes in perspective would take place.

Silent Killers

The early twentieth century ushered in a new popular medium and a new source of concern: motion pictures. Crime stories and violence were staples of the early film industry, just as they were for early publishers. But it was the nascent craft of film editing that would soon cause politicians, religious leaders and social reformers to fear the influence of motion pictures on children's morals and behaviors. Indeed, the conventions of film editing paved a clear and direct path for the creation of video games.

Many of the early commercial motion pictures consisted of a single scene or event, such as a romantic kiss or the slapstick attempts of a gardener desperately trying to control a spraying hose. (Similarly, the first video game, which was developed at Brookhaven National Laboratories in 1958, was a simple two-dimensional tennis game displayed on an oscilloscope.) As filmmakers became more sophisticated, their films started looking like scenes from stage plays, with actors on static sets.

The earliest of these minute-long films were unedited; they showed a single event from a single perspective. Within a few years, filmmakers started editing films to show the same events from two or more different perspectives. A movie about the rescue of a woman from a fire might cut between shots of the woman and shots of the firefighters. Still, the plot consisted of a single event shown from beginning to end.

While some early silent films were shown in storefront theaters, most were projected on a screen in between live acts on a vaudeville stage. For example, the Edison Company's 1899 film *Love and War* consisted of six minute-long modules that told the story of a young soldier who goes off to fight in the Spanish-American War as a private, is wounded, gets promoted for bravery, meets the girl of his dreams (a Red Cross nurse) and returns home in triumph.

Audience members could follow the young man's heroic story through each of the six acts and listen to each act's accompanying song, which was commonly played after the film segment: "Parting" ("Our Hero Boy to the War has Gone"), "Camping" ("What! A Letter from Home"), "Fighting" ("Father, on Thee I Call"), "Convalescing" ("Weeping, Sad and Lonely"), "Sorrowing" ("Come Back, My Dear Boy, to Me") and "Returning" ("The Star-Spangled Banner").

The film was a multimedia event, complete with musical arrangements for soloist, quartet or full orchestra and with accompanying stereopticon slides that could be projected on the screen during the songs. Like other early silent films, it wasn't viewed in silence. Rather than providing a piano or organ accompaniment, which would become common in later years, exhibitors added live sound effects, such as train whistles or pistol shots, to make the audience's experience more realistic and emotionally arousing.

Theater owners would show these early films in different ways. In one venue, *Love and War* could be spliced together to form a continuous narrative. In another, it might be shown in pieces throughout a vaudeville performance. In a third, each of its modules might be shown on different weeks.

The film world changed in 1903 with the release of the Edison Company's twelve-minute motion picture *The Great Train Robbery*. Unlike earlier films of this length, the producers intended it to be shown in its entirety and without interruption.

The Edison Films catalog that was sent to exhibitors promoted it vividly:

> This sensational and highly tragic subject will certainly make a decided "hit" whenever shown. In every respect we consider it absolutely the superior of any moving picture ever made. It has been posed and acted in faithful duplication of the genuine "Hold Ups" made famous by various outlaw bands in the far West, and only recently the East has been shocked by several crimes of the frontier order, which fact will increase the popular interest in this great Headline Attraction.[11]

The Great Train Robbery was seminal for several other reasons as well, not the least of which was its intense and graphic violence. The brief plot contains multiple murders, including throwing a body off a train; shooting a fleeing passenger in the back; several robberies; an attack on a telegraph operator and the subsequent discovery of his tied and beaten body by his young daughter; the dynamiting of a safe; and a square-dancing posse that sneaks up on and kills the thieves. (The square-dancing scene, which is interrupted by the injured telegrapher who'd been untied by his daughter, is apparently the writer's way of letting us know that the vigilantes who will eventually hunt down and mercilessly shoot the robbers are just ordinary folk.)

The final scene shows a close-up[12] of the mustachioed and menacing outlaw leader, Barnes, firing his six-shooter point-blank at members of the audience. Exhibitors were told by the Edison catalog that they had the option of showing this snippet at either the beginning or the end of the film.

The Great Train Robbery was a blockbuster hit that played for several years. It also popularized a new style of film editing. Instead of following a single series of events, the film took the audience to different locations in which different things were happening simultaneously. For example, the editor cut between the robbers making their escape on horseback and the telegraph operator lying bound and gagged on the floor of his office, mustering the strength to call for help.

This use of editing to allow the audience to move instantly through time and space became fundamental to the grammar of future films, and eventually to video games. It increased the emotional tension and suspense of the film because, unlike in earlier motion pictures, the scenes did not automatically play out to their natural conclusions. No longer would a movie be limited to a single plot thread. Time and perspective could be manipulated freely. The audience could know things that the on-screen characters did not. The era of the modern film had begun.

Who Put the Sin in Cinema?

As the motion picture industry grew, so did concerns about the immoral content of films and their effects on viewers, especially children. Matters came to a head in the early 1920s with the intense national publicity that surrounded two scandals.

At the height of his popularity, Roscoe "Fatty" Arbuckle was second only to Charlie Chaplin in his renown as a silent-film comedian. By 1921, he was under contract to Paramount Pictures for a reported $1 million per year. His career imploded that September when he was accused of the rape and murder of a young actress, Virginia Rappe, who had been partying with Arbuckle and some other friends from the film industry in their hotel rooms in San Francisco.

The scandal was a newspaper sensation, especially in those papers owned by William Randolph Hearst, who had been railing against "liquor-and-sex orgies" and other decadent behaviors of Hollywood actors and moguls. Given Hearst's own reputation for decadence and partying, as well as his closeness to studio heads, actors and others in the film industry, it's doubtful that his complaints grew from a sense of moral outrage. Rather, Hearst knew that sex and scandal sold newspapers. The juicier the scandal—the more sexual depravity and moral decrepitude he could describe or imply—the more money he could make. He set out to make a lot of money off the trial, even if there were few facts to back up his newspapers' stories.

The grand jury indicted Arbuckle for manslaughter, much to the disappointment of the prosecutor, who had been pushing for a charge of first-degree murder. Theaters and state film boards started banning Arbuckle's films. Protests against the film industry sprung up around the country. The director of youth programs at the National Presbyterian Temperance Board stated,

> The entire film business should be closed for at least one month and then opened only under intelligent management. Under present circumstances, I contend that cities would be justified in declaring martial law in respect to the mad mob spirit growing out of the movies.[13]

Arbuckle was tried on the manslaughter charge three times. The first two trials ended with hung juries; the third acquitted him of the charge. Indeed, that jury read him a note of apology in the courtroom stating, "Acquittal is not enough for Roscoe Arbuckle. We feel a great injustice has been done him. . . . Roscoe Arbuckle is entirely innocent and free from all blame."[14] Most historians who have studied the trials have concluded that he was innocent and that much of the derogatory speculation about him in the popular press was inaccurate. His career never recovered.

In the time between Arbuckle's second and third trials, another Hollywood scandal captured the imagination of the press and the public. William Desmond Taylor, a well-known silent-film director, was murdered at his home. The press speculated on whether Taylor's lifestyle— described in various conflicting reports as including opium use, homosexuality, multiple affairs with young actresses and throwing and attending "wild parties," as well as his attempts to help drug-addicted friends in the industry kick their habits—had led to the crime. The murder has never been solved.

These and other Hollywood scandals of the early twentieth century fueled the flames of both religious and governmental groups that wanted to protect people, especially children, from the influence of the motion picture industry as talking pictures came onto the scene. "Silent smut had been bad," wrote Daniel A. Lord, a Jesuit priest and prolific social critic at the time. "Vocal smut cried to the censors for vengeance."

In 1921, New York State established an independent commission to "review and license" films for distribution. During its forty-four years, the New York State Motion Picture Commission reviewed more than seventy-three thousand films. About three hundred were rejected in their entirety; another seven thousand were asked to make changes before they could be issued a license.[15]

In 1922, Commissioner Joseph Levenson defended the government's right to censor motion pictures:

All those who attack motion picture regulation ignore the basic reason for such regulation. The motion picture draws an enormous proportion of its trade from children of immature years, from a great many of mental defectives, and a vast number of illiterates and the ignorant. The non-English speaking foreigners contribute great numbers to every one of those classes. After all, the way these elements receive their impression of life, of moral standards, of the obligations of citizenship, will ultimately affect in great degree the welfare of the state.

More far-reaching than the schoolhouse is the motion picture theater. If one bad picture can undo years of schooling to those who receive instruction, what must be the influence of the motion picture on the minds of those who never receive any schooling; or on those who were schooled in foreign lands, and whose conception of life in America is entirely different from that of our people.

These conditions made it clear to those who gave serious thought to the subject that the attitude of many of the people in the motion picture industry that they could present to the public all types of pictures, crime-inciting, immoral, indecent, sacrilegious without restraint would result in a decided lowering of the standards of our citizenship.

A careful study of the facts convinced students of the situation that failure to regulate and supervise the work of the motion picture producers was resulting in an increase of crime in all communities, particularly among our young, and affecting the moral welfare of all classes of our people. These were the main reasons that brought about the legislation of last winter creating the Motion Picture Commission of the State of New York.[16]

Better the Devil You Know . . .

The film industry was rapidly being outflanked. Social critics, politicians and religious leaders blamed motion pictures for a wide swath of social ills. At the same time, cinema attendance was down. Some of this decline came from the influenza pandemic of 1918 and consequent public concerns about "exposure to crowds." Some of it came from the increasing popularity of radio as an entertainment medium.

A growing number of states and cities were establishing censorship boards of various types. The decision by New York State, the largest and most profitable domestic market for films, to start its Motion Picture Commission was apparently the tipping point for the industry. In an attempt to regain public confidence and to stop the growth of government censorship, the studio heads formed their own censorship board and public relations group, the Motion Picture Producers and Distributors of America (the MPPDA, now known as the Motion Picture Association of America).

Will Hays was the U.S. postmaster general at the time, a former chairman of the Republican National Committee and an elder of the Presbyterian church. With his deep political connections and savvy, as well as his flair for public relations, studio executives viewed him as a natural choice for president of the MPPDA. Hays took the job in 1922, and would soon become one of the most influential men in the history of motion pictures.

Pressures for censorship continued. Congress held hearings in 1925 and 1926 to explore establishing a Federal Motion Picture Commission. Hays attempted to fend off federal regulation by, among other things, issuing a memorandum in 1927 containing guidelines for producers that became known as the "Don'ts and Be Carefuls." The Don'ts consisted of prohibitions on profanity, suggestive nudity, use of illegal drugs, sexual perversion, white slavery, miscegenation, venereal diseases, childbirth, children's sex organs, ridicule of the clergy and willful offense to any nation, race or creed. The longer list of Be Carefuls was a hodgepodge of items that could potentially cause trouble if they were construed as vulgar or suggestive. Most of these involved violence, crime or sex.

It didn't work. The studios saw the guidelines for what they were:

suggestions with little hint of enforcement behind them. Pressure from the state and federal governments increased. Hays responded by expanding the Don'ts and Be Carefuls list into the Motion Picture Production Code, later known as the Hays Code. It gave detailed instructions for what would and would not be acceptable in a commercial motion picture:

> No picture shall be produced that will lower the moral standards of those who see it. Hence the sympathy of the audience should never be thrown to the side of crime, wrongdoing, evil or sin. . . . Theft, robbery, safe-cracking, and dynamiting of trains, mines, buildings, etc., should not be detailed in method. . . . The sanctity of the institution of marriage and the home shall be upheld. Pictures shall not infer [sic] that low forms of sex relationship are the accepted or common thing.

All of the attention paid to sex and crime in the Motion Picture Production Code hints at what was drawing audiences of all ages to their local motion picture theaters. Hollywood was happy to oblige, of course. The film industry's attempt at setting moral standards for motion pictures was fundamentally a business decision, an attempt to ward off costly distribution problems if state governments developed different standards for what could be shown in their theaters. It was an approach that would later be copied by the creators of other entertainment media, including video games.

The Public Enemy

Compared with the violent content of *The Great Train Robbery*, most gangster films of the 1920s and 1930s were relatively tame. They were also structurally more complex, with far more sophisticated acting, photography and editing. But it was probably one technological improvement that made gangster films so popular: sound.

The iconic sounds of gangster films are immediately identifiable: The screech of brakes and squeal of tires in a car chase, the smack of a closed fist against a chin or an open hand across a cheek, the rat-a-tat fire of a machine gun, the dull thud of a dead body as it hits the ground. Indeed, the first "100 percent all-talking" feature film to be released,* *Lights of New York* (1928), was a gangster film. The film was produced for a paltry $23,000. During its first run, it grossed well over one million dollars. Thus, the future of gangster movies was assured.

The plots of this first generation of talking gangster films played off the headlines of the day. Prohibition and the Great Depression had turned the likes of Al Capone, Pretty Boy Floyd and John Dillinger into celebrities. The St. Valentine's Day Massacre of 1929 had captured the public's imagination about gangland turf battles. The larger-than-life stories and characters were tailor-made for Hollywood.

Indeed, the plots of these films turned traditional morality tales on their heads. The protagonists used their wits and skills to pursue long-standing American goals of wealth, power, social status and material goods. But they did so through selfish, immoral and often violent behavior, without regard to the consequences of their actions.

Concerns over the influence of movies on children turned the book *Our Movie Made Children* by Henry James Forman into a national bestseller. It detailed a combination of supposedly scientific experiments and case histories to show how motion pictures posed a significant danger to the youth of that day. In retrospect, many of these stories, like the movies themselves, seem quaint.

> "I saw a picture, 'Me, Gangster,' " writes a high-school boy of seventeen. "This gave me a yearning to steal. . . . I went to our register and took out a quarter and went to a show. I did this in a sly manner just as in the show."
>
> Numerous minor delinquencies are attributed by boys to the movies—stealing small sums, robbing a chicken coop, a small newsboy or a fruit vendor—little is thought of these acts by the boys or even by their elders. Criminologists, however, are well aware how often this type of early minor delinquency leads to more serious acts and graver forms of crime. Experienced criminals, moreover, join the criminologists in this belief and frequently

---

*Films such as *The Jazz Singer* (1927) and *Dream Street* (1921) contained limited synchronized sound effects, songs and dialogue, and are known as "part-talkies."

condemn the movie influence and touch upon it with bitterness as a factor in their own unfortunate careers.[17]

A few pages later, a seventeen-year-old boy who was charged with burglary adds:

"I learned something from 'The Doorway to Hell.' It is a gangster picture. It shows how to drown out shots from a gun by backfiring a car." This is one of the numerous techniques learned from the movies, as one ex-convict explains it. There is a large amount of such terse testimony as to the education source—the movies— for a great many methods and techniques acquired by young criminals.[18]

Late in 1933 the *American Journal of Public Health* featured a book review of *Our Movie Made Children*. It was sandwiched between reviews of a White House conference on infant and maternal illness and the book *A Short History of Dentistry*.

Easy money, fine clothes, luxury, wild parties, sex suggestion, exert an insidious appeal. Young people report the movies a liberal education in love-making with the sex side often over-empha-sized. "The road to delinquency is heavily dotted with movie addicts and it needs no crusaders, or preachers, or reformers to come to this conclusion."

Everyone interested in the physical, mental, or moral welfare of children should read this book and take a positive stand against the evils that are exposed. Parents should consider carefully the seriousness of the facts and supervise the movie-going habits of the children as far as possible.[19]

No groups took up the cause more enthusiastically than the pro-censorship religious activists. Protestant and Jewish movie censorship groups were mostly local. The Catholic Church, however, took a national approach. They organized the Catholic Legion of Decency, inspired by a 1933 speech made by a politically savvy Italian priest named Amleto

Cicognani at a Catholic Charities convention in New York City, in which he railed against the movies' "massacre of innocence of youth." (Cicognani would eventually become the cardinal secretary of state at the Vatican.) The organization was renamed the National Legion of Decency in 1934 in an attempt to become more ecumenical, and perhaps to shed itself of the acronym CLOD. Its membership pledge read:

> I condemn all indecent and immoral motion pictures, and those which glorify crime or criminals. I promise to do all that I can to strengthen public opinion against the production of indecent and immoral films, and to unite with all who protest against them. I acknowledge my obligation to form a right conscience about pictures that are dangerous to my moral life. I pledge myself to remain away from them. I promise, further, to stay away altogether from places of amusement which show them as a matter of policy.

The National Legion of Decency came up with a film rating system that was a precursor to the current industry-sponsored rating systems for films, television and video games. The Legion assigned films ratings of A ("morally unobjectionable"), B ("morally objectionable in part") or C ("condemned by the Legion of Decency"). A slightly revised version of this ratings system is still being used by the successor to the Legion, the United States Conference of Catholic Bishops' Office for Film and Broadcasting.

Horror in the Nursery

In some ways, the crime and horror comics of the late 1930s through the 1950s were a throwback to the popular storypapers of the nineteen century. Many of the plotlines featured violence and gore. The artwork exaggerated men's muscles (if they were heroes) and women's legs and breasts. This approach to portraying women, known as "good girl art," was a natural successor to the popular pinup and calendar girl art of World War II. The term "good girl" does not refer to the morals or behavior of the subject, but to her physical features. Indeed many of these exaggerated women were shown in violent, sexually provocative, or downright ludicrous situations.

The contents of these comics were outlandish in their creativity. They both reflected and mocked the conventions and mores of the time. The cover of an issue of *Crime Does Not Pay* ("All true crime stories!") shows a sexy young woman in a low-cut red dress running away from a diner. She has a pistol in each hand, which she has clearly used to shoot several men around her. There's blood everywhere. In an issue of *Baffling Mysteries*, two green-scaled humanoids abduct a scantily clad blonde, telling her, "We have long sought a queen! You shall reign as queen of the Lizard Men!"

There were deeper metaphors as well, perhaps conscious, perhaps not. An issue of *Tales from the Crypt* features a story about a criminal who survives a prison electrocution and seeks revenge on the judge who sentenced him. Indeed, this theme of someone rising from the dead to chase down and kill his former torturers recurs regularly in the horror comics of the late 1940s and early 1950s. This was only a few years after World War II and the public's recognition of the real-life horrors of the Holocaust. Many of the editors and executives in the comic book industry were European Jews, so this theme had special resonance.

Predictably, concerns about these comics' influence on children led to articles with titles like "Horror in the Nursery" and "What Parents Don't Know About Comic Books" that appeared in national magazines. A child psychiatrist, Fredric Wertham, MD, led the charge against crime comics in his bestselling 1954 book, *Seduction of the Innocent*.

Wertham, a social activist and classically trained psychoanalyst, railed against the criminal behaviors portrayed in the stories. He also pointed out a partial image of a nude woman that was seemingly embedded in an illustration of a man's shoulder, and warned loudly and repeatedly about the influence on youth by what he claimed to be the homosexual relationship between Batman (Bruce Wayne) and Robin (Dick Grayson).

> They live in sumptuous quarters, with beautiful flowers in large vases, and have a butler, Alfred. Batman is sometimes shown in a dressing gown. . . . It is like a wish dream of two homosexuals living together. Sometimes they are shown on a couch, Bruce reclining and Dick sitting next to him, jacket off, collar open, and his hand on his friend's arm. Like the girls in other stories, Robin is

sometimes held captive by the villains and Batman has to give in or "Robin gets killed."

Robin is a handsome ephebic [adolescent] boy, usually shown in his uniform with bare legs. He is buoyant with energy and devoted to nothing on Earth or in interplanetary space as much as to Bruce Wayne. He often stands with his legs spread, the genital region discreetly evident.

In these stories there are practically no decent, attractive, successful women. A typical female character is the Catwoman, who is vicious and uses a whip. The atmosphere is homosexual and anti-feminine. If the girl is good-looking she is undoubtedly the villainess. If she is after Bruce Wayne, she will have no chance against Dick.[20]

Because of these and other concerns, at least fifty cities tried to prevent or regulate the sale of comics. The New York State legislature passed a bill to make it a crime to sell comics that might incite minors to violence or immorality, but the governor vetoed it out of concern that the ban might be unconstitutional. The U.S. Senate Judiciary Committee's subcommittee on juvenile delinquency held hearings in 1954 about the pernicious influence of comics. Its interim report stated,

It has been pointed out that the so-called crime and horror comic books of concern to the subcommittee offer short courses in murder, mayhem, robbery, rape, cannibalism, carnage, necrophilia, sex, sadism, masochism, and virtually every other form of crime, degeneracy, bestiality, and horror. These depraved acts are presented and explained in illustrated detail in an array of comic books being bought and read daily by thousands of children. These books evidence a common penchant for violent death in every form imaginable. Many of the books dwell in detail on various forms of insanity and stress sadistic degeneracy. Others are devoted to cannibalism with monsters in human form feasting on human bodies, usually the bodies of scantily clad women.[21]

Dr. Wertham's testimony at the subcommittee's hearings in New York City started with that premise and took it even further.

If it were my task, Mr. Chairman, to teach children delinquency, to tell them how to rape and seduce girls, how to hurt people, how to break into stores, how to cheat, how to forge, how to do any known crime—if it were my task to do that, I would have to enlist the crime comic book industry. Formerly to impair the morals of a minor was a punishable offense. It has now become a mass industry. I will say that every crime of delinquency is described in detail and that if you teach somebody the technique of something you, of course, seduce him into it. Nobody would believe that you teach a boy homosexuality without introducing him to it. The same thing with crime.

Wertham had similar concerns about the sexual orientation of Wonder Woman and her potential influence on the young girls who read her comics.

The homosexual connotation of the Wonder Woman type of story is psychologically unmistakable. . . .

For boys, Wonder Woman is a frightening image. For girls, she is a morbid ideal. Where Batman is anti-feminine, the attractive Wonder Woman and her counterparts are definitely anti-masculine. . . . In a typical story, Wonder Woman is involved in adventures with another girl, a princess, who talks repeatedly about "those wicked men."[22]

Following in the footsteps of Hays and the film industry, the comic book publishers set up the Comics Code Authority the same year as the Senate hearings. Highlights of that original industry code included:

❖ Crimes shall never be presented in such a way as to create sympathy for the criminal, to promote distrust of the forces of law and justice, or to inspire others with a desire to imitate criminals.

❖ If crime is depicted it shall be as a sordid and unpleasant activity.

❖ Criminals shall not be presented so as to be rendered glamorous or to occupy a position which creates a desire for emulation.

❖ In every instance good shall triumph over evil and the criminal punished for his misdeeds.

❖ Scenes of excessive violence shall be prohibited. Scenes of brutal torture, excessive and unnecessary knife and gunplay, physical agony, gory and gruesome crime shall be eliminated.

❖ Females shall be drawn realistically without exaggeration of any physical qualities.

❖ Nudity with meretricious purpose and salacious postures shall not be permitted in the advertising of any product; clothed figures shall never be presented in such a way as to be offensive or contrary to good taste or morals.

The introduction of the code marked the end of the golden age of horror and crime comic books. Many of these comics are now valuable collector's items and are even integrated into university courses on popular culture and art. In 2001, Michael Chabon won a Pulitzer Prize for his novel *The Amazing Adventures of Kavalier and Clay*, about this heyday of comic book publication.

The Largest Comic Book Collection in My Neighborhood

It comes as a surprise to many parents and educators when they learn that Jim Trelease is a big fan of comic books. After all, he's a nationally known reading consultant and the author of *The Read-Aloud Handbook*.[23] He lectures all over the world on how to improve children's reading ability and increase their love of reading. He says that studies clearly show that top students in all grades are more likely to read comic books than lower-ranked students.

"In the early 1950s, I had the largest comic book collection in my neighborhood," says Trelease, who has a framed *Call of the Wild* Classic Comic Book hanging on the wall of his office. "I had *Batman, Superman, Tarzan*—a lot of boy adventure comics. Also, *Mad* magazine and Donald Duck comics. *Mad* magazine was forbidden fruit, which made it more attractive. We were reading stuff that the adults didn't want us to read."

He's such a fan of this era's horror comics that when his son was twelve years old, he gave the boy a bound collection of them. "He loved them!" he says, adding that he's not sure his ten-year-old grandson is ready for the level of graphic violence and gore that were commonplace in those comics. As with all media, including video games, he recommends making sure that the subject matter and approach are developmentally appropriate for the child. His son was ready to handle the comics at age twelve; his grandson will still have to wait a few years.

Trelease attributes the widespread fears about the influence of comics when he was a child to parents and other well-meaning adults trying to cope with the significant social and cultural changes that took place after World War II. "The changes made them uncomfortable," he adds. "Nobody likes change. It was a way for them to fight those changes. I see a repetition of this paranoia today in some evangelicals' concerns about books like the Harry Potter series."

Broadcasting Sex and Violence

Predictably, radio and television were the next media to be attacked as destructive to children, using many of the arguments and approaches employed by earlier critics of comics, gangster films and dime novels. One would think that Wertham would have anticipated this in his writings about the dangers of comic books. Quite the contrary!

> Television is on the way to become the greatest medium of all time. It is a marvel of the technological advance of mankind. The hopes it raises are high, even though its most undoubted achievement to date is that it has brought homicide into the home. . . . Television has a spotty past, a dubious present and a glorious future. That alone distinguishes it from crime comic books, which have a shameful past, a shameful present and no future at all.[24]

Oddly, Wertham wrote this opinion at a time when, in retrospect, television programming—especially programming for children—was chock-full of gratuitous violence. Westerns, the most popular television genre in the 1950s, routinely involved multiple shootings, stabbings, scalpings and torture. Disney's Davy Crockett ("Kilt him a b'ar when he was only three!" proclaimed the hit theme song) got into a tomahawk fight in his first episode, "Davy Crockett, Indian Fighter." It also triggered a fashion and cultural craze that had millions of children suddenly wearing coonskin caps like their hero and begging their parents to buy them plastic or wooden replicas of his faithful rifle, Old Betsy.

For many Americans, an iconic photograph of suburban life in the 1950s might show a young boy with a serious look on his face, a squint in his eye and an oversized holster strapped to his leg. He's firing a cowboy six-shooter at an unseen villain or varmint, just as he'd seen on *Hopalong Cassidy* or *The Lone Ranger*. These once-ubiquitous children's cap pistols, such as the Mattel Fanner 50 and the Kilgore Buc-A-Roo, are now valuable collector's items.

Killers for hire, like Paladin on *Have Gun—Will Travel*, were portrayed as heroes on television. Marshal Matt Dillon, the protagonist of *Gunsmoke*, began each episode by gunning down a man in the street, often following that with another shooting later in the show. During the program's twenty-year run, it was also broadly implied that he was having a long-term affair with the town's saloon owner, the provocatively named Miss Kitty. The adults who watched had a good idea how she and her attractive barmaids really made their money, even if the children in the audience didn't.

Perhaps Wertham had such high hopes for television because, during the 1950s, the electronic medium of greatest concern due to its supposedly detrimental influence on children was radio, which was shifting in both tone and format. Irving Caesar, the music publisher and lyricist who wrote such songs as "Tea for Two," graphically summed up one popular perspective on why parents should be worried about the salaciousness of the new music—rock and roll—being broadcast by radio stations:

> Parents have a right, because they sense not the content but the intent. The leering clarinet, the moaning, sensuous trombone. It's interpretation. The very fact that it appeals to a certain kind of interpreter. For instance if I say, "I love you truly, truly." But if I say, "I love you truly" and weave my eyes and twist my body when

I say it, "I love you truly," you know what I intend to convey when I say, "I love you truly" that way. . . . You know the rock and roll business. It was born out of rhythm and blues and race. Written by people who didn't know the English language. Didn't know how to spell, didn't know how to play but could accompany himself on the gee-tar and so forth and that's how rock and roll was born.[25]

Déjà Vu

What does all of this have to do with video games? The parallels are striking. Until the early 1970s, access to computers was restricted to an elite class, such as programmers and engineers at corporations, government agencies and schools. These were mainframe computers, the Gutenberg presses of their day. As with those first hand-powered presses, these early computers had started a revolution that had not yet directly reached the masses.

As had happened with printing, a confluence of events—the use of new technologies, more efficient manufacturing and distribution, increased demand and cheaper raw materials—led to the development of the personal computer in its many forms, including video game consoles. What was once available only to a few people has, like printed books, become inexpensive and commonplace.

Today, an amalgam of politicians, health professionals, religious leaders and children's advocates are voicing concerns about video games that are identical to the concerns raised one, two and three generations ago with the introduction of other new media. Most of these people have the best of intentions. They really want to protect children from evil influences. As in the past, a few have different agendas and are using the issue manipulatively.

Unfortunately, many of their claims are based on scanty evidence, inaccurate assumptions, and pseudoscience. Much of the current research on violent video games is both simplistic and agenda driven.

As with Alger's books in the nineteenth century, violent video games that are associated with religion are sometimes viewed differently and with less scrutiny than other commercial games. (There are exceptions, as we'll see in chapter 6.) For example, many families embrace the violence in *Left Behind: Eternal Forces*, a video game in which Christian players score points for gunning down nonbelievers.

The video game industry, like the motion picture and comic book industries before it, has developed voluntary standards for content in an attempt to stave off state and federal regulation. Governors, legislators and presidential candidates have all chimed in with their opinions on the supposed dangers of violent video games for children, and in some cases have introduced legislation in an attempt to quash the same type of threat that our parents, grandparents and great-grandparents had been warned about regarding the new media of their times.

Throughout the rest of this book, we'll examine some of the research on video games and help you make sense of it. We'll describe our own research, discuss its implications and limitations, and suggest practical things you can do as a parent, teacher or health professional to make the most of the good and limit the potentially bad aspects of violent video games. We'll also explore the concept of differential risk: the idea that we should be more concerned about some children and less concerned about others.

CHAPTER 3

Science, Nonsense and Common Sense

More than 3500 research studies have examined the association between media violence and violent behavior; all but 18 have shown a positive relationship.

> —*"Media Violence," American Academy of Pediatrics Committee on Public Education, November 2001*[1]

It is not true, for example, that "more than 3500 research studies have examined the association between media violence and violent behavior [and] all but 18 have shown a positive relationship." . . . In fact, there are probably fewer than 300 empirical studies that try to measure the effects of violent media—with even and ambiguous results.

> —*National Coalition Against Censorship, December 2001*[2]

LET'S GO FROM HISTORY TO SCIENCE FOR A BIT. TO UNDERstand the claims made by researchers, it's useful to know how scientists approach a complex problem like the causes of violence. Scientific research is like solving a jigsaw puzzle in which you don't know if you have all the pieces; the pieces that you do have can fit together in many different ways and you're not sure what the finished picture will look like. If you're not a scientist or you don't have an interest in research, it might be tempting to skip this chapter. Some of it may be hard sledding.

We urge you to bear with us. Don't let the technical terms or the details intimidate you.

Why should you, as a parent, care about the process of video game research? As you'll see in chapter 8, academic studies turn into valuable ammunition in political battles on the local, state and national levels, with the fate of many tax dollars and careers at stake—not to mention policies designed to shape the behavior of game makers, game retailers and your children.

Our goal for this chapter is not to bore you with an exhaustive analysis of research on media violence but to address one seemingly simple question that has some surprising answers:

Why Don't the "Experts" Agree?

You'd think that things would be clear-cut by now. After all, there are so many studies. Many of the conclusions bandied about sound pretty obvious. But that's not the case. Video game violence research is highly complex for a wide range of reasons. We'll start to explore some of those in a few pages, but let's begin by examining some of the conflicting claims.

> These results clearly support the hypothesis that exposure to violent video games poses a public-health threat to children and youths [and] is positively associated with heightened levels of aggression in young adults and children, in experimental and non-experimental designs, and in males and females. . . . In brief, every theoretical prediction derived from prior research and from GAM [*General Aggression Model*] was supported by the meta-analysis of currently available research on violent video games.
>
> —*Craig Anderson, PhD, and Brad Bushman, PhD,*
> *Iowa State University*[3]

> I have read nearly all the published English-language research on electronic games, which includes video and computer games, CD-ROM and online games. Neither the quantity nor the quality of research on video games does much to inspire confidence in solid conclusions about their effects.

Nearly every study suffers from unclear definitions (of violence or aggression), ambiguous measurements (confusing aggressive play with aggressive behavior, or using questionable measures of aggression, such as blasts of noise or self-reports of prior aggression), and overgeneralizations from the data. Experiments that claim to study the effects of playing electronic games rarely study play at all.

—Jeffrey Goldstein, PhD,
University of Utrecht (the Netherlands)[4]

If you scan the chronology of research, congressional debates and other documentation that has gone into attempting to deal with media violence since 1952, you should be outraged. How is it that millions of dollars and an uncountable number of hours and energy have been put to work against TV, movie, and video game violence for decades—and things have only gotten worse?

—Lieutenant Colonel Dave Grossman and Gloria DeGaetano,
authors of Stop Teaching Our Kids to Kill[5]

On balance, given that video game play is highly prevalent among children and adolescents in industrialized countries, there is little evidence that moderate frequency of play has serious acute adverse effects. Adverse effects, when they occur, tend to be relatively minor and temporary, resolving spontaneously with decreased frequency of play. More evidence is needed on excessive play and on defining what constitutes excess in the first place.

—Mark Griffiths, PhD,
Nottingham Trent University (England)[6]

Those are pretty dramatic contrasts. How can these experts arrive at such different conclusions? Sometimes, it's a matter of timing. In 1999, when Grossman and DeGaetano published their book *Stop Teaching Our Kids to Kill: A Call to Action Against TV, Movie and Video Game Violence*, the available data on youth violence in America painted a grim picture. Keep in mind that government crime data are always a few years old. As we write this in mid-2007, the most recent data available are from 2004.

When they were writing their book in the late 1990s, the most recent crime data available to them were from the early 1990s.

Using data supplied to the Federal Bureau of Investigation by local law enforcement agencies, the U.S. Office of Juvenile Justice and Delinquency Prevention reports that the rate of juvenile arrests increased in the late 1980s and peaked in 1994. This looked like an alarming trend. Media reports at the time were filled with speculation about a new breed of "super-predator" juvenile delinquent.

Meanwhile, in 1992, *Mortal Kombat* hit the video arcades with its over-the-top, blood-spewing "fatalities." According to Jeff Greeson, who manages a Web site devoted to the game series, *"Mortal Kombat* not only stood out, it grabbed you by the shirt collar and demanded your attention. *Mortal Kombat* had the biggest and most realistic characters ever featured in a video game at that time. You wrwere literally watching digitally animated photographs of people flying through the air and beating the living hell out of each other."[7]

By 1995, *Mortal Kombat 3* had invaded the home arena on multiple fronts, including the original PlayStation, Sega Genesis, and Super Nintendo, along with other scary-sounding titles such as *Doom*. It seemed natural to connect the video game violence and the real-life violence.

But juvenile arrests declined in each of the next seven years. Between 1994 and 2001, arrests for murder, forcible rape, robbery and aggravated assaults fell 44 percent, resulting in the lowest juvenile arrest rate for violent crimes since 1983. Juvenile murder arrests reached a high of 3,790 in 1993. By 2004, arrests were down 71 percent, to 1,110.[8]

In retrospect, we can see what drove the increase in murders. We don't need to cast about for an explanation. In their 2006 report for the Office of Juvenile Justice and Delinquency Prevention, Howard N. Snyder and Melissa Sickmund of the National Center for Juvenile Justice wrote, "Ninety percent of the overall increase was murders of nonfamily members committed by males with a firearm—generally a handgun. . . . Nearly three-quarters of the increase was the result of crimes committed by black and other minority males—and in two-thirds of these murders, the victims were minority males. The decline in murders by juveniles from 1994 to 2002 reversed the earlier increase."[9]

There's no evidence that black teens' use of violent media differed significantly from that of other young people, though there is ample evidence that *as a group*, they had and still have greater exposure to other risk factors for violence. For example, as of 2002, almost one third of black Americans aged seventeen and under were living in poverty.[10] African-American youth are also more likely to witness real-life violence.[11]

Changes in social priorities and ideas about crime also affected juvenile arrest rates in the early 1990s. Fears of youth violence led some communities to increase arrests for curfew violations; arrests for marijuana possession rose—although surveys did not show increased use. Acts of domestic violence were being redefined as criminal rather than family matters. Behavior once classified as a juvenile "status" offense might now lead to arrest for assault.[12]

For whatever reason, the various experts who cited the 1990s increase in crime as evidence of harm from media violence are not rushing to take back those statements in the face of reduced crime or the more direct explanations for the temporary rise. Nor are they addressing the dramatic growth in the popularity of video games, including violent video games, during the years when violent crime rates were plummeting.

Smoke and Mirrors

Some researchers have described what they call "instructive parallels" between the relationship of media violence to youth aggression and the relationship of smoking to lung cancer.[13] By using meta-analyses that pool the results of many different studies (more on that later), they conclude that the effect size (the strength of the relationship) of the violent media-aggression link is almost as big as the smoking-lung cancer link.

We agree that there are instructive parallels here. But they don't strengthen the case for media violence increasing aggression—they *undermine* it. Here's why:

• **Lung cancer was a rare disease** before cigarette smoking became common; now it's the leading cause of cancer deaths. Aggressive behavior was not rare before electronic media became popular.

- **Lung cancer rates increase as smoking rates go up** and decrease as they go down. We can see this not only in the population as a whole, but among subgroups (men, women, rich, poor, East Coast, Midwest and so forth). No matter how you look at the group, the more smoking, the more cancer. We see nothing like this relationship when we look at violent video games and such measures of real-world violence as violent crimes committed by minors.
- **There is a well-understood physiological mechanism** for how cigarette smoke triggers cancer. The process by which violence in media leads to real-life violence still inhabits the realm of speculation and ad-hoc theory.
- **There's a dose-response relationship** between smoking and lung cancer. Although it's mediated by genes and environmental factors (such as exposure to asbestos), in general the more a person smokes, the higher his or her risk of lung cancer. It's not clear whether greater exposure to violent video games (More hours of play? More years of play? Choosing games with more blood?) is related to greater effects on children. Our surveys of middle school youth did find some interesting correlations, which we'll describe in the next chapter.
- **Lung cancer is a clearly defined set of diseases**; we know it when we see it, and experts pretty much agree on diagnostic methods and results. A pathologist looking at a cancer cell in Boston will almost always reach the same diagnosis as a pathologist looking at the same cell in Bangkok or in Barcelona. But experts definitely differ on how to define and "diagnose" aggressive or violent behavior, both in artificial (laboratory) settings and by real kids on playgrounds or in classrooms.
- **The relationship of smoking to lung cancer is obviously a one-way street, with a clear direction of causality**. People who have cancer or a genetic predisposition to cancer are not more likely than other people to seek out cigarettes! But it's likely that children who are already more aggressive than their peers prefer and seek out violent media programs and games. It's possible that time spent with a violent game or movie could help shape or trigger aggressive impulses in aggressive children. Perhaps a high level of violent media consumption could be a marker for existing aggression.
- **Exposure to cigarette smoke is easy to observe and can be measured in agreed-upon ways** (although it's tougher for second-hand smoke).

"Exposure" to video game violence is subject to argument and difficult to measure. In some ways, measuring exposure to violent video games is easier than measuring exposure to TV violence; at least you know the child is paying attention when playing a video game. But in a television program or film, everyone who watches is exposed to the same violence. In a video game, different players can be exposed to dramatically different amounts and types of violence even though they play the same number of hours.

- **The reliability (consistency) of measurement over time** is also different. Cancerous cells will still be present three hours later, while aggressive thoughts or behavior may have gone away.
- **We know that starting smoking at a young age increases the risk** of addiction, long-term use and cancer. We don't know if young people of a particular age are at higher risk from voluntary play of violent video games. For example, we might want to pay extra attention to the media use of young teens. Why? Because parents monitor them less closely than they watch younger children, just when their stage of emotional, social and brain development might make them more vulnerable to the influence of violent media.[14][15]

My Way or the Highway

The wildly divergent opinions about video game violence may partially reflect professional training and background. Different researchers and theorists sometimes see things quite differently because of their experiences and perspectives. One of the challenges faced by our own highly diverse research team was keeping track of all its members' different underlying assumptions. We soon realized that when it comes to research design, psychologists think differently than public health people, who think differently than biologists, who think differently than psychiatrists. We had to get all of our assumptions and biases out on the table, argue a little, then draw on the best of our combined training to maximize the links between our research and the real world.

In 1995, Dave Grossman wrote the book *On Killing: The Psychological Cost of Learning to Kill in War and Society*. It was based on his experience as an army ranger and as a teacher at the U.S. Military Academy at West

Point. He claimed direct connections between the training (in values and in methods of killing) that military recruits receive and what children experience through "shooter" video game play. He saw "point and shoot video games" as simulators for practicing murder. (We'll address the claim that children can literally learn to shoot from a video game in chapter 8.)

Henry Jenkins, PhD, director of the Comparative Media Studies Program at the Massachusetts Institute of Technology, has published widely on the use of video games for education. He's skeptical of the assumptions that underlie the proposed link between playing violent video games and learning to become a killer:

> Grossman's model only works if:
>
> - we remove training and education from a meaningful cultural context.
> - we assume learners have no conscious goals and that they show no resistance to what they are being taught.
> - we assume that they unwittingly apply what they learn in a fantasy environment to real world spaces.
>
> The military uses games as part of a specific curriculum, with clearly defined goals, in a context where students actively want to learn and have a need for the information being transmitted. There are consequences for not mastering those skills.[16]

Craig Anderson and Brad Bushman are experimental psychologists. In that role, they develop laboratory experiments that try to shed light on what's happening in the real world. When done well, such laboratory data can be extremely powerful, much as laboratory data using test tubes and petri dishes can give us tremendous insights into biological processes that take place in living organisms. But for a laboratory experiment to provide useful information about the real world, the assumptions (model) the researchers use have to be explicit, and have to make sense. Anderson and Bushman state:

> It is important to note that real-world aggression measures (e.g., violent crime) share few surface features with laboratory aggression measures (e.g., delivery of electric shock). However, these

aggression measures do share the conceptual features of delivering a noxious stimulus to a victim with the intent and expectation
of harming the victim.[17]

Here, the researchers fail to differentiate between aggression and
violence. Their logic assumes that the subjects in these experiments—
usually college students who participate to earn some spending money
or to get extra credit for a class—cannot tell fantasy from reality and
don't know that "punishing" a person with a mild electric shock or a 9
mm pistol will lead to different outcomes. Can someone who delivers a
brief blast of noise really be said to have the same malicious intent as
someone who shoots a convenience store clerk or stabs someone in a
bar fight?

Consider the famous experiment[18] conducted in the early 1960s at
Yale by Stanley Milgram, PhD, in which participants were duped into
believing that they were delivering painful or even life-threatening electric shocks to a person they could hear but could not see. The participants
typically showed symptoms of acute stress during these experiments—
including profuse sweating, trembling and stuttering—things not seen in
video game violence experimental research.

To understand other factors behind the standoff on video game violence's effects, we need to take a closer look at the research process.

Designing a Video Game Violence Study: A Primer

In fairness, studying the influence of violent video games is much harder
than it appears. What do researchers actually do to find out whether
media violence makes kids aggressive? Let's walk step-by-step through
some of the basic decisions and assumptions that scientists have to make
when they design and carry out a study.

WHOM WILL WE STUDY? As we've seen, much of the fuss over video
games has involved putative links to school shootings or other real-life
violence. So, why don't researchers study teens or young adults who've
committed or attempted murder? Here, we run into our first problem.
Teenage murderers and rapists may have played Mature-rated video

games, but, as you'll see in chapter 4, so have most of the law-abiding boys on your local middle school soccer team.

Violent video game play is extremely common, and violent crime is relatively rare. This makes it tough to document whether and how violent video and computer games contribute to serious violence, such as criminal assault or murder. Criminals are also much more likely to have past exposure to other factors, such as poverty, alcoholism, family violence or parental neglect, that are known contributors to violent behavior.

There are also practical and ethical barriers. Most research conducted today that involves people must be approved by institutional review boards (IRBs), also called human subjects committees. To IRBs, prisoners are a "vulnerable population" because they are subject to coercion and control. Because of past research abuses, research subjects must be fully informed about the nature of the research and must feel free to decline to participate without fear of reprisal or loss of benefits. (In the best-known case of abuse, the Tuskegee Syphilis Study, participants were so shockingly exploited that the survivors received a presidential apology in 1997.[19]) While studying felons is not impossible, getting a large and representative group to sign on would be very difficult.

What about just studying teenagers? There are lots of them around. The question then becomes, what kinds of kids do we include, and whom do we exclude? Do we want children who are at highest risk for aggression? If so, how will we identify them: A questionnaire? Interviews with teachers? Or, is there an age when children might be most vulnerable to the effects of video game violence, so that we should focus on studying that group's game play?

If we want the results of this study to help kids and want that help to be effective and cost-efficient, it's important to focus on those children who are at the greatest risk. Violent games might be a bigger influence on children who lack the protection of a nurturing relationship with a caring adult, don't feel connected to a community or are falling behind in school.

If we want to look at the effects of violent video games on young teenagers, does it makes sense to study a representative group of children under seventeen? Or could we accurately extrapolate from results of studies on high-risk kids, or even studies of college students enrolled in Psychology 101? The latter group is a popular choice, because children under eighteen are also considered a "vulnerable population" for research purposes.

Often, researchers are required to obtain a signed parent consent form for each participating child, plus a signed "assent" from the child. If you've ever helped round up signed permission forms for a class trip to the museum, you can imagine how much harder it is to get detailed research consent forms returned!*

Since school is a primary gathering place for children, researchers often try to use schools as sources of research subjects. Principals and teachers can be less than enthusiastic. With increased government mandates and testing, there is very little discretionary time in which to hand out questionnaires. They also dislike the disruption of routines, especially when there is no clear benefit to the school. In areas with many colleges and universities (such as the Boston area, where we work), many schools are overwhelmed with requests and are fed up.

Let's say that we successfully woo a principal and gain access to a school. We send out the consent forms, and even with follow-up mailings or phone calls, only 40 percent come back with parent signatures. (That's not unusual.) How do we know whether the group of signed-up children is similar to the group whose parents declined or didn't bother to fill in the form? Is their video game use the same? What about their household income, their cultural or ethnic background, their academic achievement, parental supervision of their game play, or any number of other factors that might affect the link between violent video games and aggressive behavior? This creates a problem with "generalizing" the results of our study to the overall population of children.

Another problem with studying children is: they're kids. They don't read and write as well as adults do. They get bored and make things up.

---

* Because we conducted our research under the auspices of the IRB at Massachusetts General Hospital, we were required to use the hospital's standard "informed consent" form, which covers all of its highly diverse research—most of which involves drug trials or new medical and surgical procedures. Consequently, even though we were only talking to people in an office, we were obligated to tell the participants in our focus groups that if they suffered any side effects from our conversations, they should immediately go to the nearest hospital emergency room!

They have trouble remembering or estimating potentially important things, such as how many hours they play video games during a typical week. At what age can kids be expected to fill out questionnaires or give accurate responses? Can older kids accurately recall what they did not only last week, but what they did a few years earlier?

As you can see, there are many possible answers just to the question of whom to study. Researchers make different choices based on what they want to find out (their "research question")—and frankly, on whom they can get to sign up. In the real world, time and resources are limited, and we sometimes have to make the best of things. However, researchers who study different populations may end up with divergent or even contradictory results. Studies that try to combine the results of many small studies on very diverse groups (e.g., ten-year-olds in Belgium, college undergraduates in Minnesota, and urban sixteen-year-olds who played arcade games in 1987) should be taken with a grain—make that a lump—of salt.

What Type of Study? It Depends on the Question

The design of a research study has a profound effect on what its findings can (and cannot) demonstrate. Here are three of the most common designs for research on the effects of violent media:

1. **A cross-sectional study**. This involves looking at behaviors at a particular point in time or during a relatively short period of time. We might find, for example, that children who report playing a particular type of violent video game, or who play for significantly more hours per day than their peers, are more likely to have lower grades in school. One problem with these studies is that the data only show correlations; we can't say that violent video game play *causes* poor grades, that frustration at school leads to more violent game play or that a third factor causes them both. We simply don't know.

2. **A longitudinal study**. This type of study measures children's video game play multiple times, over a long period of time. Some longitudinal studies in other fields have gone on for a half century or longer. As you can imagine,

these are extremely expensive to run. They also tend to involve smaller samples of participants, some of whom will probably drop out or move away before the study ends. Also, by the time you finish your study, social or technological changes may make your findings irrelevant. The graphics and plotlines of 1980s arcade-based games such as *Pac-Man* and the original *Mortal Kombat* bear little resemblance to the home-based violent video games of today. In a few years, games with holographic images and full-body interactivity could make today's studies less relevant.

3. **Laboratory experiments**, such as pre/post experimental studies. This is the most common type of study done in this field. Participants play a game in a controlled situation, which can range from a spare room in an after-school program to inside an fMRI machine at a neuroimaging center. After subjects are exposed to the video games, researchers measure some sort of behavior or physiological response, either immediately or after a delay. They look for relationships between the exposure (say, to a violent game versus a nonviolent game) and the behavior or response.

Because laboratory experiments are, by definition, carried out in controlled environments, one has to be careful about making the leap not only from correlation to causation (e.g., exposure to video games causes participants to feel more aggressive) but from the laboratory to the real world (e.g., that a 0.1-second difference in the length of an air horn blast immediately after playing means that this person is more likely to behave violently after playing a violent video game at home).

VIDEO GAME VIOLENCE: HOW MUCH, AND WHAT KIND? Now that we've chosen a group to study, how will we measure whether, and how much, our group is exposed to video game violence? Suppose we've settled on a cross-sectional study of real children or adolescents. We might ask them (or their parents) about games they play a lot or their favorite games. We could give them diaries and ask them to record what they play, and how long, every day for a week. We could watch them play (live or on videotape) and count how many murders of human-like characters they see per hour of game play. We could go to kids' homes and look at the number or proportion of game cartridges and discs that are rated Teen or Mature.

Each method has pros and cons and requires a set of additional decisions. For example, if we count game cartridges: Do we only include those played within the last month? Six months? At least once a week, or for at least an hour per week? What about rented games or games played at friends' houses?

Another complication is that unlike movies, video game play is non-linear; each child who plays follows a somewhat different sequence. And the more flexible the play a game allows, the more variation in exposure to violence there will be. For example, in *Grand Theft Auto: Vice City,* you can make Tommy Vercetti rampage through the city in ugly plaid golf pants, literally chainsawing through everyone in his path, or he can peacefully deliver pizzas. In this case, a child's game play would need to be observed for hours to get a sense of how much vicarious violence he or she is experiencing.

One might use ESRB ratings or content descriptors to assess levels of game violence. (Our surveys used a variation of this method.) But there is some debate about the accuracy of ESRB ratings, including how violence is defined and labeled. In a study of violent content in E-rated games,[20] researchers Kimberly Thompson, ScD, and Kevin Haninger, PhD, chose not to count routine aggressive behavior in sports games—such as tackling in football or checking in hockey—as violent, because there is no real intent to harm. As you'll see in chapter 7, parents in our focus groups shared this view. They also would probably agree with the researchers' definition of violence as "acts in which the aggressor causes or attempts to cause physical injury or death to another character."

Interestingly, the definition of "character" is where these researchers and our parents of preteens part company. The parents were bothered by violence against realistic human or at least humanoid characters. Thompson and Haninger "defined characters broadly, including personified objects that attacked either the player or other characters." Using this definition, one of the study's most violent games, in terms of percentage of screen time (72 percent), was *Kirby 64: The Crystal Shards*. Kirby is a smiling pink puffball who inhabits a number of Nintendo games. We have a hard time picturing Kirby as a violent role model.

Of course, parents of young children may be more concerned about animated violence, and researchers have every right to define terms as they see fit. Sources of honest disagreement would be easier to spot if all researchers explained their assumptions and methods as clearly as in this study.

Also, how much violence is too much? If we assume that any and all exposure to violent games is harmful, we end up treating the majority of preteens and teens as abnormal. This doesn't make sense. As Griffiths noted above, "More evidence is needed on excessive play—and on defining what constitutes excess in the first place."[21] We need to know what "normal" is so that we can meaningfully measure behaviors against it.

Finally, as you'll see in chapter 5, not all violence appears to have equal effects on game players' thoughts, feelings and behaviors.

A Rose by Any Other Name?

A key part of any research design is establishing what's known as "validity." In other words, are you really measuring what you think you're measuring? This can be tricky.

Let's begin by looking at some famous longitudinal studies. Because video games are a relatively new medium, researchers looking for evidence about their long-term effects often point to well-known studies of TV violence. One such study[22] followed children from northern New York State for seventeen years and found that young teens (and young adults) who watched three or more hours of television a day were later involved in more fights, robbery and aggressive acts in general.

However, the researchers didn't bother to measure what these children watched on TV. They assumed all content was basically the same. After all, as they pointed out, "violent acts are depicted frequently on television."

They also noted that "childhood neglect, growing up in an unsafe neighborhood, low family income, low parental education, and psychiatric disorders were significantly associated with time spent watching television at mean age 14 and aggressive acts at mean age 16 or 22." Even though researchers tried to account for these factors in their analyses, it's not at all obvious that more time with television causes more aggressive behavior. It's just as plausible that heavy TV-watching represents a poverty of options—no safe places to play outside, poorer social skills, or no access to social, intellectual or artistic activities that support healthy development.

A study of Chicago grade-schoolers[23] found that watching violent shows and identifying with aggressive characters was linked to aggressive behavior fifteen years later. Researchers asked children to choose their favorites from lists of popular programs and whether they watched these shows "every time it's on," "a lot but not always," or "once in a while."

Two raters coded the amount of physical violence in each show on a five-point scale from "no violence" to "very violent," based on "visually depicted, interpersonal acts that were intended to harm." Nature-show violence was excluded. The examples of "very violent" programs listed by the researchers were *Starsky and Hutch, The Six Million Dollar Man*, and Road Runner cartoons. (This is a great example of how changing social standards make longitudinal studies so chancy. When we describe this study in presentations, it always gets a laugh.)

Children were also asked about how much they acted like particular male or female "aggressive characters" such as the Bionic Woman or the Six-Million-Dollar Man. It's unclear why kids were not supposed to identify with these heroic figures: a tennis pro and an astronaut who overcome catastrophic injuries and pursue assorted bad guys and spies.

Measuring exposure to game violence in laboratory studies has a completely different set of challenges. If the study will compare reactions to a violent game versus a nonviolent game, how do we choose appropriate games for our tests? In some studies, an action-packed violent game goes head-to-head against a tranquil nonviolent game. In one case, researchers compared *Wolfenstein 3D* (which involves killing Nazis in the corridors of a fortress prison) to *Myst* (a surreal puzzle-solving and exploration game) on the basis that both involved a "3-D walk-through format."[24] For these comparisons to make sense, games need comparable levels of emotional excitement and physiological arousal.

In this study of college students, as in many similar studies, play times were extremely short. Participants were seated at a computer, read an instruction sheet, played for fifteen minutes—then completed a questionnaire on how they were feeling. As those of us who've struggled to survive even a few minutes in an unfamiliar game can attest, any increase in hostility or anger could easily be due to frustration over trying to learn a new game so quickly! Also, this experience is far removed from that of a typical child who plays self-selected games in a familiar environment, perhaps with friends, over a long period of time. There's also the issue of whether we can accurately extrapolate from college students to young teenagers.

WHAT IS THIS THING CALLED "AGGRESSION"—AND HOW DO WE MEASURE IT? If we're going to study aggression, we need to know it when we see it. "Violence" is somewhat easier: a person or thing gets physically attacked with the intent to injure or break it. But the definition of "aggression" can be surprisingly slippery and is another factor behind the warring interpretations of video game research.

Some researchers use "aggression" and "violence" almost interchangeably, implying that one inevitably leads to the other. That's simply not true. A common definition of aggression as used by psychologists is "behavior leading to self-assertion; it may arise from innate drives and/or a response to frustration, and may be manifested by destructive and attacking behavior, by hostility and obstructionism, or by self-expressive drive to mastery."[25] As you can see, some behaviors can be aggressive but not violent.

For most media violence studies, some aspect of aggression is the "outcome" that's measured. A classic example is the 1960s experimental studies by Albert Bandura, PhD, of Stanford University on young children's imitation of aggression.[26] He used what are known as Bobo dolls—inflatable plastic clowns several feet tall that have a weighted round bottom. If you hit or push the top, the doll topples over and then springs back up.

Children watched an adult (on film) either attacking a Bobo doll (punching it or hitting it with a mallet) or playing quietly with other toys while ignoring the Bobo doll. Children were more likely to attack the doll when they saw that behavior modeled by an adult. (One problem with this study is that there's not much you can do with a big inflatable Bobo doll other than punch it and watch it bounce back!)

Some of the most-publicized experimental studies done by other researchers use a "noise blast" as a stand-in for aggressive behavior. As one study[27] describes it, "The participant's goal is to push a button faster than his or her [nonexistent] opponent. If participants lose this race, they receive a noise blast at a level supposedly set by the opponent (actually set by the computer)." The study participants, in turn, are told to set a loudness level for the noise that their opponent will hear if he or she loses. "Aggression is operationally defined as the intensity and duration of noise blasts the participant chooses to the deliver to the opponent." This is basically white noise, the "whishing" sound you hear between channels when tuning a radio. The test is an adaptation of an earlier measure that used electric shocks instead of sound.

Christopher J. Ferguson, PhD, at the Department of Behavioral, Applied Sciences and Criminal Justice at Texas A&M International University, takes issue with the noise-blast test:

> Most people outside of research associate aggression with physically trying to hurt someone. Whether the noise blast corresponds with anything like that is very debatable. My guess is that it's actually a better measure of competitiveness, which is right in the name: the Taylor Competitive Reaction Time test. In my opinion, it's a far cry from beating someone to death, or even spanking or slapping someone, because it's not that aversive.

In science, new measures are supposed to be "validated," or proven to represent something in the real world. For example, if we developed a new questionnaire or physical test to screen for depression, we would need to show that the test scores of people who'd been formally diagnosed with depression were different from the scores of people known not to be depressed. At minimum, we'd need to compare our test results to some existing validated questionnaire. But the "noise blast" test has never been validated as a measure of aggression. Without such validation, we are simply asked to accept someone else's belief that the test means what is being claimed.

As Ferguson points out:

> The test ranges from zero to ten. But it's not, "If you score above seven you're a violent individual, below seven you're in the nor-

mal range, and below three you're a pacifist." Say that study Group A gets a 5, and Group B gets a 5.4. Does that mean that Group B is ready to go out and riot? No. Nobody knows what *any* of these scores mean. I think the noise blast test could be salvageable if put into a standardized, reliable format and subjected to rigorous testing.

As we write this, Ferguson is undertaking studies to try to validate the noise-blast test.

Some real-world studies, especially of younger children, look at aggressive behavior on the playground after exposure to violent games or cartoons. But is this really unhealthy, potentially dangerous aggression, or is it normal rough-and-tumble play?

Michael Jellinek, MD, is a professor of psychiatry and pediatrics at Harvard Medical School, the chief of child and adolescent psychiatry at Massachusetts General Hospital and the president of Newton-Wellesley Hospital. He points out:

> A normal kid on the playground who's playing army or spaceman, and pushing his friend or trying to vaporize him but never hurting him—that's normal, healthy fantasy play. It's totally consistent with the biological nature of 10-year-old boys.

Another problem is that today's aggressive first-grader may be tomorrow's thoughtful teen. According to the Surgeon General's 2001 report on youth violence,[28] most children who are aggressive or engage in antisocial behavior *do not* grow up to be violent adolescents or adults—and most violent adolescents were not notably aggressive as children.

Finally, how do we know whether kids with different personalities or behavioral styles respond differently to the same video games? What about how they're feeling just before they start to play? Several Australian researchers looked at those issues with respect to anger, which they saw as related to aggression and violent behavior:

> The results demonstrated that some people increase, some decrease and the majority saw no change in anger ratings. Unlike

past research, we also demonstrate that these changes are mediated by the player's feelings immediately prior to game play and a labile temperament—one predisposed to aggression.[29]

DO THE RESULTS MATTER? So, we've measured changes in aggressive behavior, mood or attitudes. How do we decide whether exposure to media violence has made a difference? Also, what's the effect size? That is, how much of a difference does what you're measuring really make?

For Ferguson, this is a sore point when he sees experimental results described on television and in newspaper stories:

> When these things get reported to the general public, there's no discussion of what an effect size is and what it means. It's "Study A shows a relationship between video games and aggression." And people think that's a very conclusive, important finding. But when you look at the effect size, sometimes it's near zero.
>
> For example, twin studies of antisocial or violent behavior find that about 50% of the variation [the R-squared effect size] is due to genetics. That's a pretty powerful effect. By comparison, the R-squared effect size for media violence—including television—ranges anywhere from one percent to nine percent. So you're getting anywhere from one fifth to one fiftieth the bang for the buck you'd get from a genetic effect.

If you were four percent more aggressive today than yesterday, could anybody tell the difference?

Most important: Does the new study help parents recognize whether their child is at risk of, or already has, problems related to violent video games? Academic research on video game effects is not geared to the needs of parents. You can't scan your child's brain at home, even if anything meaningful could be found that way. Parents need markers that they can observe and specific things they can do to prevent problems or catch them early.

One could make the argument, as Anderson does, that small effect sizes can be significant because of the overall long-term exposure:

If youths spent only a little time playing violent video games (e.g., less than 30 minutes per week), or if only a few youths spent a lot of time playing such games (e.g., 1 in 10,000), then the overall cost to society would likely be fairly small. But . . . a lot of youths are playing violent video games for many hours per week. When large numbers of youths (including young adults) are exposed to many hours of media violence (including violent video games), even a small effect can have extremely large societal consequences.[30]

It's absolutely true that across a population, small things can add up to a big difference. Consider salt intake and cardiovascular disease, for example. But we don't assume that all people are equally affected by a medical risk and that the same remedy is good for all. Some people are not salt sensitive and would give up better-tasting food for no benefit; others might be healthier with a little extra salt. One glaring problem with most studies of violent game effects is their failure to consider which groups are most at risk and should therefore lower or monitor their time spent playing games, which groups are probably at little or no risk (at least with moderate use) and whether any groups might even benefit from a little downtime with a joystick.

Violent Video Games and the History of the Bathtub

Now there's an odd juxtaposition! But it's relevant as a cautionary tale when you hear published research results being bandied about. One of the most important skills you can use as both a scientist and as a parent is skepticism.

During World War I, the eminent journalist H. L. Mencken wrote an article in the *New York Evening Mail* that purported to give a history of the bathtub. It was a joke, designed to provide his readers with some respite from the awful news of the day. Mencken later described his article as "a tissue of absurdities, all of them deliberate and most of them obvious."[31] These included descriptions of physicians calling the bathtub dangerous and laws passed against it in Massachusetts and Pennsylvania.

His essay struck a chord. It was reprinted in newspapers across the country. Then Mencken started noticing something strange. His intentionally absurd claims were being quoted in reputable publications as undisputed facts. "They began to be cited by medical men as proof of the progress of public hygiene. They got into learned journals. They were alluded to on the floor of Congress. . . . Finally, I began to find them in standard works of reference. Today, I believe, they are accepted as gospel everywhere on earth. To question them becomes as hazardous as to question the Norman invasion."[32]

Take another look at the quote at the beginning of this chapter, the one about the "3500 research studies." It doesn't make any sense. But it's cited all the time. Where did that number come from? We decided to trace it back as far as we could.

The list of citations at the end of the American Academy of Pediatrics policy statement gives the book *Stop Teaching Our Kids to Kill* as the source. That book, in turn, lists a 1998 article published in Sweden by the United Nations Educational, Scientific and Cultural Organization (UNESCO), which states, "Over the past forty plus years more than 3,500 research studies on the effects of television violence on viewers have been conducted in the United States."[33] There is no information given about how the authors arrived at that number.

In all fairness, we should point out that the media researchers in the next quote who claim that "there are probably fewer than 300 empirical studies that try to measure the effects of violent media" don't demonstrate how they came up with that number, either. But it sounds much more logical.

NOT ALL STUDIES ARE CREATED EQUAL There are even fewer studies about the effects of violent video games on aggression. In a 2001 review, John L. Sherry, PhD, of Purdue University found "32 independent studies in which violent video game play was the independent variable and some measure of aggression was the dependent variable."[34] He concluded, "There is a small effect of video game play on aggression, and the effect is smaller than [that of] violent television."

In a separate review published the same year, Anderson and Bushman found thirty-five reports (some with multiple studies) in a psychology research database.[35] Their analysis included many of the same studies used by Sherry. Yet their conclusion was different: "These results clearly support the hypothesis that exposure to violent video games poses a public health threat to children and youths."

We decided to take a closer look at the studies reviewed by Anderson and Bushman. Unusually, there is no listing of these studies in their paper; instead, the reader is directed to a Web site. We reviewed the list and tracked down full-text copies of as many of those studies as we could.

Of the twenty-one experimental and thirteen correlational studies included, about one third are dissertations or other unpublished research, making descriptions difficult to obtain. Across the peer-reviewed correlational studies, subjects and measures varied widely. Many focused on time spent playing games and did not ask about content; those few that did ask about content used vague measures such as a stated preference for aggressive games. Outcomes had little to do with real-world aggressive behavior (perhaps the closest being teacher observations of free play). Some studies were from the 1980s, when children still primarily played video games in arcades. Study samples were small. (The largest is a survey of 278 Dutch children.) There is little or no information on response rates or other means to assess the characteristics or the representativeness of the samples. (One sample included students at a high school for "disturbed young people.") The study that came closest to looking at effects of violent games on children's aggressive behavior (a British study of two hundred and four students aged twelve to fourteen) found that "aggression scores were not related to the number of games with aggressive content [children] named among three favourite games."[36]

As we said at the start of this chapter, this is not an exhaustive review of research on video game violence but an attempt to examine why experts disagree about its effects. However, it seems clear that despite the worrisome conclusions that appear in the popular press, there are very few studies involving current violent video games and real children.

Statistical Significance vs. Real-World Significance

The term "statistical significance" refers to the odds against something occurring simply by chance. Let's say that you claim that you have supernatural powers and can use them to blindly select an ace from a full deck of cards. You know this because you tried it once and picked an ace.

How could we decide whether your supernatural powers are real? Let's leave aside issues of research design such as making sure that you agree on what an ace is, that the cards are adequately and randomly shuffled and that no one is cheating, and focus on interpreting the results.

In a standard deck, four of the fifty-two cards (one in thirteen) are aces. That means that you'd choose an ace, on average, one out of every thirteen tries simply as a matter of chance. But what if you were able to select two aces in a row? Would that prove that you have supernatural powers? What if you did it twice, then failed the next twenty-eight times, and then were successful again?

Statisticians can look at those different success rates and calculate the odds that the results are occurring simply by chance. That's what a test of statistical significance is. It's usually expressed as a probability or "p value." If the difference between your actual performance (you selected three aces out of thirty-one tries) and your expected performance that's attributable to chance or dumb luck (you select three aces out of thirty-nine tries—one in thirteen) is described as significant at the $p < .05$ level, that means that there's less than a 5 percent chance that you've simply been lucky. If it's significant at the $p < .01$ level, then the odds that it's a fluke are less than one in a hundred.

There are two technical things to keep in mind here. The first is that the more people you're dealing with—that is, the larger the sample size—the more you should be looking for higher levels of significance. For example, in our survey of over 1,200 teenagers, we didn't focus on findings at the $p < .05$ level; we looked for findings at the $p < .01$ or $p < .001$ levels before we paid serious attention to them.

Also, some statistically significant differences may be mathematically sound but irrelevant to the real world. For example, an experimental study may find small but consistent differences in the heart rates of game players exposed to violent vs. nonviolent games. The findings may be significant at the $p<.05$ or even the $p<.01$ levels. But that doesn't mean that those differences actually make a difference in predicting a person's future or even immediate behavior.

META-ANALYSES AND THE "FILE DRAWER PROBLEM" The two research reviews mentioned above used a statistical method called "meta-analysis." It is a very powerful and respected technique when used as intended, gleaning important information through synthesizing studies that are too small or otherwise problematic to rely on individually (such as studies of the best drug treatment for a particular heart problem, or among people of a certain age group). But as one how-to article on meta-analysis puts it, "Even though the statistics used in meta-analysis are quite sophisticated, the end product will never be better than the individual studies that make up the meta-analysis."[37] In other words: garbage in, garbage out.

Goldstein raises another important issue that affects meta-analyses: the "file drawer problem":

> Published research in scholarly journals does not represent all the research on electronic games. Studies that fail to find statistically significant results are less likely to be accepted for publication. So the published record is an unknown fraction of all research, and it tends to consist of those studies with statistically significant results. This is known as the "file drawer problem" because studies that do not find any effects of video games remain unpublished, locked away in the researcher's files.[38]

The file drawer problem is an open secret among academic researchers. The editors of academic journals generally think that positive results are more interesting and more likely to be cited by future researchers, which is one measure of a journal's influence and prestige.

They're more likely to publish research that finds a relationship or a significant difference between two things than a study that shows no relationship.

If findings don't fit the hypothesized results, researchers may assume their study was somehow flawed in methods or analyses and keep trying for a more acceptable outcome. Or they may simply decide to bury undesired or embarrassing results.

The existence or extent of publication bias in a given body of research can be estimated using advanced statistical methods. In a recent meta-analysis,[39] Ferguson found a pattern of missing studies, particularly for experimental studies of aggressive behavior and nonexperimental studies of aggressive behavior and thoughts.

> The problem is this focus on statistical significance testing—this sort of black-and-white, either-you-have-it-or-you-don't kind of thing. You get these tiny, tiny little effects that become statistically significant the bigger your sample size is. But how meaningful are those results?

Our point is simply this: be skeptical of claims about violent video games. You don't need a degree in statistics to judge research for yourself. When you hear about a new study that "proves" the link between video games and aggressive or violent kids, ask yourself:

❖ Whom did they actually study?

❖ How did they define "violence" in video games or television programs?

❖ How did they measure exposure to video game violence?

❖ How did they define "aggression"? What did they use as a measure of aggression? How do they justify the relationship of this measure to real-world aggression or violence?

❖ Does that measure pass the common-sense test?

In the next chapter, we'll describe some findings from our own research and what they mean to you as a parent. We urge you to apply these questions to our research as well.

Justified Violence

Imagine the following gruesome plot: A mob rapes and beats a concubine all night. They leave her bloodied corpse on a doorstep to be discovered in the morning. Her master takes her home, carves her body into twelve pieces and incites another mob to seek revenge. They do, killing tens of thousands of men, women, children and animals, and destroying a city.

It sounds a bit like a violent video game. It's not; it's a story from an obscure passage in the Bible (Judges 19-21) that was used in two interesting studies of the influence of religious beliefs and attributions on responses to violent media. Half the participants who read the passage were told of its Biblical origins. The other participants were told that the text was from an ancient scroll. In each group, half were given a version that included two sentences from the original text in which God commands the mob to undertake the violent retaliation; the version that the other half read did not include the commands from God.

In the first study, the participants were students at Brigham Young University, of whom 99 percent said that they believed in God and in the Bible (the religious group). In the second study, they were students at Vrije Universiteit in Amsterdam, of whom 50 percent said that they believed in God and 27 percent said that they believed in the Bible (the nonreligious group).

The researchers measured differences in the intensities of noise blasts on a competitive test conducted immediately after reading the material. (Note that this design suffers from the same weaknesses as other research using these noise blasts as stand-ins for violent behavior, as we described above. It also only measured immediate effects, not long-term effects.)

They summarize their research results: "We found compelling evidence that exposure to a scriptural depiction of violence or to violence authorized by deity can cause readers to behave more aggressively. . . . Aggressive responses were greater when a violent depiction was attributed to a scriptural source than when it was attributed to an ancient scroll and were also greater when the violence was said to be sanctioned by God than when God was not mentioned. . . . Even among our participants who were not religiously devout, exposure to God-sanctioned violence increased subsequent aggression. That the effect was found in such a sample may attest to the insidious power of exposure to literary scriptural violence."[40]

We should note that the lead author of this research article, Brad Bushman, PhD, is well known for his research on the potentially harmful effects of video games, and we commend him for exploring this "politically incorrect" topic. But we also note that in their conclusion, the researchers offer advice that is quite different from that offered by many video game researchers, including Bushman, who found less-compelling results when measuring the effects of that medium:

"Does this ultimately mean that one should avoid reading religious canon for fear that the violent episodes contained therein will cause one to become more aggressive, or that individuals who read the scriptures will become aggressive? Not necessarily. Violent stories that teach moral lessons or that are balanced with descriptions of victims' suffering or the aggressor's remorse can teach important lessons and have legitimate artistic merit."[41]

Unfortunately, the story they used in their experiments does not teach any moral lessons. (To the contrary, the full text describes murder, capturing women as slaves and ways to get around promises that you've made.) There is very little description of the victims' suffering aside from the insult felt by the master of the concubine. Nor is there much remorse for their acts of genocide. So it's difficult to see what important prosocial lessons are being taught.

The authors tie this finding to the behavior of contemporary terrorists who are religious fundamentalists, stating that reading selected violent scriptures might partially account for their behaviors. In essence, they say that this type of violent religious story will have a good effect on most people, but a bad effect on a population that's at greater risk of violent behavior due to other causes. But video game opponents argue the opposite when it comes to that technology: the games are dangerous because their influence over real-world aggression and violence extends to a broad range of people.

What's sauce for the goose should be sauce for the gander.

CHAPTER 4

Grand Theft Childhood?

For every problem there is a solution that is simple, neat and wrong.

—*H. L. Mencken (1880-1956)*

WE FOUND THE SOMEWHAT SARCASTIC QUOTE ABOVE reprinted in the unlikeliest of places: a federal government report called *The School Shooter: A Threat Assessment Perspective*,[1] published in 2000 by the FBI's National Center for the Analysis of Violent Crime. The report was written in response to the Columbine High School shootings in Littleton, Colorado, and was derived from detailed analyses of eighteen actual or successfully foiled school shootings.

At the time, politicians, pundits and school officials were calling for draconian actions to stanch the supposedly dramatic increase in school violence. Many of those crying the loudest lay blame for the school shootings on violent video games. At the FBI, cooler heads prevailed:

One response to the pressure for action may be an effort to identify the next shooter by developing a "profile" of the typical school shooter. This may sound like a reasonable preventive measure, but in practice, trying to draw up a catalogue or "checklist" of warning signs to detect a potential school shooter can be short-sighted, even dangerous. Such lists, publicized by the media, can end up unfairly labeling many nonviolent students as potentially dangerous or even lethal. In fact, a great many adolescents who will never commit violent acts will show some of the behaviors or personality traits included on the list. . . .

At this time, there is no research that has identified traits and characteristics that can reliably distinguish school shooters from other students. Many students appear to have traits and characteristics similar to those observed in students who were involved in school shootings.[2]

The FBI report mentions violent video games only in passing and within the context of pathological behaviors and personality types. It drives a metaphorical stake through the heart of the "violent video games cause school shootings" myth.

But school shootings are extremely rare events. Could playing violent video games promote aggressive behavior, increase fear, or desensitize children to violence? If the answer is "yes" or "maybe," then which kids are at greatest risk? Does the amount of time spent playing games matter, or who kids play with? Are there particular types of games that are worse for kids? And what can we do as parents to protect our kids?

Since 2004, we've been researching the answers to questions like these. In this chapter, we'll share findings from our survey of 1,254 middle school students in Pennsylvania and South Carolina. We'll also draw on comments from in-depth focus groups with middle school boys from Massachusetts who play violent video games.

How We Gathered Our Data

We ended chapter 3 with a list of questions you can use to judge the value of any video game violence study. In fairness, we should begin by answering those questions about our own study of middle school kids.

Whom did we study? We conducted detailed, written surveys in the classrooms of seventh and eighth graders in two middle schools in Pennsylvania (664 students) and South Carolina (590 students) during a Language Arts/English period. Nearly all of the participants were twelve to fourteen years old; half were thirteen.

We chose these schools because they gave us a good mix of kids— Northeastern and Southern, boys and girls, white and black, suburban and small city, richer and poorer—to make our results more applicable to American teens in general. Just as important, the principals and teachers were enthusiastic about working with us on the research. (Latino and Asian teens were underrepresented among the children we studied. We will include more of them in future research.)

We received approval from our human subjects committee at Massachusetts General Hospital to use "opt-out" consent forms. That meant that we could let parents know how to contact us if they didn't want their child included. Only a handful of parents and/or their children opted out of the survey. This meant our response rate was unusually high; virtually every eligible child who came to school that day took the survey. (School administrators exempted a few classrooms because the children had limited English skills or had disabilities that were serious enough to prevent them from participating.) To make the kids more comfortable and to encourage honest answers, their teachers never saw or touched the surveys.

How did we define "violence" in video games? At first, we planned to use Entertainment Software Rating Board "content descriptors"—the short phrases that appear on the back of the game box, under the letter rating. We developed a scale that rated violence from 0 to 3:

3 (high): "intense violence" or "sexual violence"
2 (moderate): "fantasy violence," "realistic violence" or "violence"
1 (low): other violence-related descriptors (e.g., "mild realistic violence," "cartoon violence")
0: no violence-related descriptors.

Unfortunately, these content descriptors were not designed to be rank ordered, so we weren't sure whether a 3 might be worse than a 2, and if so, by how much. They also didn't tell us anything about the context of violence, such as whether violent behavior is rewarded, which could affect the potential for imitation.

Parents in our focus groups seemed most concerned about games rated M (Mature, for ages seventeen and older). Virtually all games assigned this rating have substantial violent content; some have sexually suggestive content or nudity. Many proposed state and federal policies aim to keep M-rated games out of the hands of children under seventeen. So, to make the clearest and most useful distinction, we focused on children's exposure to M-rated games.

How did we measure exposure to video game violence? We asked participants to "list five games that you played a lot in the past six months." This was a straightforward way to find out which ones had recently spent a lot of time with M-rated games. All survey questions were about "electronic games," which we defined for them as "computer games, video games (Xbox, PlayStation, GameCube, etc.) and handheld games (Game Boy, etc.)."

Of the 1,254 kids who filled out surveys, 1,126 wrote down at least one game title, and most listed five. Our research assistants spent days combing through the survey forms, entering game titles into a database and matching them with ESRB ratings. (In cases where a child wrote a game series name, and that series had some recent titles with different ratings, we assigned the lower age rating to that child's game.)

Since the kids listed more than five thousand game titles or series, we merged titles from series with similar content and mode of play (e.g., *The Sims*) into single categories for analysis, ending up with about five hundred unique titles of games or game series. Over half were listed by only one child; 119 were listed by five or more children.

To help their memories, we also gave them a list of several hundred of the most popular games. As a check on the validity of their reporting, that list included some realistic titles of nonexistent games. No one selected a fake game title. All of the titles written down by the participants actually existed. This provides evidence that they were responding honestly.

How did we define "aggression"? What did we use as a measure of aggression? We reviewed existing research to find the best survey questions related to aggressive behaviors and attitudes, and to being a victim of aggression. We also asked about problems at school (such as getting into trouble with a teacher or principal) and delinquent behavior (such as damaging property for fun).

To make it easier to compare our results to those of other studies, we adapted or used questions from validated surveys designed for children or teens, including the Olweus Bully/Victim Questionnaire,[3] the Profiles of Student Life: Attitudes and Behaviors survey,[4] the Youth Risk Behavior Survey,[5] and other public-domain questionnaires compiled by the Centers for Disease Control.[6]

How did we justify the relationship of this measure to real-world aggression or violence? We asked kids about real-world behavior and experiences. We didn't ask about violent crime; we didn't expect that to be common among kids going to regular public schools, and we didn't want to ask kids to incriminate themselves.

How meaningful are the results? The differences between groups were large enough to make our results statistically significant. But were they of practical significance? As you'll see, in some cases, kids who regularly played M-rated games were two or three times more likely than others to have certain problems or experiences.

However, a cross-sectional study design can't prove cause and effect; it can only show correlations. In other words, a one-time survey can't tell us if, for example, playing M-rated games actually encouraged or triggered aggressive behaviors. It could be that kids who got into fights or suspended from school were more attracted to violent games, or that some third factor influenced both the violent game play and the aggressive behaviors.

Because of these limitations, we focused on identifying unusual patterns of play that could be markers of increased risk for aggression, or for other behavioral or emotional problems.

What's Normal?

To understand which children might have problems with video games, we first need to know what typical game play looks like. A few studies have looked at how much time children and teens spend with video games. In 2005, the Kaiser Family Foundation surveyed over two thousand kids in grades three to twelve.[7] On average, young teens spent seventeen minutes per day on computer games, thirty-two minutes on console games, and twenty minutes on handheld games.

The chart below shows some of the most common and striking game play habits of the boys and girls in our survey. Just seventeen children out of 1,254 had never played video or computer games; sixty-three others had not played during the six months prior to the survey. (Those eighty students were left out of our analyses.)

It's clear that typical video game play for seventh- and eighth-grade boys is very different from the norm for girls. When we asked children how many days per week they usually spent playing electronic games,

GAME PLAY HABITS	BOYS	GIRLS
Plays less than an hour per week	8%	32%
Plays 6 or more hours per week	45%	14%
Plays 15 or more hours per week	13%	2%
Plays 1 day per week	9%	23%
Plays 6 or 7 days per week	33%	11%
Usually plays games only on weekends	37%	43%
Plays games on at least 2 of these: computer, console, handheld device	84%	73%
Often/always plays alone	63%	46%
Often/always plays with multiple friends in the same room	33%	13%
Often/always plays games with friends over the Internet	11%	12%
Often/always plays games with strangers (people they'd never met in person) over the Internet	10%	5%

the most common response for girls was one day per week; for boys, it was six or seven days per week.

Half the girls and three-quarters of the boys said they often or always played video games at home. It was also common for boys in particular to play at a friend or relative's house.

Video games seem to have a more central role in the social lives of boys than of girls: although most boys played games alone at times, most also routinely played with one or more friends. Just 18 percent of boys and 12 percent of girls said they always played alone.

How Many Kids Are Playing Violent Games?

When we began planning our research studies, our son was in his last year of middle school. *Grand Theft Auto: Vice City* had recently come out. Our son mentioned that he was getting a little tired of hearing the boys at school, including the younger ones, brag about how they just got the game or talk excitedly about getting it soon. We thought he was exaggerating; after all, some of these kids were just eleven or twelve years old. This was a game rated M, for ages seventeen and up. How could so many of them be playing that game? We figured that maybe a few kids with older brothers at home would see it.

When our survey results came back, we learned that our son had been, if anything, understating the situation.

Games Thirteen-Year-Olds Play

Monthly and annual sales figures for video and computer games are tracked by corporations such as the NPD Group and are easy to find

Game Popularity: Frequency (%) of Games Among the Five Played Most Often by Boys in the Previous Six Months

GAME RANK	TITLE AND ESRB GAME/SERIES RATING	# OF BOYS LISTING ONE OR MORE IN THAT SERIES	ESRB CONTENT DESCRIPTORS
1	*Grand Theft Auto* (M)	242 (44%)	Blood and Gore, Intense Violence, Strong Language, Strong Sexual Content, Use of Drugs
2	*Madden NFL* (football) (E)	189 (34%)	No Descriptors
3	*Halo* (M)	154 (28%)	Blood and Gore, Violence
4	*NBA* (E)	111 (20%)	No Descriptors
5	*Tony Hawk* (skateboard) (T)	90 (16%)	Blood, Crude Humor, Language, Suggestive Themes, Use of Alcohol, Violence
6	*NCAA* (E)	85 (16%)	No Descriptors
7	*Need for Speed* (racing) (E or T)	76 (14%)	Mild Language, Suggestive Themes
8	*ESPN* (sports) (E)	56 (10%)	No Descriptors
9	*Medal of Honor* (T)	40 (7%)	Violence
10	*The Lord of the Rings* (T)	28 (5%)	Violence

Game Popularity: Frequency (%) of Games Among the Five Played Most Often by Girls in the Previous Six Months

GAME RANK	TITLE AND ESRB GAME/SERIES RATING	# OF GIRLS LISTING ONE OR MORE IN THAT SERIES	ESRB CONTENT DESCRIPTORS
1	*The Sims* (T)	177 (32%)	Crude Humor, Sexual Themes, Violence
2	*Grand Theft Auto* (M)	112 (20%)	Blood and Gore, Intense Violence, Strong Language, Strong Sexual Content, Use of Drugs
3	*Super Mario Brothers* (E)	73 (13%)	No Descriptors
4	*Tycoon* games (simulations) (E)	69 (12%)	Comic Mischief, Mild Violence
5	*Mario* games (unspecified) (E)	64 (11%)	No Descriptors or Mild Cartoon Violence
6	*Solitaire* (E)	63 (11%)	No Descriptors
7	*Tony Hawk* (skateboard) (T)	57 (10%)	Blood, Crude Humor, Language, Suggestive Themes, Use of Alcohol, Violence
8	*Dance Dance Revolution* (E)	55 (10%)	Lyrics, Suggestive Themes
9	*Mario Kart* (racing) (E)	53 (10%)	Mild Cartoon Violence
10	*Frogger* (E)	45 (8%)	No Descriptors

online. Unfortunately, there is no list of top-selling games by age of purchaser or player. That's why we need to ask children directly about what they play. In our survey, most game titles that kids listed (58 percent) were rated E; 20 percent were rated M. But some M-rated games were extremely popular.

Almost half of these middle school kids played at least one M-rated game "a lot": 68 percent of boys and 29 percent of girls. There was no difference by age group; about as many twelve-year-olds played M-rated games as did fourteen-year-olds. Ten percent of children played predominantly M-rated games (at least half of the games they listed were rated M).

The intensely violent, satirical *Grand Theft Auto* series was number one among boys and number two among girls; 44 percent of boys and 20 percent of girls routinely played one or more *GTA* games. The top five M-rated game series (based on the number of children who had at least one game in that series on their five-most-played list) were: *Grand Theft Auto* (listed by 359 children), *Halo* (185), *Def Jam* (52), *True Crime* (37) and *Driver* (34).* The average (mean) number of M-rated games played was similar in Pennsylvania and South Carolina.

Since we only asked about "five games played a lot," many more children had probably played a popular M-rated game at least once or twice. The Kaiser Family Foundation's 2005 media survey asked kids if they had ever played a *Grand Theft Auto* game; three-quarters (77 percent) of boys in grades seven to twelve said that they had.[8]

Are children who regularly play Mature-rated games different from children who don't? We compared children who had at least one M-rated title on their list of five games they played a lot to children who listed only games rated E or T.

As a group, children who played M-rated games spent more time with games. They were significantly more likely to play almost every day and to play fifteen or more hours a week. They were also more likely to play with several friends or to play with an older sibling. Teens who had a game console and computer in their bedroom were also more likely to play M-rated games.

Now that we have a glimpse at what typical video game play looks like, what patterns of play are less typical and may require watching by parents? First, most young adolescents who play M-rated games also play less-violent games. Playing M-rated games almost exclusively at that age is unusual enough to be a potential warning sign.

Also, boys were much more likely than girls to have played at least

---

* Note that because a few children skipped the survey question about gender, these totals are a little different than the numbers in the game popularity charts.

Portrait of the "M-Rated Game" Player

	PLAYED AT LEAST ONE M-RATED GAME "A LOT"	NO M-RATED GAMES ON THEIR "PLAYED A LOT" LIST
Plays 15 or more hours per week	11%	3%***
Plays 6 or 7 days per week	33%	14%***
Often/always plays with multiple friends in the same room	32%	16%***
Often/always plays with an older sibling	22%	12%***
Often/always plays games with friends over the Internet	14%	11%**
Often/always plays games with strangers over the Internet	11%	4%***

** STATISTICALLY SIGNIFICANT DIFFERENCES AT THE P<.01 LEVEL.

*** STATISTICALLY SIGNIFICANT DIFFERENCES AT THE P<.001 LEVEL.

one M-rated game "a lot in the past six months." They were also far more likely to play fifteen or more hours per week. This significant gender difference indicates that parents might keep an eye on girls who are frequent players of violent games.

Boys who never play video games are extremely unusual. Since game play is often a social activity for boys, this could be a marker of social problems that bear looking into. Contrary to parents' fears, M-rated game use was linked to playing with friends and was not associated with more time spent in solitary play. Many children have game consoles or computers in their bedrooms, and this is linked to greater amounts of play in general and more M-rated game play in particular.

Finally, we found that children who played M-rated games were twice as likely to play often or always with an older brother or sister. Given this correlation, if you have older teens or young adult children who are often at home, it might be wise to ask them to be careful about exposing younger siblings to mature content.

Do Violent Games Lead to Behavior Problems?

We asked boys in our focus groups whether the shooting, fighting and blood in the games they played might affect their behavior. Most said no; a few were concerned.

> Eric: "Yeah, definitely. 'Cause you might not want to fight a lot, and then when you play one of these games, you might want to fight more, so you might get in trouble a lot more."
>
> Researcher: "Has that ever happened to you?"
>
> Eric: "No, not really."
>
> Researcher: "Has anybody you know gotten into trouble because they play a lot of violent games?"
>
> Eric: "No, not really."
>
> Researcher: "But you just figure it's logical, or . . . ?"
>
> Eric: "Yeah, it could happen."

When pressed, not one boy could point to anyone they knew whose behavior was noticeably influenced by violent games. The same held true for the parents we spoke with. While some expressed concerns or repeated stories they'd read and heard, not one said that they actually knew someone who'd been affected. Perhaps the urban legends and histrionic news reports of video game players suddenly going on real-world shooting rampages had caused them to focus on the wrong behaviors. Or perhaps the effects are more subtle.

We noted earlier that violent crime has steadily decreased since the mid-1990s, over a period when video games—including violent ones—became increasingly available to children. But the pattern is different for less visible aggressive acts. For reasons not yet understood, arrests for simple assault (actual or attempted attack, without a weapon) increased by 106 percent for boys and 290 percent for girls between 1980 and 2004.[9]

Bullying at school also seems to be increasing in the United States, although it's hard to tell how much because of changes in how survey questions were worded. In 2005, about 28 percent of students aged twelve to eighteen said they'd been bullied at school (from being made fun of or excluded to being pushed, tripped or spat on) at least once in the past six months. About 9 percent had been physically bullied in some way; a quarter of that group said they'd sustained cuts or bruises, chipped teeth, or worse. Young teens were most likely to be victimized.[10]

The focus on school shootings had diverted attention from these everyday problems young people face. Studies conducted in twenty-five countries found broad variation in rates of bullying, but surprisingly similar problems were associated with it. Young teens who are bullies or victims are at greater risk for a range of problems involving emotional adjustment, peer relationships, and physical health. They are also more likely to carry weapons. Worse, these problems can persist into adulthood. Bullying is no longer seen as a trivial and temporary predicament of childhood, but as a public health problem.[11]

Could violent video games have a role in encouraging bullying, or other aggressive or delinquent behaviors? To answer this question, we need to know if there's any real-world relationship between those behaviors and children's exposure to violent video games.

Along with questions about video game play, our middle school survey asked children how many times they'd been involved in any of a dozen undesirable behaviors or situations during the past twelve months: from beating up someone, to getting in trouble at school or with police, to being victimized. We divided the group into kids who'd been involved at least once in the past year and kids who had not been involved. In line with previous research,[12] we set a higher bar for bullying; to be counted, it had to occur at least two or three times a month over the last couple of months.

We then compared children who had any M-rated games on their "played a lot in the past six months" list to children who listed only E- or T-rated games, to see if these two groups were equally likely to be involved with problem behaviors. They were not.

Girls who played M-rated games were significantly more likely to be involved in seven of the twelve problem behaviors. For boys, six of the twelve problem behaviors were significantly more likely among M-game players.

Brace yourself for a bit of mathematics here. In the end, it will be worth it. The next two tables and the statistical analysis contain a wealth of information.

Problem Behaviors and M-Rated Game Preferences: Girls

PROBLEM AREA	TYPE OF BEHAVIOR PREVIOUS 12 MONTHS	OVERALL PERCENTAGE OF GIRLS INVOLVED IN BEHAVIOR	PERCENTAGE OF M-GAMERS	PERCENTAGE OF NON-M-GAMERS
AGGRESSION AND BULLYING	Been in a physical fight	20.9%	40%	14%**
	Hit or beat up someone	34.5%	49%	29%**
	Took part in bullying another student[†]	4.4%	6%	4%
DELINQUENT BEHAVIORS	Damaged property just for fun	7.9%	15%	5%**
	Got into trouble with the police	1.8%	2%	2%
	Stole something from from a store	9.8%	14%	8%
SCHOOL PROBLEMS	Got poor grades on a report card	23.7%	37%	20%**
	Skipped classes or school without an excuse	10.8%	20%	7%**
	Got into trouble with teacher or principal	35.5%	49%	31%**
	Got suspended from school	8.4%	16%	5%**
VICTIMIZATION	Been threatened or injured with a weapon	9.0%	14%	7%*
	Been bullied at school[†]	6.9%	8%	6%

* STATISTICALLY SIGNIFICANT DIFFERENCE WITHIN GENDER BETWEEN M-GAMERS AND NON-M-GAMERS AT THE P<.05 LEVEL.

** STATISTICALLY SIGNIFICANT DIFFERENCE WITHIN GENDER BETWEEN M-GAMERS AND NON-M-GAMERS AT THE P<.01 LEVEL.

[†] THIS BULLYING OCCURRED AT SCHOOL AT LEAST TWO TO THREE TIMES PER MONTH OVER THE PAST FEW MONTHS; OLWEUS BULLY/VICTIM QUESTIONNAIRE DEFINITIONS.

Problem Behaviors and M-Rated Game Preferences: Boys

PROBLEM AREA	TYPE OF BEHAVIOR PREVIOUS 12 MONTHS	OVERALL PERCENTAGE OF BOYS INVOLVED IN BEHAVIOR	PERCENTAGE OF M-GAMERS	PERCENTAGE OF NON-M-GAMERS
AGGRESSION AND BULLYING	Been in a physical fight	44.4%	51%	28%**
	Hit or beat up someone	53.2%	60%	39%**
	Took part in bullying another student[†]	9.2%	10%	8%
DELINQUENT BEHAVIORS	Damaged property just for fun	18.6%	23%	10%**
	Got into trouble with the police	4.9%	6%	2%
	Stole something from from a store	10.5%	13%	6%*
SCHOOL PROBLEMS	Got poor grades on a report card	31.6%	35%	23%**
	Skipped classes or school without an excuse	11.2%	13%	8%
	Got into trouble with teacher or principal	52.9%	60%	39%**
	Got suspended from school	20.1%	22%	15%
VICTIMIZATION	Been threatened or injured with a weapon	12.6%	15%	6%**
	Been bullied at school[†]	10.2%	8%	15%*

* STATISTICALLY SIGNIFICANT DIFFERENCE WITHIN GENDER BETWEEN M-GAMERS AND NON-M-GAMERS AT THE P<.05 LEVEL.

** STATISTICALLY SIGNIFICANT DIFFERENCE WITHIN GENDER BETWEEN M-GAMERS AND NON-M-GAMERS AT THE P<.01 LEVEL.

[†] THIS BULLYING OCCURRED AT SCHOOL AT LEAST TWO TO THREE TIMES PER MONTH OVER THE PAST FEW MONTHS; OLWEUS BULLY/VICTIM QUESTIONNAIRE DEFINITIONS.

What These Data Mean

Let's take a look at the first chart for a minute. Among all the girls we surveyed who played video games, 20.9 percent said that they'd been in at least one physical fight during the previous year. Among those girls who included at least one M-rated game on their "most played" list (M-gamers), 40 percent reported being in a fight. This compares with 14 percent of those girls who played games, but who didn't include any M-rated games on their list (non-M-gamers). This difference between M-gamers and non-M-gamers is statistically significant at the p<.01 level; the odds of a difference that big occurring by chance is less than one in one hundred.

Among boys, 51 percent of the M-gamers and 28 percent of the non-M-gamers reported getting into a fight during the past year. This difference is also statistically significant at the p<.01 level.

We found significant relationships between M-rated game play and a broad range of aggressive or problem behaviors among middle school students. In fact, M-gamers were more likely to be involved with every one of these problems than non-M-gamers—with one exception (see below). Some of these associations, especially for less-common issues such as getting into trouble with police, were only trends; a few others were only significant at the p<.05 level (i.e., odds of one in twenty that those results occurred by chance). We'd need to repeat this study with more kids to see if those trends might turn out to be significant associations. What's more, in most cases the odds of engaging in these behaviors at least once during the previous year increased with the relative "dose" of M-rated game exposure: the more M games on children's lists, the greater the relationship.

Again, playing M-rated games may not be the cause of such problems as lower grades in school; it may be that children doing poorly in school are attracted to these games so that they can be successful at something. There may be other factors influencing both.

Problems Among Boys

Compared to other boys who regularly played video games, boys reporting frequent play of at least one M-rated title (M-gamers) were much more likely to get into physical fights, to hit or beat up someone, to damage property for fun, or to steal something from a store. They were also much more likely to report poor school grades, to get into trouble with a teacher or principal and to report being threatened or injured with a weapon such as a gun, knife or club. The odds of boys' involvement in all of these behaviors increased with each additional M-rated title on their "frequently played" game list.

Bullying

The picture was different for boys' involvement in bullying. While the differences between the two groups of boys were not statistically significant at the $p < .01$ level, being the victim of a bully was the only measure on which M-gamer boys were less likely to have a problem. They were also less likely to be victims with each additional M-rated title played. Although boys who listed one or more M-rated games were not significantly more likely to report bullying others at school, they were significantly more likely to be bullies with exposure to more M-rated titles.

Why were the boys who played M-rated games less likely to be victims of bullying? We know that children who play M-rated games are more likely to play in groups. It may be that the teenagers who play M-rated games have better social skills and therefore have a broader repertoire of responses to bullies. It may also be that these teens have more friends, so they're less likely to be picked on. At this point, we simply don't know. It's an area worth exploring to see if this difference holds up.

Problems Among Girls

Many of these relationships between problem behaviors and M-rated game play were even stronger among girls. This probably reflects the fact that M-rated games were played by a minority of girls but the majority of boys. M-gamer girls were significantly more likely to have hit someone or been in a fight, damaged property for fun, gotten poor grades, skipped school, been in trouble with a teacher or principal, and been suspended from school.

Now that we know a relationship exists between violent video games and some problem behaviors, the next step is to find out what's behind that relationship. We can make logical guesses, but we can't be sure from our research whether violent game play led to these behaviors or vice versa;

whether each aggravates the other; or if a third (or fourth or fifth) factor partially or completely explains the relationship. To know more, we'd need to conduct a larger study that follows a group of children over time.

It's also important to note that the problems we studied are common among teens. For example, over half of boys and one third of girls in our sample had hit or beaten up someone at least once during the previous year. This doesn't mean they are bad kids or are likely to be violent adults.

Aggressive Behavior and Time Spent on Games

We noted that the more M-rated games on children's "most played" lists, the more likely they were to be involved in problem behaviors. But what about the effects of time spent playing video games in general? (Since playing M games is correlated with more time spent playing games, this gets a bit complicated.)

TIME SPENT PLAYING ANY VIDEO GAMES	PERCENTAGE OF CHILDREN CLASSIFIED AS BULLIES
< 1 hour/week	1.4%
1–2 hours/week	4.1%
3–5 hours/week	7.7%
6–8 hours/week	11.7%
9–11 hours/week	12.1%
12–14 hours/week	8.0%
15+ hours/week	10.5%
0 days/week	2.8%
1 day/week	1.0%
2 days/week	5.0%
3 days/week	7.0%
4-5 days/week	7.4%
6-7 days/week	11.6%

We found that girls who played games nearly every day, regardless of game content, were significantly more likely to report bullying others. They were also more likely to report physical fights or trouble with teachers. Among girls, a pattern of very frequent game play appears to be a marker of higher risk for aggressive behavior. For boys, only one problem behavior—hitting or beating up someone—was significantly linked to near-daily game play, regardless of M-rated game play.

However, as days per week of play went up, both girls and boys were significantly more likely to be bullies. Girls who played games nearly every day were significantly more likely to be bullies than other girls (12 percent vs. 3 percent), *and* more likely to be victims of bullying (17 percent vs. 6 percent).

Although boys and girls who play electronic games a lot (in hours per week and days per week) are significantly more likely to bully others, it's important to note that *most children who play these games are not bullies.* Just 10.5 percent of children who played fifteen hours or more per week, and 11.6 percent of children who played nearly every day, admitted to bullying someone at school more than once or twice in the past couple of months. And of course, not all bullies or victims play violent games.

We need to look more closely at how the relatively small percentage of heavy game users who are bullies may differ from the majority of heavy game users who are not bullies. For example, there may be differences in the types of games they play, their family relationships, school failure, etc., that would help us better identify children at risk for problems from heavy game use. A larger study is needed to sort this out.

One unexpected finding: boys who didn't regularly play video games (i.e., not at all, or zero days during a typical week) were more likely than even boys who played M-rated games to get into fights, steal from a store, or have problems at school. There were too few boys in this category for us to delve into it further.

Since game play is the norm for boys, nonplayers are by definition abnormal. Girls who didn't play games were not noticeably different from others in terms of problem behaviors (a bit better behaved in some categories); this makes sense, since gaming is not as central to girls' daily life and social relationships.

Are Aggressive Kids More Likely to Play Violent Games?

From the moment they are born (and, according to some researchers, perhaps even earlier), children have behavioral styles that persist throughout childhood into adulthood.[13] Some babies are pretty easy to manage and are quick to figure out ways to calm themselves. Others are easily overwhelmed, overreact to new or noisy situations and need more time to be soothed.

As infants grow into toddlers, traits such as shyness and aggressiveness become more apparent. This means that the behavioral effects of watching a scary movie on a shy three-year-old or seven-year-old might be quite different from the effect on a preschooler who is already showing aggressive tendencies or a first-grader who is known for her daring behavior.

Media researchers have tried to take traits into account, particularly in laboratory studies of aggression. Some studies have found greater effects of violent content in video games among subjects high in trait hostility; others did not.[14] An Australian study that tried to reconcile these differences found that a player's emotional state before starting to play a violent game (*Quake II*) influenced how he or she felt afterward. The researchers looked at subjects' responses to a questionnaire about traits to see if they could find a difference between those who felt angry after play and those who didn't. The angry-after-play group had higher trait anger and aggression.[15]

We might also see inconsistent effects between studies because they leave out other important factors that influence aggression. Feelings of closeness to parents and connectedness to school, for example, are known to buffer the effects of exposure to real-life violence on violent behavior.[16] Children's temperament and behavioral styles will also influence how they are treated and affected by peers, parents and school.

Children with high trait hostility and aggression seem to be drawn to more violent activities, whether those be contact sports such as football or wrestling, more aggressive schoolyard play or more violent media.[17] We don't yet know how these activities might affect aggressive kids differently. For some, playing football or a violent video game might reinforce and worsen their aggressive behavior; for others, these activities might be socially acceptable ways to work through and get rid of hostile feelings.

Attitudes Toward Violence

Another charge often made against violence in video games and other media is that it may desensitize children to real violence. The fear is that constant exposure to gory virtual violence, without seeing the consequences that would accompany such violence in real life, could make children less sensitive to suffering caused by violence and reduce their empathy for its victims. They might fail to help people in distress. Thirteen-year-old Alex put it this way:

> If you watch lots of violent movies, you can get it into your head that violence isn't a very bad thing, because you see it all the time, and your sense of it is kind of dulled. So when you see someone in a movie get their arm cut off or something, then you don't, like, cry for an hour, 'cause you've seen it before. If you've never seen a movie like that, you'd probably be really sad, but after [you've seen] ten. . . .

Desensitization is not always a bad thing. For example, it's used in psychotherapy all the time to help people overcome phobias and disturbing thoughts. Jeanne Funk, PhD, professor of psychology at the University of Toledo, adds, "It's also something that occurs on a daily basis; it helps us manage life stresses. If we didn't get desensitized to tragedies, we couldn't function."

Funk became concerned that violent media could subtly desensitize children: "Over time, we could develop a group of kids who won't care about other people. Playing violent video games could be one risk factor."

A related concern is that violent video games could make physical aggression a more appealing or first-choice solution for personal conflicts. Constantly practicing aggressive behavior through video games might add to the risk.

Picture a twelve-year-old playing a first-person shooter game, fighting soldiers, aliens or zombies. The player advances through a dim corridor where enemies may lurk around a corner, pop out from alcoves or come up from behind. To stay "alive," the player must be hypervigilant for attacks and be ready with an almost automatic aggressive response. Researchers such as Funk are concerned that constant repetition of these behaviors in violent games could lead to the development of "aggressive scripts": automatic responses to certain types of situations. At question is whether the conditioned response of pressing a button in a game will generalize to reacting violently in the real world.

In theory, a nonthreatening real-life event, such as an accidental bump in a school hallway, could be seen as a threat and trigger a scripted aggressive reaction. A child who has been desensitized to violence by seeing it over and over in video games or movies might find it harder to suppress an automatic aggressive response.[18]

To investigate these concerns, Funk conducted a series of studies with more than three hundred children in elementary and high school. For example, in one study, children filled out surveys to check their attitudes toward violence, level of empathy and exposure to violence in real life. Funk also asked how many hours per week children played video games, watched television and movies and used the Internet, and their favored type of content for each. She concluded that exposure to video game and movie violence was associated with stronger proviolence attitudes, but only video game violence was linked to lower empathy.[19]

Funk would like to see more longitudinal studies that look at how factors including age, gender, personality and intelligence may interact with exposure to violent media. "My guess is that kids who already have problems with aggression are at higher risk for being affected by violent video games, such as bullies or bully victims," she notes.

Our own survey included a set of eight questions designed to explore children's beliefs about aggression (e.g., "If people do something to make me really mad, they deserve to be beaten up") and whether they consider alternatives to fighting (e.g., "I try to talk out a problem instead of fighting"). We found that boys who regularly played at least one M-rated game had significantly lower belief in the use of nonviolent strategies and significantly more positive perceptions of aggression. This was also true for girls who played M-rated games. Again, we can't say that M-rated games created these attitudes, nor do we know the real-world significance of this.

Michael Jellinek, MD, professor of psychiatry and pediatrics at Harvard Medical School and the chief of child and adolescent psychiatry at Massachusetts General Hospital, sees little evidence of children being desensitized by violent media. "I've seen kids who were exposed to domestic violence learn to numb themselves or to dissociate. I've seen kids in gangs learn to minimize it. Most kids, when they see someone injured on the field or when they come into the emergency room, there's a whole different tone—very realistic—to how they feel about that than when someone's hurt in a video game."

Violent Video Games and Feeling Safe

Marcy told the other parents in her focus group that her concerns went well beyond the contents and immediate effects of violent video games. "I think it also creates for children—and they may not admit it—a real sense of terror, an underlying sense that life is just violent; that awful things happen all the time to people."

Could violence in games or on TV make children feel less safe and see the world as a scarier place? A quarter of the children we surveyed (24 percent of boys and 26 percent of girls) reported being afraid of getting hurt by someone at school at least once in the previous month. One in three girls and almost one in four boys didn't feel safe walking alone in their neighborhood at night. However, we didn't find any significant link between game play and perceived danger.

Boys in several of our focus groups were more concerned about violence on television news than about gore in video games. For some, TV news violence could make video game violence more upsetting.

Ryan: "I don't really think video games will influence kids as much as, like, the news. That can influence kids, and that's real."

Shawn: "Yeah."

Researcher: "How do you think kids who watch a lot of news might feel different about the world?"

Ryan: "Like, I don't like to watch the news."

Shawn: "I don't either."

Ryan: "I'll tell my dad to shut it off, if I'm in the same room, or I'll just leave."

Researcher: "But how does that make you feel, when you watch the news?"

Ryan: "Well, I play video games, and I go, 'Oh, that stuff won't happen.' And if I see it happen on the news, it kind of freaks me out, 'cause, like, I just . . ."

Researcher: "Like, 'Oh, but it's not a fantasy after all'?"

Ryan: "Yeah."

Shawn: "It's scary, 'cause you don't feel safe."

Parents don't generally think about news as harmful to children or that children even watch news programs. But surveys show that children and teens watch TV news regularly; sometimes, they just happen to be in the room when an adult turns the news on.[20] A child who sees a lot of violence on television, whether it's *Law and Order* reruns or news programs, is more likely to see the world as a scary place with lurking dangers far out of proportion to reality.[21] But realistic depictions of violence, such as those on the news, are thought to be more likely to scare or desensitize children. As one child told us, "In video games, you know it's fake."

Given that older children and teens believe that news represents reality and that TV news programs increasingly show graphic or sensationalized violence, there is a real risk of harm.[22] Parents can help by keeping track of their kids' exposure to TV news and helping them put it into context—for example, stories get on the news because they are rare, and that events on the news, whether it's losing your house to a tornado or winning the lottery, are not likely to happen to them.

Research on television coverage of war shows that children of different ages are upset by different aspects, with younger ones more bothered by the visual images and teens by the complex issues, such as morality and justice, that are raised by news events.[23]

Violent Games and Criminal Violence

Is there any evidence for a link between violent crime and video game play? So far, there's not much to go on. But we may get some hints from the decades of research on violent television.

Joanne Savage, PhD, of American University's School of Public Affairs reviewed the research on how television violence is related to criminal violence.[24] When we go beyond laboratory measures of aggression and play-fighting among children and look at real-world crime—the outcome we worry about most—there are surprisingly few studies. There are even fewer studies that look specifically at violent media content (rather than assuming that more media use means more exposure to violence) and give enough detail about their methods to judge whether they make sense.

For example, one study she cites compared audience sizes for violent television shows in different U.S. media markets to local violent crime rates. It found a significant relationship, but not in the expected direction. It turned out that the more viewing of violent programs, the *lower* the violent crime rate.

Studies of violent criminals that looked back at their earlier media use (retrospective studies) didn't rule out the possibility that violent children preferred violent media, or the studies found that lots of TV watching in childhood only made a difference when kids also were exposed to violence at home.

Longitudinal studies of childhood TV watching and adult aggression had various problems, such as not actually measuring children's exposure to violent TV, using measures of adult aggression that focused more on obnoxious behaviors than on violent crime, or finding no effect when controlling for children's initial level of aggressiveness.

Savage concludes: "Because legislators and other policymakers make frequent calls to reduce media violence, this line of research, spanning over forty years now, is still relevant and topical and bears further scrutiny. At this point it must be said, however, that there is little evidence in favor of media violence as a means of remedying our violent crime problem."

She does note, and we agree, that lack of good evidence so far doesn't mean there's nothing to find. The key is to focus more specifically on which children in which situations are at greatest risk from which types of media violence. We need large long-term studies that (1) have good measures of violent behavior and of violent media exposure, (2) have a well-matched control group of kids who don't use violent media, and (3) take other important influences into consideration, including child factors (such as violent behavior and trait aggressiveness at the start of the study), parent factors (such as their supervision, abuse, and neglect of the child) and environmental factors (such as poverty, schooling and access to other activities).

CHAPTER 5

Why Kids Play Violent Games

Researcher: "What attracts your son to the violent video games?"

Marie: "I don't know. I don't know. I probably should know!"

—A mother in one of our focus groups

ONE OF OUR RESEARCH ASSISTANTS, A YOUNG WOMAN who had recently graduated from college, was taken aback at the response when she asked thirteen-year-old Charlie about his favorite part of *Grand Theft Auto*. "It's where you're in the limo, and you have to pick up all the people and have a meeting. And then the gang comes after us and then we all shoot them and stuff, and blow their heads off. I think it's funny when their heads fall off." Other boys in the group chimed in, sharing their enthusiasm for that scene's shooting techniques, the color of the blood, and the dying victims' reactions ("and they're twitching after!").

"So, you like what happens when they die and get hurt?" she asked. This sent the boys into spasms of laughter: "Die and get hurt!" "Violent!"

What's going on here? Should we be worried? Or is this simply normal behavior for boys this age?

To understand how media violence might influence children, we need to see things from their perspective: What attracts them to violent video games, and what does that violence mean to them? In our surveys and focus groups, we did something that surprisingly few researchers have

111

done before: we asked the children why they play video games—especially violent games.

After reading the research literature, debating among ourselves and talking with young game players, our team came up with seventeen likely reasons for playing video games and included them in our middle-school survey. In that survey, we asked children whether they agreed or disagreed (on a four-point scale) that each reason applied to them. (An option to write in additional reasons generated very few responses, which told us that our list was pretty good.) Here are the reasons:

- My friends like to play.
- It's something to do when I'm bored.
- It helps me relax.
- I like to teach other kids how to play.
- I like the guns and other weapons.
- It helps me feel less lonely.
- It helps me make new friends.
- I like to learn new things.
- I like to create my own world.
- It's just fun.
- I like to compete with other people and win.
- I like the challenge of figuring the game out.
- It helps me get my anger out.
- It helps me forget my problems.
- There is nothing else to do.
- I like to "mod" games (change the game using computer code).
- It's exciting.

The survey results showed that both boys and girls find inspiration, joy and relief in video games. Some are motivated by fun, excitement and challenge, while others are just passing time when there's nothing to do. Boys were more likely than girls to agree with almost every reason for play.

Using a statistical technique called factor analysis, we found that children's reasons for playing games clustered into four general categories:

- **Excitement and fun.** These kids enjoy competing and winning, and the challenge of figuring out a game.

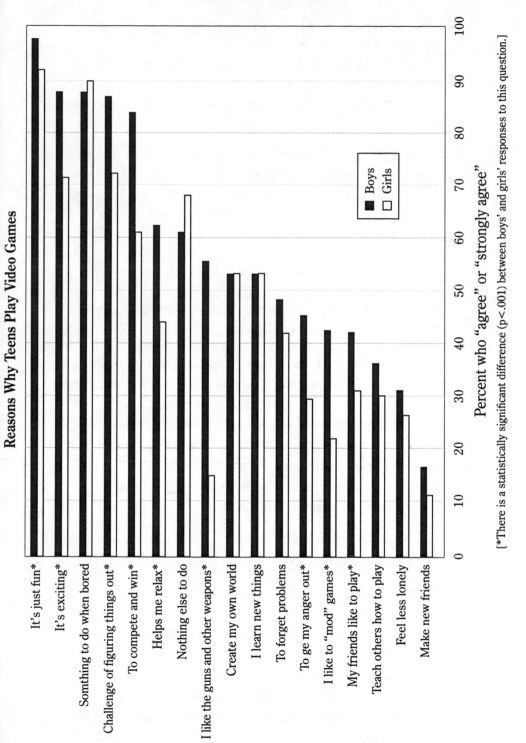

Reasons Why Teens Play Video Games

Percent who "agree" or "strongly agree"

[*There is a statistically significant difference (p<.001) between boys' and girls' responses to this question.]

- **Sociability.** This group plays because their friends like to play and perhaps to make new friends.
- **Emotions.** This group often plays to get out anger, forget problems and feel less lonely.
- **Boredom.** These kids turn to video games when there's nothing else to do.

But what about the children who say they like playing violent or M-rated video games? Do they give different reasons? Compared to children with no Mature-rated games on their lists, boys and girls who'd played any Mature-rated game "a lot in the past six months" were significantly more likely to agree with these four reasons for play:

- I like to compete with other people and win.
- It helps me get my anger out.
- I like to "mod" games (change the game using computer code).
- I like the guns and other weapons.

More than half of all the boys we surveyed agreed with the statement "I like the guns and other weapons." This response is hard to interpret. In retrospect, we should have phrased it more clearly since some of these boys lived in areas where hunting is popular and they may be thinking about real hunting rifles. However, it probably represents enjoyment of action, explosions and colorful graphics more than their love of actual weapons. The top-rated motivations for M-game players were similar to those of other players their age.

In this chapter, we'll explore the facts and theories behind these remarkably diverse motivations for children's video game play. We'll look at:

- The real and often surprising reasons why children are drawn to violent games.
- Why children value games for being realistic and utterly divorced from reality—often at the same time.
- Why boys and girls like different things about games, but often not in the ways or for the reasons that adults assume.
- What kids' motivations for play can tell us about their problems, goals and needs.

- How kids with learning or emotional difficulties may be helped or harmed by video games.

Excitement and Sensation-Seeking

One of the games discussed in the focus groups was the fourth install-ment in the *Resident Evil* series *Code, Veronica X.* The main character, Claire Redfield, battles decomposing zombies while searching for her missing brother. During one focus group, thirteen-year-old Justin picked a screenshot from *Resident Evil* out of a pile of pictures and said it was one of his favorites. Why?

"I like shooting zombies," Justin stated. "You have to go around col-lecting items, go through certain phases. Sometimes if you're bitten by a zombie, you can find a little herb. If you eat it, it heals you. And you never know what's going to happen next, what zombie is going to pop out where. So that's just why I like it. I love scary games."

At any amusement park there's always a cadre of kids clamoring to ride the roller coaster again and again. Visit a movie theater and you'll see a group of teens lined up for the latest gore fest—and other teens who won't go near it. This thrill-me-scare-me group is what psycholo-gists call sensation seekers.

In theory, everyone has an optimal level of arousal or stimulation, a comfortable space on the continuum between excitement and boredom. A young teen who rates high in sensation seeking may enjoy scary or shocking video games or movies that might repel or upset someone else.[1] High sensation seekers like novelty, thrills and unpredictability. There seems to be a genetic basis for sensation-seeking, but it's also influenced by culture. For example, a study in the 1970s found that American women ranked higher than British women (although men in both countries were similar).[2] Sensation seeking is thought to increase from childhood to adolescence and then decline.

A number of studies have found that sensation seeking is associated with a higher risk of experimenting with alcohol, drugs and cigarettes, and doing those things at earlier ages.[3] But in most cases, an occasional scary or gory game is probably nothing to worry about. In fact, as we'll see later in this chapter, it may be helpful.

Is the Blood Green?

When we asked her what attracted her preteen son to violent games, Roberta noted, "I think he would say that he wants to see the blood and guts. . . . It's something that in his world you don't see in real life. If the dragon gets his head cut off, he wants to know, is the blood red? Is it blue? Is it green?"

The term "morbid curiosity" implies an unhealthy attraction to grisly things, but the appeal of violent video games is more likely related to normal sensation-seeking and to testing the limits of acceptability. Matthew put it bluntly: "You get to see something that, hopefully, will never happen to you. So you want to experience it a little bit without actually being there."

For many children, the fact that something is taboo is reason enough to be interested. Jamie observed this type of curiosity in her son. "*Vice City* came out when he was ten and a half or eleven. . . . Some of the comments and jokes and situations were over his head. But there's nothing more fun at that age than having the older brother explain what a lap dance is, right? The little boys are laughing their heads off; now they know stuff that parents don't know. So I think there was part of that in [the appeal of] *Vice City*. Had he been a bit older, I think his reaction would be different. But the only time I saw him with it, it was just giggle-puss."

What Makes a Video Game Realistic?

Thirteen-year-old James had strong opinions about the video games he enjoyed. "I think the really violent games like *Vice City* where you can just go around killing anybody, they're less realistic. The environment, the people are real, but not the actions."

James was not the only teenager to parse his words this way, describing some parts of games as "real," but not "realistic." Steven Malliet, PhD, of the Catholic University of Leuven in Belgium, conducted a series of structured interviews with thirty-two gamers, mostly boys aged sixteen to nineteen, to understand their perceptions of video game realism.[4] At first, these teens talked about things like colors, landscapes and facial features. But it soon became clear that realism is about more than advanced computer graphics. He identified five dimensions of perceived video game realism: factuality, authenticity (whether game events could plausibly happen somewhere, or even happen to you), a sense of virtual experience, involvement with characters and graphical realism.

Although teens knew that games overall were not factually accurate, incorporating facts did make games feel more real. These could be anything from geographical locations and historical events to weaponry, procedures (such as aspects of training in *America's Army*) or outcomes (such as characters dying if shot in the head).

Even though game events were not seen as plausible or likely to actually happen, some players commented on the sense of emotional authenticity that comes from better-developed characters. One teen, describing a scene in *Baldur's Gate* in which an orphaned child searches for his teddy bear in a graveyard, noted, "In some games you have the impression of, damn, it's just like somebody has been through this in real life."[5]

A game with the freedom to make a lot of choices, versus one with a more structured story, increased the intensity of experiencing the game's virtual world. Players also liked to see how those choices affected the evolution of their character over time.

Finally, features that increase identification with characters also increase a game's realism. Things like shaping the story through interactivity, a first-person point of view (seeing game scenery and actions through the eyes of your character) and customizing a character's name, appearance, or personality could help engage some teens' emotions as much as or more than a good movie or novel.

The Purpose and Value of Story

Video games have evolved well beyond the point where the goal is simply to beat a series of levels or opponents. Popular games increasingly focus on complex stories. Given what we know about the context of violence, what are the potential effects of adding a story line to a violent game?

For example, one study of college students who were experienced gamers found that they felt more involved while playing action games that had a story, such as *Half-Life*, than while playing similarly exciting games without much story line, such as *Quake 2*. Students also identified more with their characters when they were part of a story line.[6] Identifying more closely with a character may encourage them to justify (or rationalize) their violent behavior within that game.

To see whether stories made video games more attractive to young teenagers, we asked the 1,254 middle school students we surveyed whether they:

- preferred playing games that follow a story line (i.e., *Final Fantasy, The Legend of Zelda*)
- preferred playing games that do *not* have a story (i.e., *Quake, Tekken, Super Smash Bros.*)
- didn't have a preference

We found that nearly twice as many boys as girls (39 percent versus 20 percent) preferred games with a story, and girls were more apt than boys to prefer games with no story (25 percent vs. 14 percent).

As you saw in chapter 4, many game series that made the girls' top-ten list don't have stories, including *Dance Dance Revolution, The Sims*, solitaire and various Mario games. Many of the violent series in the boys' top ten, including *Grand Theft Auto, Halo, Medal of Honor* and *Lord of the Rings*, have strong and complex stories. It's possible that the available story-based games, which include many war-themed titles (on Earth and in space), have less appeal to girls.

Is There Such a Thing as Good Violence?

The threads of violence are woven throughout the fabric of children's play and literature from a very early age. We sing them to sleep with lullabies that describe boughs breaking, cradles falling and babies plummeting helplessly to the earth. We entertain them with fairy tales in which a talking wolf devours a girl's grandmother and an old woman tries to roast children alive in her oven. Even religious instruction is replete with stories about plagues, pestilence, jealousy, betrayal, torture and death.

While the stories and songs may be different, the underlying themes are generally the same in cultures throughout the world. Ogres, monsters, sexual infidelities, beheadings, thievery, abandonment, cannibalism, drownings—such was the stuff of children's literature long before video games.

We can see these themes in children's play as well. A five-year-old is far more likely to point his finger at a playmate and say, "Bang! Bang! You're dead!" than "Let's be cooperative!" Why?

Philosophers and developmental theorists have pondered this for a very long time. One conclusion is that children are drawn to violent themes because listening to and playing with those frightening images helps them safely master the experience of being frightened. That is an important skill, perhaps even a life-saving one.

The physiological and emotional arousal caused by the stories and games give the child experience with those strange sensations at a time and place where they know that they are safe. It's like that attraction of a roller-coaster ride at an amusement park or the horror movie at a theater that draws in the sensation seekers; they know that it's scary, but they also know that they'll be just fine at the end.

Many of these classic children's stories are also filled with sexual content. While the later versions of the Brothers Grimm story *Rapunzel* describes her being visited chastely by the prince, the first edition of their collection of fairy tales told a different story. Rapunzel used her long hair to allow a lover to climb up to her room. She inadvertently reveals her pregnancy when she naively asks the witch why her clothes no longer fit.[7]

An early Italian version of *Sleeping Beauty* involved the girl being raped by the prince, kept unconscious throughout the resulting pregnancy and awakened only after one of her babies mistakenly sucks on her finger and dislodges the pin that had kept her asleep. (For some reason, Disney chose not to use that plotline in its famous animated movie.)

In a French version of *Little Red Riding Hood*, the wolf—this time a *bzou*, or werewolf—kills the grandmother and then gets the girl to eat her. The family cat cries out, "She is a slut who eats the flesh and drinks the blood of her granny."[8]

What's going on here? Why are children's stories seemingly filled to the brim with what these days are euphemistically called "adult themes"? In fact, that's a telling descriptor. Children's stories give them a glimpse at adult secrets, the things we talk about with our voices low-ered or behind closed doors. They allow them to explore sex, death, rage, violence and primal fears.

So it should come as no surprise that some of the video games teenagers like to play involve those themes as well. It gives them a chance to examine what they perceive as an adult world of power, sex and mystery.

All of this raises the question of whether violent media are inherently bad or, at the very least, problematic. We can get some hints from the National Television Violence Study,[9] conducted in the mid-1990s. This three-year study involved over three hundred people working at four universities. They sought not only to document the amount of violence on television, but also to assess the way violence was presented—the context, goals and targets of violence—and when it might encourage or discourage children from learning to behave violently.

They found that during a typical week, 61 percent of programs con-tained some violence; the greatest amount of violent programming at that time was on premium cable channels, particularly in movies. The consortium of researchers agreed that exposure to violence had the potential to adversely affect children and that the risk of learning aggres-sive behavior increases when

- the perpetrator is attractive
- the violence is seen as justified
- the violence is seen as realistic, involving a real-life weapon
- the violence is rewarded, or at least not punished
- the violence has little or no harmful consequences, and/or
- the violence is seen as funny

Exposing children to violent programs that included a combination of these factors was of particular concern: "A high-risk portrayal for learn-ing [aggressive behavior] is one that features an attractive character who engages in violence that is sanctioned and that does not result in any serious consequences to the victim."[10]

For example, our son and his friends used to play James Bond games such as *GoldenEye* and *The World Is Not Enough*. Those T-rated games met many of the criteria for teaching violent behavior: an attractive perpetrator, violence that was both justified and rewarded, realistic guns and fists used as weapons and few harmful consequences—no blood was shown, and the many dead bodies simply dissolved away within seconds.

Yet neither our son nor the friends who played the games with him are violent. Clearly, exposure alone is not sufficient to change their behaviors significantly in the real world. That shouldn't be surprising for a behavior as complex as violence. We would expect some children to have greater vulnerabilities to the influence of media and others to be more resistant and resilient. Equally important, we would expect the level of influence (the effect size) of media exposure to be relatively small when compared with other factors in the children's environment.

In most television violence studies, and video game studies as well, all violence is treated as equivalent. When differentiations are made, such as the use of the ESRB content descriptors that we'll describe in chapter 7, the emphasis is on the level or style of violence, not on its context.

"It's very simplistic to say that the content creates the motive," says Michael Jellinek, MD. "It may shape the way it's expressed, but the core meaning of that violence and aggression is in the child, not in the video game." In other words, exposure to a video game may influence the plot when the child reenacts a battle in an alien world with his friends, but the violence in that fantasy play is driven by other, more fundamental experiences.

"Let's take a ten-year-old boy on the playground who's playing army or spaceman. That's playful, normal and healthy fantasy play. But if the child has been abused at home or has seen domestic violence, he may play differently. He may be much rougher and may hurt himself or his playmate."

I'm Important!

Video games give free rein to fantasies of power, glory and freedom. That's quite different from the mundane lives of most children. Most of the day, adults tell them what to do—and it's usually not the things they'd rather be doing. It's no wonder that they crave the experience of being the virtual quarterback of an NFL team, leading hundreds of warriors into battle, running an empire or knocking off a few zombies. We can see this in how the boys in our focus groups described their favorite video game characters, special powers and weapons.

Rob: "I like Tommy Vercetti [the main character in *Grand Theft Auto: Vice City*] because he never gives up and he never quits or anything. And he's played by Ray Liotta, one of my favorite actors."

Mike: "I wouldn't like to go around killing people [like Tommy Vercetti], but to be the highest man in the town, the strongest man and stuff, it would be actually pretty cool. Everybody looks up to you. You're not the scum, you're someone that's important."

Terry: "The swords in *Mortal Kombat* are fun to use, and they look cool."

Lenny: "I wish I could be stronger, so if someone's afraid of me— not that I want them to be afraid of me—but they won't try to start something with me. And I want to be famous."

Randy: "My favorite character in *Metal Gear Solid* is like a ninja; he can sneak around places without people seeing him. And he can get people out of the way, but without killing—he can lock them out. It's cool. He has all this agility.

"[If I had that] when my teacher catches me doing something, before she can call the principal, I'd put everything back in place without her seeing it. Then she won't have any proof that I did it. I would be in the bathroom saying, 'What are you talking about? I was in the bathroom the whole time!' "

Boys understood that acting like these favorite game characters would have very different consequences in the real world. When asked what he'd do if he woke up tomorrow as Mitsurugi from *Tekken*, Alex said, "I don't know, because if I took the sword out in public, then I'd get arrested!"

Austin enjoyed imagining waking up as Tommy Vercetti of *Vice City*, because "he kills people and has fun with it." As Tommy-for-a-day, he would "Kill people. Anybody . . . anybody that's walking the street."

When asked what would be fun about that, Austin thought about it for a moment. "I don't think it would be fun in real life."

Other boys made similar comments:

> Patrick: "I'm kind of scared to do that stuff [from *Grand Theft Auto*]. If I shoot somebody and they die, then I'll go to jail for a long time, so I don't want to do that."

> Barry: "The whole thug thing seems kind of cool. But in real life, I wouldn't really want to have that life. In [*Grand Theft Auto*], you don't mind just getting out of your car and killing somebody, because you're not going to get in trouble for it. You can just turn off the game system and you're done. But I don't really admire these people too much."

The *Grand Theft Auto* series of video games is satire. Unfortunately, preteens and even some young teenagers have difficulty recognizing satire when they see it. This is a matter of brain development. One mother in a focus group expressed her concerns about this quite vividly: "It's actually a very clever game. But it really should be limited to adults. You start seeing the prostitutes, and it's a riot, *if* you are looking at it as an adult. But I step back and go, 'Hey, my thirteen-year-old has never seen that!' He doesn't have the background information."

If a child takes these game characters and behaviors seriously, is there greater potential for harm? Developmental psychologist Laurence Steinberg, PhD, of Temple University, is not concerned. "Kids start understanding satire around age twelve. Younger kids need more contextual cues to understand when something is satirical," he notes. "But even if they don't get the satire, I don't think that it will motivate kids to do something that they otherwise wouldn't do."

Does It Have to Be Violent to Be Fun?

The boys in our focus groups made it clear that while some of the games they liked were violent, many were not. In fact, they described some violent games as boring. So what makes a game fun to play more than once?

Justin: "I like adventure games because you don't only play for twenty minutes and then beat it. I like a game that takes time and focus to do it."

Mike: "I like games that, like, you beat it and you could come back and do a whole different story line and beat it again and then there might also be another story line you can go through. Also, you could go exploring."

When asked whether violence makes a game more fun, many boys who regularly played violent games agreed that it did. Some mentioned the over-the-top fantasy appeal of the violent games.

Patrick: "It's stuff that you can't do in real life, like kill people. So you could just, like, go crazy with the games."

Matthew: "I like sports games a lot, and when I do play a violent game it's fun too, because I like the action and stuff. I think there's a little more action in violence games than there is in non-violence games."

Justin: "Without violence it gets kind of boring after a while because you're sitting around doing nothing basically. But in a violence game, it's kind of fun because you actually go around, actually get to do violence stuff."

Others thought some nonviolent games were just as much fun and just as challenging.

James: "I think a game could have no violence at all and still be really good, because I like the realism and the challenge and stuff."

Daryl: "You can never actually get bored of [*Mario Party 5*] because new stuff comes out everywhere."

Mike: "I can't really explain it but [*Super Mario*] is just fun to play, because there's a lot of levels and it's an adventure game and you can beat it—and it feels good to beat a game."

Others mentioned sports games, racing games, or older games such as *Pac-Man*, pinball, or online checkers. They especially liked nonviolent games that featured realistic sounds or actions, such as choosing draft picks as a coach in *Madden NFL*.

The Joy of Figuring Things Out—Before the Other Guy

In our survey, more than half of boys strongly agreed that they played games to "compete and win" and for "the challenge of figuring the game out." (Among the girls, one in four found competition very appealing, and one in three relished the intellectual challenge.) These results are not unique to our survey. Nick Yee, PhD, of Stanford University, has conducted surveys of older teens and adults who routinely join others in online role-playing games. He found that achievement was a major part of the appeal.[11] But achievement was not simply getting a high score. It included *advancement* (progressing through the game while gaining powers and symbols of wealth or status), *competition* (challenging and competing with others) and *mechanics* (enjoying analyzing the underlying rules and system of the game, to improve one's performance).

Jeanne Funk, PhD, of the University of Toledo, conducted one of the few interview-based studies of video game players, comparing the responses of children in grades four through six with those of college students.[12] She told us, "The kids focused on pride and competition in terms of psychological gain. They said that they had more confidence: 'I feel like I did something right.' "

Mods R Us: Games and Self-Expression

Creativity and self-expression are important to some players. In our survey, over half of boys and girls agreed with the statements "I like to create my own world" (one in four strongly agreed) and "I like to learn new things." In addition, 42 percent of the boys and 22 percent of the girls agreed that they liked to "mod" games. Mods, or modifications, can be new items, weapons, clothing, characters, story lines or other features added to computer games by game players. Some games come with modding tools built in, so that players with less-advanced computer skills can have fun with them. A *Sims 2* player can create custom clothing or change the eye, hair or skin color of a character, for example, or download mods created by others from the Web. Mods are generally benign and often quite creative. But a child might occasionally write (or more likely, download) an objectionable mod such as a "nude patch"—which removes a game character's clothes.

One parent in our focus groups observed that many violent games allow creative options for play. "You can actually change your objective and strategy," Clara noted. "And now with these new weapons, it's a whole other game." Asked why she thought her son plays violent games, she added, "I think that he'd probably say, 'Mom, because it's so cool. Look, now I can use this Uzi instead of this one. And I can even throw a dagger from there!' "

I Like the Gore: Aesthetic vs. Representative Emotions

When Joe selected a screenshot of *Mortal Kombat* to discuss, the first thing he said was that he liked "the gore." His favorite thing to do was "the 'fatalities.' At the end, when you're going to beat them, you do a special move and kill them. Like, thunder god Raiden, he grabs you and hits you until you blow up."

It's startling and a bit upsetting to hear comments like this from young teenagers. Does this kind of admiration of gore signal a disturbing desensitization to violence? Not necessarily.

Some researchers have distinguished emotions that are related to admiration of artistry (aesthetic emotions) from feelings related to experiences in the game world (representative emotions) or even in the real world. As Jeroen Jansz, PhD, of the University of Amsterdam, wrote, "In playing a violent video game, [aesthetic] emotions may occur, for example, when a gamer admires the way in which a specific gruesome scene was staged."[13]

About the fatalities in *Mortal Kombat*, Joe added, "They made the graphics good. It's not realistic; it's like, fancy and fun."

The Appeal of *Grand Theft Auto*

In our survey of middle school youths, more boys listed a *Grand Theft Auto* game among their most-played games than any other game or series. Among girls, it came in second. *Grand Theft Auto* is one of those games that is shown in gruesome thirty-second clips before state and federal legislatures as an example of why video games should be regulated. If the violence is what makes these games popular, things look bad for the future of our civilization.

But is it really the violence? Says game designer John Feil, who's on the board of directors of the International Game Developers Association, "If it were just about the blood and guts, then you'd just have [games like] *Postal*.* In *Grand Theft Auto*, it's about the world you can explore."

In fact, comments from boys in our focus groups support Feil's view that the open environment is the primary source of the game's appeal.

"I personally think *Grand Theft Auto: Vice City* is a great game," said Barry. "Along with exploring the city, you can just get out of your car and beat up somebody. And that starts a series of things, like the cops come and then you run away from the cops. I like doing the missions, but apart from that, if I get caught up in something in the city, I keep doing that. I can do my own thing."

Other kids in the room agreed. "*Grand Theft Auto* games were, I think, the first where instead of doing certain levels, you can just walk around, blow up cars and escape the police," Martin noted. "Or work for the police, if you happen to get a police car, or a tank, or a fire truck, or ambulance or whatever. You press a button, and all of a sudden, you're working for them. You can catch criminals, or drive people places, or put out fires. It's more creative than just walking around, than shooting people and doing a mission when you feel like it."

"And you can be a good guy and a bad guy at the same time!" added Shawn.

---

* Here is a description of *Postal* from the review site Gamespot.com: "Moving from one surreal landscape to the next, you must make use of the twelve weapons at your disposal in order to dispatch anything with a pulse. Men, women, children—it doesn't matter if they're shooting at you or not, fill 'em full of lead! . . . As anyone can see, this is most certainly not a game for the kiddies." Not one child in our survey listed *Postal* among his or her frequently played games.

When Girls Play Violent Games

Justine Cassell, PhD, directs the Center for Technology and Social Behavior at Northwestern University. In the late 1990s, she and Henry Jenkins, PhD, organized a conference at the Massachusetts Institute of Technology called From Barbie to *Mortal Kombat*: Gender and Computer Games. The topic proved so popular that it led to a book of the same name.

"When I first started working on this, in 1997 or 1998, there was this assumption that girls didn't like violence," Cassell recalls. "Henry Jenkins and I interviewed serious girl gamers. And they said, 'What's your problem? We like violent games. Other games don't have a plot, they're not active, they don't allow you to do anything.'" In essence, some girls were attracted to the same elements of games such as *Grand Theft Auto* noted by boys in our focus groups.

"For a long time, there's been a misunderstanding about what girls like in games," says Cassell. "Companies would make games without violence, but also without a plot or characters. Girls are disdainful of an industry that doesn't understand their abilities. And when boys played the games for girls, they'd say, 'This game's so dumb, even girls won't play it!'"

Cassell recently contributed to a follow-up volume, *Beyond Barbie and Mortal Kombat*. "What's amazing is how little things have changed over a decade," she says. "Many games for girls are still so dumb, and game makers still think girls don't like action.

"I'm not surprised girls play violent games because there are some very fun things about them. That fact that we're surprised tells us about the images we have of girls in our society, that are not always positive. Being an innocent all the time is not fun," she adds.

Structured interviews with preteens, teens and young adults conducted for the British Board of Film Classification also showed differences between boys and girls in that part of the world.

> Female gamers are in general much less interested in fast action, first-person shooter, "swords and sandals," "hack and slash" games than males. Young boys are prone to boast about having played 18+ [*Mature-rated*] games, but girls appear not to regard these

games as cool in the same way. Girls and women rarely play football games, whereas these are popular amongst many males, and girls/women seem in general to be less interested in keenly competitive games.[14]

Perhaps things will change as today's teens become tomorrow's game developers. As we note in the next chapter, the number of female action game protagonists is still small, but appears to be growing. And despite the domination of today's games by macho male characters, at least some boys appear to have no problem taking a female perspective.

Earlier, we mentioned that Justin enjoyed being scared by the horror-adventure game *Resident Evil: Code: Veronica X*. In this game, the player takes on the role of a woman who is searching for her brother.

When asked what he liked about Claire Redfield as a character, Justin said, "It's usually a guy going around shooting them, but now I just like having girls because it seems like girls aren't brave enough to do this, but all these girls are chilling in this game and actually do this stuff. So that's why I like it."

Mike agreed: "I think Claire is a pretty good character. It's fun to play, like he said. Usually it's all boy characters. In this one it's a girl. It's showing that, like, I don't know, girls can be strong too, and brave too, not just boys."

Teaming Up: Violent Games and Friendships

"We absolutely had no video games in our house," said Wendy in a parents' focus group. "We had a 'no video games' rule for years. When my son was in fourth grade, we finally broke down and got a video game system, because he kept coming home from school saying, 'I'm completely out of the conversation. I don't have anything to talk about. I don't have anything to add.' "

Academic research on video games and kids has typically focused on games played in isolation. Yet for many young teens in our surveys and focus groups, friendship was a major factor in their video game play. Forty percent of middle school boys and almost a third of girls agreed that one attraction of video games is that "my friends like to play."

Roughly one third of both boys and girls said that they enjoyed teaching others how to play video games.

> Bill: "Most of the interaction my son has with his buddies is about solving situations within a game. It's all about how do you go from this place to that place, or collect the certain things that you need, and combine them in ways that are going to help you to succeed."

> Wendy: "Jody and Alex talk constantly in the car and everywhere else about the games and the characters, so it's part of their friendship, part of what they do and what they like to play. . . . And they give each other help sometimes when they get to different levels."

Research conducted for the British Board of Film Classification found differences in the ways in which boys and girls approach playing video games. "More broadly, the social rewards of gaming—talking about how you are doing, playing together, helping or beating each other—are less a part of the attraction for females than males."[15]

Nick Yee's surveys of (mostly adult) online game players also found that socializing was an important motivator. They enjoyed being part of a team, helping others and forging solid relationships.[16] This suggests that video games could play a role in healthy friendships for children and adults.

But what about violent games? The image of a friendless child holed up in his bedroom, practicing his sniper skills on a bloody video game, is a parent's nightmare. Our survey found that children who play Mature-rated games are not more likely than other children their age to play games alone. In fact, compared to children who don't play M-rated games regularly, M-game players were significantly *more* likely to play games in social settings, with one or more friends in the same room.

According to researcher Jeffrey Goldstein, PhD, "Violent entertainment appeals primarily to males, and it appeals to them mostly in groups. People rarely attend horror films or boxing matches alone, and boys do not often play war games by themselves. These are social occasions, particularly suitable for 'male bonding' and communicating a masculine identity to your mates."[17]

Boys often use rough-and-tumble play-fighting to explore aggression. They aren't out to hurt each other, but to establish dominance and a social pecking order.[18] Video game play could serve as another arena to continue that healthy battle for status among one's peers.

C. J., age twelve, comments: "Usually me and my friends, when we're over at each others' houses, they're like, 'Oh, I'll kill you in *Madden NFL.*' It's fun to beat them."

In early adolescence, boys also use play-fighting as a way to test budding relationships with girls.[19] This could easily translate to play-fighting in video games. We'd like to see studies done to explore this and how video games might be used to promote healthy boy/girl friendships as well as same-gender friendships.

Even though "I like to compete and win"—a very popular reason for video game play—could refer to beating one's personal best or a computer-generated foe, challenging and defeating a real person has definite pluses when it comes to helping young teens figure out social relationships. "I like to play with a friend better because then when you win, you can gloat," said Mike. "But then, if you lose then they gloat, too. So it's fun, and it's pretty even matched, when you play versus a friend. And I like playing versus a friend better 'cause you can talk. You can't talk to the PS2 or the Xbox or anything."

Boys also gain status among peers by owning or mastering a popular game. "My twelve-year-old son isn't a particularly good athlete," says Richard Falzone, MD, a child and adolescent psychiatrist in the Boston area. "But he's very competitive on video games. It gives him a certain social status and a certain respect among other kids. And it expands his peer group."

> Roberta: "One of my son's biggest pleasures is to have a couple of guys sleep over and ask me to take them to the video store and rent a game that they've never played. You'll see them all sitting on the couch together almost having a conference, and they'll take turns manipulating the figures."

W. George Scarlett, PhD, a psychologist at Tufts University who's an expert on children's play, has two sons who are video gamers. "Video games are a foundation for many kids' relationships. It impresses me how one kid can be playing a video game and as many as five kids can be around him and participating in what's going on."

In our survey, relatively few children chose "to make new friends" as a reason they played video games. But in focus groups, several boys mentioned that video games helped them structure conversations with potential friends.

"You say, 'Do you own a system, a game system?'" explained Carlos. "If he says 'yes,' then, 'What kind? PS2, GameCube, Xbox?' Like that."

"When kids first meet, they'll often ask, 'What games are you into?'" adds Falzone. "The common language and common experience is an instant icebreaker. It allows them to be interested in somebody else and to share a part of themselves. It's a vehicle for connection."

We've observed the icebreaker role of games in our own family, at holiday gatherings. Cousins who had been apart for months (an eternity for a child) could settle in with a video game and quickly resume their friendship.

Given the role of video game play in starting and maintaining friendships, there is potential for games to help socially awkward children gain acceptance and self-esteem. Game developer John Feil described how a friend's child, who was born prematurely and suffered a number of problems with overall health and coordination, has benefited from involvement with video games. "He had trouble walking for many years. But he's smart intellectually. Getting him video games let him be Batman and Superman. It helped him feel empowered," says Feil. "It also let him feel competitive, without having to develop a lot of physical strength."

Internet Play

A number of boys (including some from low-income neighborhoods) mentioned playing games over the Internet—sometimes teaming up with friends and other times with players from different cities or countries to play against other virtual teams.

> Josh: "[It] makes me friends, like that you don't even know; all I know is by computer. Never met them. . . . You talk to them [on the headset] as you play, 'Oh, go this way and I'll go that way.'"

"Video games allow kids to have virtual play dates," notes child psychiatrist Falzone. "They're playing games together, each from his own house, all the while talking to each other. There's lots of communication and problem-solving together."

In our survey, about one in eight children regularly played games over the Internet with friends; one in ten boys and one in twenty girls played with people they didn't know. Given that most new game consoles as well as computers allow Web-based play, socializing over the Internet is likely to increase.

While playing with strangers on the Internet sounds scary, there are virtually no reports of children being approached by predators through online games. Game chat is limited and focuses on coordinating play. Also, as Northwestern University's Cassell points out, studies show that the risk of sexual predators on the Web is overblown.[20]

"Basically, there aren't predators in the number we think there are," says Cassell. "And when there are predators, the horrifying thing is they are as likely to be family members as strangers."

Video Games and Learning Disabilities

Our survey of middle schoolers included seventy-eight students with mild learning disabilities who could fill out the survey with extra time or assistance from staff (while still keeping their answers private). As a group, these kids tended to play games for more hours per week than others. They were more likely than other children to play games to feel less lonely, to get their anger out and because they liked "the guns and other weapons."

They were also more likely to be victims of bullying and to report being left out or excluded by their peers. Their overall top reasons for playing games reflect their needs to connect with friends and cope with feelings: they played because their friends did, to make new friends, to teach others or because they were bored and games are exciting.

Child psychiatrists and psychologists have found that children with attention deficit disorder (ADD) are often particularly attracted to media, including television, video games and computers. Surveys, including ours, support the idea that kids who have problems paying attention or sitting still spend more time with video and computer games.[21] Some parents worry that video games are a cause of ADD symptoms or make them worse. But it's more likely that for kids who already have ADD, games have greater appeal.

Many of these children find school stressful, demanding and—even with an individualized education plan—not very supportive of their self-esteem. One of the things they value about electronic games is that they offer interaction without criticism.

"That feels great for most of us," says Michael Jellinek, M.D., "but it's especially important to kids who have learning disabilities. A lot of people don't appreciate how much these kids get criticized and how self-critical the kids themselves are. They don't understand how liberating it is to be in control of something like a computer where they can pause and start over, where their work comes out neat and organized instead of messy. They don't understand how much of a relief this is. The computer is unconditionally accepting, while most parents and teachers aren't."

Our middle school survey gave other hints about how children with attention or hyperactivity problems use video games. We incorporated five questions from a standardized survey used by pediatricians to screen for behavioral and other problems.[22] Boys whose responses put them over the threshold level for ADD symptoms were more likely than others to use games to cope with angry feelings. Among girls with ADD symptoms, twice as many (almost one in four) played games to make new friends compared to other girls. In moderation, these are probably healthy uses of video games.

Because skill with video games or computers can be an important source of self-esteem for a child with ADD, Jellinek encourages parents to support this. He notes that coming home from school and immediately starting on homework can be too much for these kids; some kind of after-school activity, such as a sport, can help. Once children are home, video games can serve as a useful transition to or break from homework.

At Northwestern University, Cassell and Andrea Tartaro have studied using a "virtual peer" to teach social skills to children who have autism and related disorders.[23] A virtual peer is a life-size computer-generated animated "child" projected onto a screen. The virtual child, named Sam, can interact with a real child by sharing toys (which appear both on the screen and in a real toy castle in front of the screen) and taking turns telling stories. It's a different way to use video game technology and is part of what's known as the Serious Games movement.

"We know that many children with autism and Asperger's really enjoy playing games and will play for long periods of time," says Cassell. "But that's not exposing them to the kind of social interactions that may bring them benefits. A lot of learning happens through social interactions. So we've been building a virtual child who can sit and tell stories, and model and elicit social interaction behaviors."

For example, to let the real child know it's his turn, Sam will direct her gaze at the child and use language ("She, umm . . . then she . . .") to hint that the child should pick up the tale. If he does, Sam encourages the process, saying, "And then what happens?" or "Wow!" or "Cool." Tartaro and Cassell hope this research will lead to the design of other methods to help children better connect with the social world.

Like children diagnosed with ADD, developmentally delayed kids may use video games to pass the time, especially when they have few social relationships. Parents of children with developmental delays need to keep a closer eye on media use, however, because these children may have more trouble than their peers with distinguishing a fantasy game world from the real world. This could lead them to mimic language or behavior from a game in socially inappropriate ways, possibly getting themselves into trouble. When using age-based ESRB ratings to choose games, parents need to consider their child's developmental age as well as his or her calendar age.

Handling Anger

Many boys in our focus groups described using violent games to cope with feelings of anger, frustration or stress. Based on our survey findings, young teens often use games to manage their emotions, particularly boys; 62 percent of boys played to "help me relax," 48 percent because "it helps me forget my problems" and 45 percent because "it helps me get my anger out." Among those boys who strongly agreed that they played for an emotional reason, about one in four used games to relax or cope with anger, and one in five used games to help forget problems. One in eight boys strongly agreed that they played games to feel less lonely.

In focus groups, boys talked about using games with violent content in particular as an outlet for emotional expression or as a form of distraction. For example:

> Randy: "Getting wrapped up in a violent game, it's good. 'Cause if you are mad, when you come home, you can take your anger out on the people in the game."

> Eli: "If I had a bad day at school, I'll play a violent video game and it just relieves all my stress."

> Patrick: "Last week, I missed one homework and my teacher yelled at me. . . . When I went home, I started playing *Vice City* and I did a cheat code to get a tank and I ran over everybody. And I smashed a lot of cars and blew them up. . . . I was mad, and I turned happy afterwards."

Lenny described coping with a real-life conflict by role-playing it in the game: "Say some kid wants to fight you, and he talks trash about you. When you go home and play, you're like, 'This is the kid that I hate,' and you beat him up and stuff."

Asked if playing the game might help him avoid a fight, Lenny said, "Maybe. 'Cause if I don't play a game or if I don't do nothing, it gets me even angrier, real mad. If I play a game, it's, 'All right, I beat him.' Then it feels like I really did something and I'm done, man."

A smaller but still substantial proportion of girls also clearly use electronic games to deal with feelings. Ten percent of girls strongly agreed that they played to get out anger, 16 percent to forget problems, and 13 percent to relax.

Interestingly, in her focus groups comparing views of elementary-age and college-age students, Jeanne Funk found that only the older students mentioned using games to cope with feelings—particularly relieving stress and boredom. One said, "Of people I know, video games are a tool to act out their aggression as opposed to doing it in real life."[24]

Video Games and Depression

Aside from a few studies on ADD,[25] there is almost no research on video games and children with emotional or mental health problems. As a first step in this direction, our survey included five questions from the screening tool used by pediatricians concerning symptoms of depression (feeling sad, hopeless and worried, having less fun and feeling down on themselves).[26]

About two thirds of kids who met the threshold for depression agreed that they played games to forget their problems. Depressed children were more likely than other kids to play in order to feel less lonely or to get out anger. Two-thirds of depressed girls said they played to "create my own world," compared to just one third of other girls. Depressed kids did not play video games for more hours per week than other kids, but they were more likely to play alone.

Unfortunately, we don't know enough to say whether these uses of video games to manage emotions are healthy or unhealthy for depressed children in general or any child in particular. It may be that temporary or intermittent immersion in a game is therapeutic, while playing games alone for hours most days after school makes matters worse.

CHAPTER 6

Sex, Hate, Game Addiction and Other Worries

The most politically incorrect video game ever made. Run through the ghetto blasting away various blacks and spics in an attempt to gain entrance to the subway system, where the Jews have hidden to avoid the carnage. Then, if you're lucky, you can blow away Jews as they scream "Oy Vey!" on your way to their command center.

—Promotional material from a Web site selling the game Ethnic Cleansing[1]

THE SIMPLISTIC BELIEF THAT EXPOSURE TO MEDIA VIO-lence will lead directly to individual violence is clearly wrong. So what, if anything, should we as parents, teachers and public policy makers be concerned about? Based on our own research as well as the research of others, we believe that many of the true risks to our children share several characteristics:

❖ They're subtler than the issue of violence, which means that they may be overlooked by casual observers who are focused primarily on game content, such as drugs, sex, crime and so forth.

❖ They don't affect all children in the same way. Some children are at significantly greater risk; others are likely to be unaffected.

❖ Biological and developmental issues, such as children's abilities to understand other people's hidden motives, play a significant role in determining which children are at risk. So do the psychological states of children and their emotional connections to adults and peers inside and outside their families.

❖ There are practical things that parents can do to limit many of these risks. We'll go into greater detail on some of those in chapter 9 as well as throughout this chapter.

The content of some of the games readily available to children will likely give pause to even the most ardent supporters of free speech. Like earlier generations of media critics and social reformers described in chapter 2, it's tempting for parents and politicians to focus on rare and extreme examples of troublesome games, like some of the neo-Nazi recruitment games we'll describe later in this chapter. However, this may lead to two unintended negative consequences for society in general and for our children in particular.

First, this approach gives those "outlier" games the recognition and publicity that their makers crave but otherwise wouldn't get. It legitimizes them and makes them appear more popular and mainstream than they actually are. Second, it shifts our focus away from finding effective ways to address the underlying problems, such as racism, sexism, anti-Semitism, poverty, drugs and social isolation. It's much easier to blame a game (or a comic book or a film) than it is to examine complex social issues.

Also, by focusing our attention on dramatic and upsetting content, we run the risk of glossing over some potentially significant but much more subtle problems. Are video games being used to market unhealthy or otherwise inappropriate things to our children? Are games shifting our children's perceptions of normal or appropriate behavior and healthy relationships?

Video Games, Sex and Teens

It's easy to leap to the conclusion, as so many parents and politicians have, that the sexual content of video games has significant and deleterious effects on the sexual attitudes and behaviors of the teenagers who play them. So why not just restrict it in the name of protecting children?

Even setting free speech issues aside, researchers are much more cautious in assigning blame for what teenagers do and believe when it comes to sex. In a major article published in 2005 in the prestigious medical journal *Pediatrics*, public health researchers point out that the proportion of high school students who have had sex has actually declined over the past decade. They add:

> Data regarding adolescent exposure to various media are, for the most part, severely dated. Few studies have examined the effects of mass media on adolescent sexual attitudes and behaviors: only 12 of 2522 research-related documents (<1%) involving media and youth-addressed effects, 10 of which were peer reviewed. None can serve as the grounding for evidence-based public policy.[2]

A few recent studies of television and popular music suggest that, as with violent media content, the influence of sexual media content on teen behavior may depend in large part on the context of the sexual talk or images. Two longitudinal studies of teens aged twelve to seventeen found that:

- Watching TV shows that talk about or show sexual activity makes teens more likely to engage in earlier sex, but this effect was reduced for some teens if programs showed the risks and consequences of sex.[3]
- Frequent listening to music with sexually degrading lyrics hastened teen sexual activity, whereas other sexual lyrics did not.[4]

Parents concerned about their children's exposure to sexual content in video games should keep in mind that, among ESRB-rated games, the content descriptors are not all as intuitively obvious as "Sexual Violence" and "Mature Humor." For example, "Lyrics" and "Strong Lyrics" can refer to sexual content.

And Now a Word from Our Sponsor

Let's begin with what is perhaps the most American of mass media tools: advertising. You won't find the game *Prom Paranoia*, featuring Capitán Cool and his female sidekick Super Silky, on game store shelves. Nor will you find *Sneak King, Bratz Kidz Racing Starz* or *Buzz's Adventures: The Mumbee's Curse*. Most of these games, which are aimed at children and teenagers, have no ESRB rating, although almost all would clearly be rated E (Everyone).

They are examples of a growing advertising and marketing tool known as "branded immersive advertising" or "advergames": commercially produced, simple video games distributed for free or at low cost to promote a product, brand or idea and to gather marketing and contact information, often from children. As with all marketing to children, these games raise the question of whether the target audience understands the underlying motives and goals of the sponsor.

They also raise questions about the effects they'll have on the game players. Unlike commercially produced fantasy games, most advergames have a well-defined behavioral goal: getting players to ask for or to purchase a product. They also help make a Web site "stickier," which means that visitors stay there for a longer time. This stickiness metaphor seems especially apt for the children's game *Buzz's Adventures: The Mumbee's Curse*, underwritten by General Mills's Honey Nut Cheerios cereal.

The player begins by reading, "After tracking the mumbee's movements, Buzz [an animated bee] and his pals find themselves in a system of lost catacombs nestled deep within the hive. Maybe the key to the recent disappearance of golden honey used to make Honey Nut Cheerios so irresistible is down here?" In the next panel, one of the bees says, "I don't know what's scarier—breakfast without Honey Nut Cheerios, or this creep-tastic cave!" The cereal's logo is clearly visible throughout the game.

This heavy-handed marketing approach (and ham-handed writing) is common among advergames aimed at children. Current advergames remind us of children's programming during the early days of television. Many of those shows, especially the ones produced by local stations, contained repeated product mentions and other plugs by the hosts between the commercials. It was common for television programs of that era, like the radio programs of an earlier generation, to contain the sponsor's name in their titles: *Texaco Star Theater*, *Mutual of Omaha's Wild Kingdom*.

To play upon teenagers' acute sensitivities about how they look, Procter and Gamble's Head & Shoulders shampoo sponsored *Prom Paranoia*, a Spanish-language advergame. It's set in the futuristic Caspita ("dandruff") City, where Capitán Cool and Super Silky patrol the skies in their Head & Shoulders-branded spaceship. They receive a message that three teenagers (Jorge, Gabriela and Miguel) are having problems with—you guessed it—dandruff on their prom night. The players can select and guide either Capitán Cool or Super Silky as they battle sebaceous flakes, fungi and other adolescent scalp horrors.

Children are offered a free sample of the shampoo if they complete an online form giving their mailing address, e-mail address, telephone number and other information. Filling in the form also allows them to compete with other players to have their high scores on the game posted on the sponsor's Web site.

Sneak King takes a different approach to marketing. It was one of a trio of inexpensive Xbox 360 games created for Burger King restaurants in 2006 and offered for sale exclusively at those restaurants. The games were promoted through a national advertising campaign and were rated E by the ESRB.

This game, like the cereal-sponsored game mentioned earlier, is little more than an extended advertisement since the Burger King mascot is the protagonist. The premise for the game is painfully strained:

> It takes a special person to sneak up on someone with a hot, delicious sandwich. It takes an even more special person to get away with it. And only the King can pull it off with vigor, finesse and a royal flourish. . . . So step right up and into the royal shoes. Sneak down alleys, roads and sidewalks to surprise innocent bystanders with a burger. If you do it well, you'll be rewarded.[5]

In addition to distributing the game, Burger King offered several tournaments at which being rewarded (receiving a prize of an Xbox gaming system) was not a function of doing well in the competition; prizewinners were selected at random from entrants. To participate in the tournament, however, children had to register by providing their name, date of birth, e-mail address and cell phone number. (The notice at the top of the registration page read, "Okay, so we need some information from you. It's no big deal really. Just fill out the form below to get e-mail or mobile alerts from BK® and BKgamer.com. All vital information, right? So sign up today."[6])

Rules for the tournament, which are in tiny type on a separate page, state that participants must be at least eighteen years old at the time they enter. (Would anyone over the age of eighteen be interested in such a game? We doubt it.) A few paragraphs lower, Burger King adds, "If a potential winner is a minor, his/her parent or legal guardian will be required to sign the Affidavit/Release on the potential winner's behalf."[7] Clearly, they're aware of their real audience.

For sponsors, a key attraction of advergames is that they provide a means and excuse to obtain contact and demographic information on children who are prospective customers so that they can be approached directly. Parents should be concerned about any Web site that asks children to submit personal information for inclusion in any database.

In the United States, the Federal Trade Commission regulates gathering information online from children under the age of thirteen through the Children's Online Privacy Protection Act (COPPA).[8] That act requires the posting of privacy policies on Web sites, limits the use of data collected, and defines those circumstances in which Web site operators have to obtain permission from parents to gather or use data from each child. In many cases, Web sites will automatically "lock out" a child whose birth date shows that she's younger than thirteen, eighteen or whatever cutoff they've chosen.

But kids are smart. After a few experiences like this, they learn quickly that they should submit a birth date that makes them appear to be over twenty-one. When the Burger King Web site locked us out after we submitted a birth date claiming that we were twelve years old, it only took us a few seconds to remove the lock and resubmit the same information, changing only the birth date to claim that we were now suddenly fifty. The second try was immediately accepted. Clearly that lock is not very strong.

The growth in e-mail, instant messaging on computers and SMS text messaging on cell phones opens new frontiers for marketers and advertisers trying to reach children with sales messages. Young children and even teenagers may not be aware of why marketing firms are collecting their contact and other personal information.

The situation is disturbingly similar to that of lonely, elderly people whose cognitive abilities are no longer up to par and who are targeted by telemarketers. As a result, some of those people are financially and emotionally exploited. The same could happen to children who cannot put the marketing and sales messages they receive into perspective.

Keeping "Buy Me" at Bay

There's no doubt that playing some advergames can be a lot of fun. However, it's not a good idea to let your children play them unchecked. What you should do will depend upon the age and sophistication of your child.

Protect your child's privacy. Children should know never to put personal information such as their name, address, e-mail or birthday on a computer form unless it's for school or for health care. This applies to any request for information on the Web or elsewhere, not just those associated with games. They should know to check with you first.

Children in elementary and middle school are especially vulnerable to this type of marketing. They're used to taking directions from adults and often cannot fathom the true goals of marketers and others in gathering such information. They're also easily lured by the promise of a gift or membership in a special club.

As a parent, you should act as an intermediary between all of these materials and your child. If your child insists on filling out a form that requires personal information, use *your* e-mail address and other contact information so that you can screen what gets sent by the company before relaying any of it to her.

Teenagers are savvier than younger children about company marketing strategies and motives. This is a reflection of their brain development. You can use this to your advantage in helping them become more media literate. (We'll go into this in greater detail in chapter 9.)

Talk with your kids about why companies use advergames. The level of your discussion will be determined largely by your children's age. Point out how sponsors make their product more attractive by having game characters say and do certain things. Point out logos and other marketing materials embedded in the game. Help them understand what the sponsor hopes to get children to feel, believe or do.

Be wary of downloading games. Spyware and other software that tracks your child's online activities can be embedded into games. So can computer viruses. Make sure your computer has up-to-date virus and spyware protection programs.

Social Marketing Games

Social marketing, also known as cause-related marketing, focuses on such important and noble issues as youth smoking prevention, organ donation, wearing seatbelts in cars and the benefits of good nutrition. We've both worked as consultants in this field of communication for many years. The things we've observed in other media also apply to video games.

Most people who engage in social marketing are filled with the best of intentions. They really do want to make the world a better place. Unfortunately, much of the material produced for these campaigns is strikingly ineffective and, all too often, stunningly inappropriate. Video games, especially advergames, are now a part of that morass. Here are a few examples:

Hallway Hurdles, which was sponsored by the Ad Council and the U.S. Army, is a rather bizarre bit of social marketing designed to encourage teenagers to stay in school. Players get a choice of assuming the roles of " 'A-Plus' Alice" or " 'True Fact' Jack" as they make their way toward graduating from high school. Oddly, they do this by engaging in many of the behaviors that real schools frown upon. Players can only succeed if they run through the halls; get into frequent fistfights with oversized orange gang members and green drug dealers (apparently the Bloods and Crips of this animated world); leap over desks that symbolize detention, bottles that symbolize alcohol abuse and overflowing garbage cans that apparently symbolize overflowing garbage cans; and receive grades of "A" simply by being in the right place at the right time.

There is nothing in the game that bears any resemblance whatsoever to the academic skills or emotional resilience needed to graduate from high school. None of the behaviors that are rewarded in the game, such as getting into fistfights with drug dealers and gang members, make any sense at all in the real world. What did the designers of this game think this running-jumping-punching race would accomplish as part of a program to prevent high school students from dropping out? It is bizarre, to say the least.

Similarly, MTV has promoted its online *Darfur Is Dying* game as a way that players can help stop the genocide in the Darfur region of western Sudan:

Darfur is Dying is a narrative-based simulation where the user, from the perspective of a displaced Darfurian, negotiates forces that threaten the survival of his or her refugee camp. It offers a faint glimpse of what it's like for the more than 2.5 million who have been internally displaced by the crisis in Sudan.[9]

A faint glimpse, indeed! To start the game, the player selects one of several children who must forage for water and bring it back to the camp. The instructions warn:

You risk being attacked and possibly killed by Janjaweed militias when you leave the confines of your camp, but you must do it in order to provide water for your community. Navigate by using the arrow keys to move and the spacebar to hide.[10]

The pathetic-looking child grasps a water can tightly in her hands as she runs through the desert, sometimes hiding behind the occasional cattle carcass or bush. Meanwhile armed militiamen in four-wheel-drive vehicles hunt her down. When the player is caught, the following message appears:

You have been captured by the militia. You will likely become one of the hundreds of thousands of people already lost to this humanitarian crisis. Girls in Darfur face abuse, rape and kidnapping by the Janjaweed. . . . As someone at a far-off computer, and not a child or adult in Sudan, would you like a chance to try again?[11]

Dig Beneath the Surface

The problem with these types of social marketing games is that they may give us, as parents and as children, the unwarranted sense that we're actually accomplishing something when we're not. This can have the unintended and dangerous consequence of our not paying attention to the real issues that underlie what makes a child drop out of school or what can be done to help the victims of genocide. (Some cynics have referred to this approach to solving social ills as "slacktivism.") You may feel good for a moment or two, but you accomplish nothing.

Talk to your child about the underlying problems that inspired the game. Let the game naturally trigger conversation. Keep things light; don't turn it into a lecture.

Explore ways of becoming involved in these issues outside of the game. That may be as simple as looking up more information or finding out how a problem affects your community.

Portrayal of Women

The "good girl" drawings in the 1950s comic books that we mentioned in chapter 2 can't hold a candle to many of the images of women in video games. There is nothing inherently wrong with this; many drawings in fantasy games are, like the drawings in comics, creative, over-the-top caricatures. The exaggerated eyes and mouth of the chef in *Cooking Mama: Cook Off* are as unrealistic as the exaggerated breasts and fangs of the half-vampire in *BloodRayne*.

These omnipresent buxom, wasp-waisted video game women—even those who don't sport fangs—draw the ire of social critics who say that they promote superficial definitions of beauty and impossible physical proportions. They may be right.

But the real issue of concern is both less obvious and more complex. While there are a few heroines in these games, such as the impossibly proportioned Lara Croft in the *Tomb Raider* series and Rayne in the *BloodRayne* series, most game protagonists—especially adventure game protagonists—are men. This is probably because boys and men constitute the majority of game players. Thus, many adventure game heroines fit stereotypical male fantasies. There are exceptions, such as Kate Walker, the attorney-turned-adventurer in the *Syberia* series. Also, there is some evidence that the proportion of video game heroines is increasing.[12]

The greater problem may be that most of the women in most of the current games are adjuncts to the plot, not main characters. They're like the "Bond Girls" in the movies: they're known primarily for their looks, they often need to be rescued and they are surrounded by many men who have much more power, money and influence. The James Bond movies also had exceptions to this rule, of course, but they are largely noticed *because* they are exceptions: exotic temptresses who could deliver a lethal punch, kick or squeeze.

Of the sixteen major characters in *Grand Theft Auto: Vice City*, for example, only one (Auntie Poulet, a voodoo chemist and the elderly leader of a Haitian gang) is a woman. A few more women are minor characters. As with films and comics, this male-female discrepancy is still the norm for adventure video games. This leaves girls without many nonviolent video game heroines with whom they can identify.

Explore Role Models

It became clear during our focus group interviews with middle schoolers that they identified strongly with the characters in the commercially produced games that they played. Some even fantasized about what life might be like if they could become that character in the real world.

Talk about different characters' roles in the games. Let your child do most of the talking. See what he thinks about a character's personality and values as well as his goals. Find out what he likes and dislikes about the character's apparent values.

Use games to trigger conversations about your child's own aspirations and dreams. Don't take these too literally, of course. And don't be surprised if he hasn't thought much about them or is reluctant to talk. Just let him know that it's an open topic.

Express your opinions clearly but gingerly. If you think that a game is sexist, point that out but don't harp on it. Because children identify with these characters, they're likely to defend them out of a sense of loyalty. If you attack an issue like this too hard, your children will probably feel so defensive that they won't listen.

Flash Dance

The easy availability of Flash and other inexpensive software and integrated development environments has spawned the creation of many thousands of games. Most of these are obviously innocuous: in *Frisbee Dog*, the player guides a dog that's riding a skateboard. The goal is to have the dog catch either a ball or a Frisbee with his mouth and to avoid catching the occasional flying hand grenade.

This is fairly typical of the types of homemade games available on the Internet: simple, single-task-oriented tests of skill, coordination, timing and luck. Amateur developers can create more sophisticated games by purchasing a "game engine"—customizable software that forms the core of a game's graphics and action. These powerful programs are inexpensive, with some available for free and others costing only a few hundred dollars or less for noncommercial game developers. They have allowed hobbyists and organizations to create much more graphically and structurally sophisticated games than they otherwise could. Consequently, children have access to a growing number of video and computer games that are created and distributed outside the bounds of traditional retail channels.

Addressing Uncomfortable Topics

Take a moment to do a Web search using the terms "racist games" or "porno games." As of mid-2007, each of these resulted in more than two million hits, which gives an idea of how common games with these themes have become. The number of actual games in each category is far less, of course, and they still constitute a small minority of games. But in each case, the actual number of racist or pornographic games is likely to be in the hundreds, if not the thousands.

This shouldn't be surprising. Sexual content has been a mainstay of many new media, including the Internet, video, comics, film, photography, books, sculpture—even ancient European and Asian pottery.

Similarly, fringe political groups have tended to embrace new media earlier and more enthusiastically than more mainstream groups. The Library of Congress maintains an impressive collection of hand-printed broadsides published by radical groups and individuals in the mid-eighteenth century calling for the American colonies' independence from Great Britain. These single sheets of paper, sometimes filled with graphics and caricatures, were the mass media of their day.

Coming across sexual material in games, or adjacent to games that are played on the Web, can be upsetting and confusing to young children. That's another reason why it's a good idea to supervise any online game playing.

Games with a Social or Political Agenda

Today there are a lot of games—many of them available for free—that make no bones about spewing racist, sexist, homophobic and anti-Semitic beliefs, often wrapped in attempts at humor. Many are quite simple. In *Kaboom: The Suicide Bombing Game*, players use a computer mouse to direct an Arab suicide bomber along a city street, timing the explosion to maximize the carnage. After each explosion, the scoreboard lists the numbers of men, women and children killed and injured by the blast. The start page of the game shows a caricature of the late Yasir Arafat; all of the people killed on the street except the suicide bomber are white.

Border Patrol has slightly more sophisticated graphics and related themes. The game is set along what is presumably the Rio Grande on the border between Mexico and Texas. A sign, filled with bullet holes, is stuck in the sand. It says, "Welcome to the United States." In the American flag depicted below those words, the fifty stars have been replaced by a large Star of David, thereby awkwardly combining anti-Semitic and anti-Mexican sentiments. A nearby handwritten sign points the way to the "Welfare Office."

The player points a rifle sight at any of three types of caricature cartoon targets as they run across the desert: an armed "Mexican Nationalist," a "Drug Smuggler," or a "Breeder"—a pregnant woman dragging two young children behind her. When a player hits a target, it spurts blood for a second and then disappears from the scene. With each killing, the player gets a higher "wetback" score.

There are hundreds of similar games: *Virtual Drive By 2* ("Feel what it's like in the ghetto"), *Watch Out Behind You, Hunter* ("Shoot the fags before they rape you"), *NES KKK* ("The original Mario Brothers with a good ol' Ku Klux Klan twist"), *Amor Caliente* (an animated low-budget porn film).

Link to the Real World

You should expect your children to run across these games, either by themselves or with the help of their friends. As with all generations of children, there's a particular thrill in doing something that you know your parents don't want you to do. (We'll see how one group is exploiting that feeling in the next section.)

Don't assume that playing these games occasionally reflects your child's true beliefs. More likely, he's exploring what it might feel like to be someone who has different values from his own and different perceptions of the world. It's like using a major league baseball video game to see what it's like to be a manager, or a flight simulator to try out being a pilot.

Talk to your child about the values being promoted by the game. Listen more than you lecture. Explain why you disagree with the assumptions built into the game and the actions taken by the characters. Encourage your child to think about why someone might find these games funny or rewarding.

Link the games to real-world problems. Illegal drugs and drug culture, for example, are routine themes of homemade games and even some commercially produced games. If you find your child playing *Drug Pusher*[13] online, use that as an opportunity to talk about the larger issue.

We Want YOU: Recruitment Games

The National Socialist Movement (NSM), an American neo-Nazi organization, offers links to free downloads of several games, including *Concentration Camp Rat Hunt*, in which the player shoots Jewish "rats" inside the Auschwitz death camp. The NSM Web site promotes these games specifically to children:

Yes, these free computer games will drive teachers and parents crazy, because they are politically incorrect, and even downright

NS [neo-Nazi]. So much the better! Some people just don't know how to have a good time. But YOU do! So do your friends.

These free computer games are real collector [sic] items. Let's face it, the retail stores do not carry these computer games. And you won't see them advertised on TV or in your local papers.

The NSM in joint cooperation with the NSDAP/AO [National-sozialistische Deutsche Arbeiterpartei/Auslands-Organisation, the National Socialist German Workers Party/Foreign Organization] are launching a mass literature distribution of flyers announcing these video games.

All Pro-White groups and activists are urged to assist in this project and get the word out to the Public. Any NSM or NSDAP/AO activists willing to pass out these leaflets in large amounts are urged to contact us asap. Hail Victory![14]

We quoted some of the marketing material for *Ethnic Cleansing* at the beginning of this chapter. The game is produced and sold by Resistance Records, which is a division of the National Alliance, another neo-Nazi and white-supremacist group in the United States. The premise for *Ethnic Cleansing* is outlined at the beginning of the game:

The Race War has begun. Your skin is your uniform in this battle for the survival of your kind. The White Race depends on you to secure its existence. Your peoples [*sic*] enemies surround you in a sea of decay and filth that they have brought to your once clean and White nation.

Not one of their numbers shall be spared. . . .

Unlike other games of this ilk, which can be downloaded for free, this one is sold for a token amount of money. While the money received by the National Alliance is relatively small, much greater value comes from being able to build a list of contact information from children and adults who purchase this material. Indeed, recruitment is a key goal behind this type of game development.

Using games to recruit adolescents into organizations is not limited to neo-Nazi, white-supremacist and skinhead groups. The U.S. government does it, too. Since July 2002, the U.S. Army has used a series of *America's Army* video games as recruitment tools. These games and their promotional materials combine video images with sophisticated graphics. The introduction to *America's Army—Virtual Army Experience* begins:

> The Virtual Army Experience (VAE) provides participants with a virtual "test drive" of the Army, with a focus on operations in the Global War on Terrorism. The core of the 10,000+ square foot VAE is the America's Army: Special Forces (Overmatch) computer game, rendered with state-of-the-art Army training simulation technology to create a life-size, networked virtual world. The VAE highlights key Soldier occupations, Army technologies, operating environments and mission profiles, within a fast-paced, action-packed, information-rich experience that immerses visitors in the world of Soldiering in the U.S. Army. Participants employ teamwork, rules of engagement, leadership and high-tech equipment as they take part in a virtual mission to capture an HVT (High Value Target).[15]

The Web site refers to real-world army recruiting fairs across the country as "upcoming missions." Players have the option of participating in formal competitions, such as those run by the Hostile Tactics Gaming League.[16]

Palestinian groups have developed games to recruit teenagers in its intifada (uprising) against Israel. In *Under Ash*, the player assumes the role of Ahmed, a young Palestinian stone-thrower who battles the Israeli army and settlers. The game publisher's Web site states in fractured English:

> A nation in Palestine is being uprooted: their houses are being devastated, their establishments are being destroyed, their lands are being occupied, their trees are being pulled out, their property is being confiscated, their cities are being besieged, their schools are being closed, their sanctuaries are being violated, their sacred structures are being made permitted, their children are being beaten, their hands are being broken, their bones are being crushed and they are imprisoned, tortured and slain. They are

even prevented from crying and moaning. The whole world is plotting to ignore them. None hears them moan. None sees the trains of their martyrs. None says a word of support to their rights. . . .

UnderAsh is a call to justice, realizing truth, preventing wronging and aggression.

This idea, accompanied by the best available technology, is still handy to our youth, trying to dry up their tears; heal their wounds; remove all the feelings of humiliation, humbleness and wretchedness from their souls, and draw the smile of hope and the sense of dignity and efficiency on their faces.[17]

A more recent game by the same publisher, AfkarMedia, called *Under Siege*, is more sophisticated. Despite the protestations of the publisher that "it does not include shooting at civilians or abusing them, nor does it include suicide bombing or any terrorist simulation,"[18] its "teaser video" includes scenes of a child's teddy bear being crushed by a tank, a Palestinian father being executed on the street, and Israeli soldiers firing at a Red Crescent (Red Cross) ambulance.[19]

Welcome to Our (Scary) World

Video games can be extremely powerful lures, especially when they're trolled in front of teenagers. One of the hallmarks of adolescence is that children this age feel invulnerable. The games allow them to take risks in the virtual world without consequences in the real world.

There's nothing wrong with that. In fact, that's what adventure games are all about. But we know that it's unlikely that we'll soon be battling aliens or zombies; the scenarios for recruitment games are much closer to our world, emotionally if not physically.

This relates to the issue of relevance discussed in chapter 1. Game fantasies can be particularly engaging and appealing when they offer a child or teenager someone at whom they can direct their real-world anger. He or she might even consider adopting some of a game character's behaviors and attitudes as his or her own behaviors and attitudes in the real world.

This doesn't mean children will turn into neo-Nazis or join the army because they choose to play games that attempt to convert or recruit. The games allow them to see themselves in different roles, and often with significantly more power in the virtual world than they have in the real world.

These simulations are of necessity and purposely incomplete. The same could be said of college recruitment brochures aimed at adolescents and their parents; they focus only on select positive aspects of an experience rather than a complete picture. Children and teens are likely to be unaware of this, and sometimes, that's exactly what the game developer is counting on.

As parents, you can help your children fill in the missing parts of the picture. How is the game different from reality? What things are glossed over during the game play? What are the underlying premises—the things that the game designers are asking you to assume are true for the game to make sense? Are those things true?

Video Game Addiction: It Turned Into a Battle of Wills

Richard Falzone, MD, is a child and adolescent psychiatrist in suburban Boston who specializes in treating teenagers who have substance abuse problems. Most of the time, they use alcohol or street drugs. Some abuse prescription drugs. A growing number, he says, act as if they're addicted to video games.

"I'm seeing a fifteen-year-old boy who has been hospitalized for depression and for cutting himself. He's bombing out of school, not because he wasn't smart, but because he couldn't cut down on the time he spent playing *World of Warcraft*. He would spend ten to twelve hours a day playing the game; he would play until somebody made him get off the computer. His parents would put controls on the computer to limit its use, but he would figure out ways to bypass them. He would pretend to go to sleep and get up in the middle of the night to play. It turned into a battle of wills. He would get very upset and angry until he got his fix. Sometimes he wouldn't make it to school and would sleep through the day because he's been playing video games all night."

Clearly this young man has significant problems that are interfering with his life. But is it really an addiction? That's a term bandied about freely; we describe some people as "addicted to food" and others as "addicted to eBay." There are three diagnostic hallmarks of an addiction:

- A compulsive, physiological craving for a substance
- Increased tolerance (needing a higher dose to get the same effect) following early use
- Well-defined and uncomfortable physiological symptoms during withdrawal.

Among drug addicts who use heroin, for example, these three hallmarks are obvious. We also see them clearly among alcoholics. With these and other classically addictive substances, we can see changes in the brains of addicts in response to both the substances' introduction and their withdrawal.

Does this hold true for video games? The best answer today is: we don't know. Playing video games that involve a lot of action has been associated with increased levels of two neurotransmitters in the brain, dopamine and norepinephrine, that help brain cells send messages to each other. These neurotransmitters are involved in both learning and addiction.

Some of the children labeled as addicted to video games may be struggling with a compulsion similar to an obsessive-compulsive disorder. Their game playing behavior may be out of their control and interfering with their lives, but the underlying mechanism may be different than that of someone addicted to a drug. Others said to be addicted to games may simply be responding to the powerful reinforcements they receive every so often (a "variable-ratio reinforcement schedule") when they play. These children may have more in common with recreational lottery players and casino gamblers than with drug addicts.

Some supposedly addicted game players may be behaving normally— but not in the ways that the adults around them believe to be normal. For example, many young children and preadolescents have difficulty making the transition from one activity to another, especially when the initial activity is pleasurable. We can see this when a parent asks a child to stop playing a game or to stop watching television in a minute and get ready for dinner. The child promises to do exactly that and makes that promise with great sincerity. But ten minutes later he's still playing the game or watching TV, unaware that so much time has passed.

Is this a sign of addiction? No. It's normal. In fact, it's a reflection of brain development. But parents sometimes interpret this type of behavior as anything from spite to laziness. It's not.

Finally, as parents we may unconsciously apply different standards to different behaviors. If a child plays basketball or plays the piano for four hours per day, we may describe him as a dedicated athlete or musician. A teenager who knows all the game statistics and trivia about a local professional football team, and who spends a lot of money buying jerseys and other memorabilia, is considered a true fan. It's a socially acceptable hobby; in fact, it's encouraged. But if that child takes the same approach to playing video games, spending hours each day at the computer and reveling in the details and strategies of play, we may worry about an addiction.

This concern leads parents and clinicians to focus on easily measured behaviors, such as the amount of time the child spends playing video games, instead of more useful indicators of a potential problem. Is your child finishing his schoolwork? Is he establishing balanced and reciprocal friendships with peers?

The danger in calling some children's behavior a video game addiction if it's not is that we might miss underlying problems such as depression. That's a classic case of treating a symptom (e.g., a fever) and not the disease (e.g., a bacterial infection). On the other hand, if we don't identify the behavior as a video game addiction when that's what's really going on, we may be distracted by other behavioral problems and miss the opportunity to treat the underlying cause.

Did Video Game Addiction Trigger This Suicide?

On Thanksgiving morning 2001, Shawn Woolley fatally shot himself in the head.[20] He was twenty-one years old. His mother, Elizabeth Woolley, found him sitting at his computer surrounded by notes about *EverQuest*, a game he had been playing increasingly and even obsessively for several years. Mrs.

Woolley, who later founded the self-help organization On-Line Gamers Anonymous, blamed the game for her son's death.

Her seemingly logical argument is that her son had become addicted to *EverQuest*. (Indeed, some of the game's aficionados playfully refer to it as *"EverCrack,"* comparing its seductive quality to crack cocaine.) She had noticed that Shawn had become increasingly isolated and had spent most of his last days sitting at his computer, playing the game.

Whatever the cause, Shawn Woolley's suicide was a tragedy. But his mother's post hoc, ergo propter hoc ("after this, therefore because of this") logic does not tell the whole story. Concluding that video game addiction led to the death of an otherwise healthy young man may unintentionally lead other parents and clinicians to miss opportunities to save lives.

In fact, Shawn Woolley was not otherwise healthy; he had a long history of neurological and psychiatric problems. He had been diagnosed with depression and with schizoid personality disorder, a mental illness characterized by an avoidance of close social relationships and a preference for solitary activities, among other things.

Shawn had recently quit his job and been evicted from his apartment. After moving back in with his mother and then being admitted to and leaving a group home, he rented another apartment despite his mother's objections and started playing the game non-stop. He purchased the gun he used to shoot himself a week before he took his own life.

Major depressive disorders are closely associated with suicide, especially among young people. Having a schizoid personality disorder would make Shawn seek ways to withdraw socially and to isolate himself. It would also make him less likely to seek help from others for his problems.

It's much more likely that his obsessive video game playing was a reflection of his other, more profound problems—a way he tried unsuccessfully to handle the intense emotions and stress he was feeling—and not the root cause of his suicide.

So what's going on with the fifteen-year-old boy being treated by Dr. Falzone? We know that a significant number of children his age use video games to help them cope with their negative emotions, especially depression, anger and anxiety. It's a form of self-treatment or self-medication, similar to people who eat chocolate or drink alcohol when they're feeling sad. In this case, playing video games may be a coping mechanism. (Whether they're an effective or an appropriate coping mechanism is a separate question.)

We also know that this boy has a history of a significant mood disorder. He's been hospitalized for depression. He's cut himself repeatedly—a type of self-injury that's associated with feeling emotionally overwhelmed. Paradoxically, self-injury is a way that these children try to help themselves feel better.

Is his use of video games simply the best way he can think of to handle his overwhelming feelings? If so, then labeling his behavior an addiction might be a red herring and could lead to focusing on the wrong issues. Or might it be a true addiction that's compounding his other problems? If so, then treating it as an addiction might help him handle his depression and self-injury behaviors as well. At this point, we simply don't know.

This lack of clarity about video game addictions and other computer-related addictions hasn't stopped well-intentioned therapists and entrepreneurs from developing and selling treatment programs. Often these programs market their services by offering nonvalidated behavioral assessments that are quite broad (e.g., "Have your child's grades gone down?" "Has your child preferred to play a video game rather than spend time with a friend?"). Consequently, many people's responses portray them as potentially addicted.

There are at least several reasons why we may be reading and seeing much more about video game addictions. Despite significant progress in the diagnosis and treatment of mental illness over the past few generations, our culture still associates it with significant stigma. Many people still view mental illnesses as the result of a weakness of will, a defect in character or bad parenting. As parents, we may view a child's mental illness as a reflection of our own competence and worth, something we would never do if our child had a disease that affected a different organ.

No rational person would tell a child who has diabetes to "just try harder" to make insulin. ("Your brother's pancreas makes great insulin! Why can't you be like him?") Yet we tell people—especially children and adolescents—who suffer from depression to "just get over it." ("Everyone feels sad at times. It's no big deal. Snap out of it. These are the best years of your life!")

Describing our child's aberrant and even self-destructive activities and demeanor as the result of a video game addiction is a way for us to distance ourselves from stigmatized behaviors. It's the game's fault, not ours. It's self-protective for us as parents, but it may not help our child. We may focus on limiting his access to a computer but not help him cope with his underlying mood disorder or thought disorder.

Also, fears surrounding new technologies create new markets for services. Video games are no different. While some treatment programs may be both appropriate and successful for some children, teens and young adults, other programs will offer little more than repackaged nineteenth-century snake oil. What are needed, of course, are well-designed scientific studies of both the video game addiction diagnosis and various treatments. Impassioned beliefs and slick marketing materials are never a good substitute for strong data and rigorous analysis.

CHAPTER 7

I'm from the Video Game Industry and I'm Here to Help

The continual increase in adult content, the failure to use the AO rating, and the "hot coffee" scandal of 2005 all point toward the deep flaws in the ESRB rating system.

—National Institute on Media and the Family's Tenth Annual MediaWise Video Game Report Card, November 29, 2005[1]

NIMF's attack on ESRB ratings has nothing to do with whether a rating is accurate and everything to do with the real agenda of NIMF, which is to ban the sale of games it does not like.

—Entertainment Software Rating Board Comments on MediaWise Video Game Report Card, November 29, 2005[2]

IF YOU THINK IT'S DIFFICULT TO DESIGN GOOD VIDEO GAME research and to interpret it accurately, try putting together a rating system! The video game industry has learned a great deal from previous industry-imposed rating systems for films, comic books and television. However, they face an additional challenge: unlike those other media, video games are nonlinear. In almost all cases, you don't simply start at the beginning and proceed along a predefined path to a conclusion. Like chess or Monopoly, different players have different experiences, and each player can take multiple paths through the game. Each path exposes the player to different things.

In this chapter, we'll look at the agendas behind comments like those that opened this chapter. We'll explain how the ESRB system is supposed to work and compare it to systems used in other countries. Drawing on our survey of 501 parents, as well as focus group discussions, we'll look at what parents want from ratings and how they use ratings to make decisions about what games to buy or rent for their children. Finally, we'll make a few recommendations both for how parents should use the current system and how it should be improved.

In the United States, the rating systems for movies, television, music and electronic games are designed by their respective industries to help parents select age-appropriate media for their children. Most provide general age guidelines and additional information in specific content categories. As we described briefly in chapter 2, these systems arose in response not only to pressure from the public, legislative bodies and government agencies, but also to stave off potential direct government oversight and censorship.

In 1994, a consortium of game producers founded the Interactive Digital Software Association, now known as the Entertainment Software Association. This group, in turn, created and funded the Entertainment Software Rating Board (ESRB), which issues the ratings printed on each game's box and advertising.

While participation in the ESRB rating system is voluntary for publishers, having an ESRB rating makes it significantly easier for a game to be sold in traditional retail outlets. Publishers who participate sign a contract that binds them to follow ESRB rules and to fully disclose the content of the games being rated.

Beyond the Reach of the ESRB

"The recent release of *V-Tech Massacre*, a sick game which exploits the Virginia Tech University tragedy, is a painful reminder of the culture of violence which has severe consequences on our youth and society," said New York State senator Andrew Lanza in a May 2007 press release.[3] "The emotions and behaviors of our children are far too often shaped by the virtual reality of violent movies and video games. It is imperative that we find a way to prevent these virtual realities from continuing to fuel and teach the violent behavior which is corrupting our youth."

Lanza sponsored a bill meant to "crack down" on video game violence, including a review of the ESRB's system and effectiveness. The game he refers to, *V-Tech Rampage,* is a crude home-brew affair. It reenacts the killings at Virginia Tech, with the player taking the role of Seung-Hui Cho. "It was meant to be offensive, so me and my friends and people like [us] could have a laugh," said the young Australian who created it.[4]

The problem with Lanza's logic, however, is that games like *V-Tech Rampage* have nothing to do with the game industry or the ratings system. It's available for free on the Internet, not sold in stores. Regulations designed to restrict sales of ESRB-rated, industry-produced games would have no effect on these types of games.

The ESRB ratings comprise two components[5]: an age symbol that's placed on the front of the game box, and as many as five or six content descriptors that are printed next to that age symbol on the back. The standard ESRB age symbols are:

- EC: Early Childhood. Suitable for all children age three and older.
- E: Everyone. Suitable for everyone age six and older.
- E10+: Everyone 10+. Suitable for everyone age ten and older.
- T: Teen. May be suitable for ages thirteen and older.
- M: Mature. May be suitable for ages seventeen and older.
- AO: Adults Only. Contains content that should only be played by persons eighteen and older.

Some advertisements for games display a rating of RP, for "rating pending." This refers to a game that's undergoing ESRB review before its release.

Games rated E, T and M are by far the most common. The difference between a rating of M (17+) and AO (18+) is more than just the difference in one year, as we'll explore later in this chapter.

In addition to the rating, the ESRB assigns any of more than thirty content descriptors designed to give prospective purchasers a sense of both the content and the tone of the game. These range from "Crude Humor" ("Depictions or dialogue involving vulgar antics, including 'bathroom' humor") to "Use of Drugs" ("The consumption or use of illegal drugs"). In the area of violence alone, the content descriptors include:

- Animated Blood—Discolored and/or unrealistic depictions of blood.
- Blood—Depictions of blood.
- Blood and Gore—Depictions of blood or the mutilation of body parts.
- Cartoon Violence—Violent actions involving cartoon-like situations and characters. May include violence where a character is unharmed after the action has been inflicted.
- Comic Mischief—Depictions or dialogue involving slapstick or suggestive humor.
- Fantasy Violence—Violent actions of a fantasy nature, involving human or nonhuman characters in situations easily distinguishable from real life.
- Intense Violence—Graphic and realistic-looking depictions of physical conflict. May involve extreme and/or realistic blood, gore, weapons and depictions of human injury and death.
- Language—Mild to moderate use of profanity.
- Lyrics—Mild references to profanity, sexuality, violence, alcohol or drug use in music.
- Mild Violence—Mild scenes depicting characters in unsafe and/or violent situations.
- Sexual Violence—Depictions of rape or other violent sexual acts.
- Strong Language—Explicit and/or frequent use of profanity.
- Strong Lyrics—Explicit and/or frequent references to profanity, sex, violence, alcohol or drug use in music.
- Violence—Scenes involving aggressive conflict.

Are all of these variations really necessary? When does "Cartoon Violence" become "Comic Mischief"? Is "Blood and Gore" more intense than "Blood"?

ESRB president Patricia Vance told us that this array of descriptors grew over time in response to demands for more nuance and detail on violent content, the category of greatest interest to most parents. ESRB raters and staff sometimes suggest new descriptors when the existing ones aren't specific or detailed enough.

The meaning of or standards for a descriptor can change with the age rating. A violence descriptor in a T-rated game, for example, will refer to milder content than that same descriptor assigned to an M-rated game. Also, to avoid overcrowding the game box, milder descriptors such as "tobacco reference" might be left off a game rated M, on the assumption that a parent is unlikely to base his or her decision to buy a Mature-rated game on whether cigarettes are mentioned.

A Tempest in a Coffee Pot

As we mentioned in chapter 1, ESRB raters don't actually play the games to assign a rating. Rather, they watch videos supplied by each manufacturer containing representative excerpts from the games and sometimes supplement this by looking at scripts or listening to soundtracks to get an accurate picture of game content. Although there have been calls from critics to make the ESRB raters play all sections of a game to see everything that it contains before assigning a rating, this is impractical and will become even less feasible as games become more sophisticated and complex. There are simply too many potential paths for a rater to follow in a reasonable amount of time.

The ESRB relies on publishers to submit accurate representations of their games on video. One basis for this reliance is simple economics: having a game reclassified to a more restrictive level after it is published would be prohibitively expensive for a publisher, not just because of the fines levied by the ESRB, but also because of the cost of recalling and repackaging copies of the game that have been manufactured but not yet sold.

This was the case with the 2005 furor over the "hot coffee" scenes in *Grand Theft Auto: San Andreas*. (The word "coffee" is used within the game as a euphemism for sex; a woman who is dating the protagonist, CJ, may invite him to her house for "coffee.") Sexually explicit material that was hidden in the game and controlled by some disabled code was accessed by a Dutch game "modder," who shared the news of his discovery and the code necessary to play it through the Internet. Although the publisher was seemingly unaware of the hidden minigame (which looked like it had been abandoned by the programmers early in its development and simply programmed around in the published version), its revelation turned into a financial and public-relations disaster.

Politicians lined up to criticize the company, Rockstar Games, which had already been the subject of public lambasting for the *Grand Theft Auto* series. Senator Hillary Clinton, in calling for an investigation by the Federal Trade Commission, stated, "The disturbing material in *Grand Theft Auto* and other games like it is stealing the innocence of our children, and it's making the difficult job of being a parent even harder."[6]

Ironically, the disturbing material in *GTA* first came to public notice when then–California Assemblyman Leland Yee issued a public statement about it, followed by a "national parental warning" circulated by the National Institute on Media and the Family. (We'll have more to say about them in a few pages.)

According to the administrator of GTAGarage.com, a site for *GTA* modding fans that hosted the controversial code, "Before NIMF and Yee 'warned' everybody about Hot Coffee, we had only a couple of thousand downloads on the mod. After the media panic, over a million!"[7] Few if any children would have been exposed to the graphic material without this publicity.

Because of the furor, the ESRB changed the game's rating in July 2005 from M to AO. The Australian rating board, the Office of Film and Literature Classification (OFLC), banned the game from the country. *Grand Theft Auto: San Andreas* was pulled off U.S. retailers' shelves until a replacement version, without the hidden "hot coffee" scenes and with its M rating reinstated, was distributed a month later. Take-Two Entertainment, the parent company of Rockstar Games, lost $28.8 million that quarter, a significant part of it attributed to the cost of recalling and modifying the game.

The ESRB has taken action against other games as well. In 2006, the ESRB re-rated an already-released game, *Elder Scrolls IV: Oblivion*, from T to M. It learned that the PC version of the game included files that could be unlocked using third-party code to make the female characters topless.

Other Rating Systems

The United States is unusual among major nations in its use of voluntary, industry-sponsored ratings. Other countries use government regulation, such as the Australian government's Office of Film and Literature Classification, or joint ventures between government, industry and consumer groups, such as the Pan-European Game Information (PEGI) rating system for interactive games. Let's look at a few of these systems and how they differ from the ESRB.

The PEGI rating system, established in 2003, is used in more than two-dozen European countries. Its five age labels are similar to those used in the United States: 3+, 7+, 12+, 16+, 18+. (Most games rated T [13+] by the ESRB receive a 12+ rating from PEGI.) However, there are only seven content descriptors, each represented by a black-and-white icon: Language, Drugs, Sexual Content, Violence, Gambling, Fear ("may be frightening or scary for young children") and Discrimination ("game contains depictions of, or material which may encourage, discrimination").

There are no visible distinctions made between levels or types of violence. However, the eight-page PEGI rating guide[8] gives intriguing behind-the-scenes detail on how those age ratings and icons are assigned. Some content automatically leads to a higher age rating. For example, "glamorization of crime . . . where the depiction of criminal acts could encourage the game's player to think that 'crime pays' or has no negative repercussions" by itself warrants a 16+ rating. So does a scenario "where the character gains advantage in the game by the use of tobacco or alcohol." (The ESRB has its own rating questionnaire, of similar length, but does not generally share these details with the public.)

The Japanese CERO (Computer Entertainment Rating Organization) system uses stylized depictions of letters: A (everyone), B (age twelve and older), C (fifteen and older), D (seventeen and older), Z (eighteen and older). Z is similar to the ESRB's AO rating, but with government regulation of sales rather than voluntary restriction by retailers. The content descriptors are also more limited: Love, Sexual Content, Violence, Horror, Gambling, Crime, Use of Alcohol or Tobacco, Use of Drugs and Language. *Grand Theft Auto 3* and *GTA: Vice City* received the Z rating.[9]

Germany has its own system that assigns age ratings: 6+, 12+, 16+ and Adults Only. Games cannot legally be sold to minors without a rating. Germany's USK (Unterhaltungssoftware Selbstkontrolle) rating board employs three full-time testers who are asked to play through each game, using cheat codes and walk-through instructions provided by the publisher. The testers then present their findings to several "video game experts" randomly selected from a board of over fifty raters. These experts focus narrowly on whether any game element, from graphics to plot, could negatively affect children under a certain age, and rate accordingly.[10]

Australia goes a step farther than Germany and legally forbids selling games even to adults without a rating by their Office of Film and Literature Classification. Publishers are asked to provide a detailed synopsis of the game and information that will allow the review board of up to twenty people to play through it if they wish. The OFLC game rating system uses color-coded icons which, for the most part, are identical to those it assigns to films: G (general viewing), PG (parental guidance recommended), M (mature audiences), MA15+ (children under 15 are not allowed to purchase) and RC (refused classification, not allowed to be sold in the country).[11] Ultraviolent games like *Postal* have been designated RC and prohibited from being distributed.

There are no separate content descriptors in the Australian system. However, the age ratings are derived from six "classifiable elements" in each game: Theme, Violence, Sex, Language, Drug Use and Nudity. For example, to qualify for an M rating, "Moderate violence is permitted if justified by context. Sexual violence should be very limited and justified by context. Sexual activity should be discreetly implied, if justified by context."[12] To qualify for an MA15+ rating, "Violence should be justified by context. Sexual violence may be implied if justified by context. Sexual activity may be implied."[13]

The differences between these systems reflect the different sensibilities and priorities of the cultures in which they're used. The European system contains information about discrimination and fear that is ignored by the American system. The Japanese system also pays attention to horror and differentiates between love and sex.

The Australian system is surprisingly vague to American eyes, with assignments to categories subject to much interpretation of the context of each game's contents. Australian entertainment ratings are based on a terse set of principles:

(a) Adults should be able to read, hear and see what they want;
(b) Minors should be protected from material likely to harm or disturb them;

(c) Everyone should be protected from exposure to unsolicited material that they find offensive;

(d) The need to take account of community concerns about:

    (i) depictions of violence that condone or incite violence, particularly sexual violence; and

    (ii) the portrayal of persons in a demeaning manner.[14]

Australia and Germany are more likely than other Western countries to ban certain game titles outright. In an interview for Gamasutra.com, the head of the USK summed up the difference between the German system and the ESRB: "In America, sex and bad language seems to be the focus of discussion. . . . Here in Germany, violence dominates our concerns, and too much violence can get a game banned."[15] Because of this concern, game developers may change red blood to green, or severed body parts to gears and springs.[16]

Are the T and M Ratings Backward?

One of the largest concerns parents have about violent video games is that they will inspire young children to imitate the violent behaviors they see on the screen. We may be able to gain some insights from studies of other media.

As we mentioned in chapter 5, the National Television Violence Study looked at what aspects of on-screen violent behaviors made them more likely to be copied by kids who watched them. Among these aspects were:

- There were few "pain/harm cues." That is, the effects of the violence on the victim were unrealistic.
- The violence was portrayed as humorous.

Those two factors are taken into account by the ESRB when it decides whether to assign a game a T rating or an M rating. The criteria for a T rating state that these games "may contain violence, suggestive themes, crude humor, minimal blood, simulated gambling, and/or infrequent use of strong language."[17] A game that's rated M "may contain intense violence, blood and gore, sexual content and/or strong language."[18]

This raises an interesting paradox. By limiting games in the T category (and even the E category) to violence in which the consequences to the victims are intentionally not shown—the blood is green or bodies disappear after they are shot—the ESRB may be unintentionally providing younger children with violent on-screen behaviors that they are *more* likely to imitate! The interweaving of humor into the violent act may compound the problem.

The television violence researchers acknowledged this counterintuitive problem:

> Policy-makers, as well as television critics and others, often voice concern about "graphic" or "explicit" violence. . . .
>
> Our high-risk analysis demonstrates that portrayals that are not necessarily explicit but that present violence as attractive, rewarding, and painless pose a significant threat of increasing children's aggressive behavior.[19]

Does this mean that playing T-rated games is more likely to lead to violent behaviors than playing M-rated games? Absolutely not. But it does demonstrate the complexity and subtlety of the issue. It also raises some interesting questions.

Are we causing unintentional problems by not showing the realistic consequences of violence in these games? Are children more desensitized to real-world violence if the games they play show green blood or puffs of smoke instead of realistic gore? What are the emotional consequences, if any, of simply having dead bodies disappear, as is frequently done in T- and E-rated games?

The answer to the question of whether the ESRB has its T and M ratings backward is "probably not." But it's not as clear-cut as many opponents and proponents of violent video games might have us believe.

Parents' Concerns About Ratings

Our focus groups with parents found that while they were aware of the ESRB rating system, they didn't always pay attention to it. Some focused exclusively on the content descriptors. Others looked at the artwork on the packaging or spoke with a store clerk to make a rental or purchase decision. Several had M and T ratings confused, thinking that T-rated games contained more sex and violence than M-rated games. Some relied on their children's own judgment about which games would be appropriate.

Most acknowledged that while they might have strict rules at home prohibiting certain types of games, their children might easily play those games at another child's house. As one parent succinctly put it, "We don't allow him to play *Grand Theft Auto*, but somehow he seems to know the names of all of the characters and what they do!"

What came through most clearly in our parent focus groups was frustration that they weren't able to get the information they wanted and valued from the ratings. Sometimes that information was already printed on the box, but the parents didn't know how to interpret it. They were confused by the content descriptors and wanted other information as well.

Danielle: "I can imagine that the M game, by definition, would not have things like nudity, or would not have things like—I pray to God—like drugs. Or, it would not have excessive violence. But I don't know; I've never seen one."

Clara: "I think when they show blood, it's automatically in . . . not necessarily into the M range, but definitely out of the E."

Jeff: "I'm looking at the packages and the nudity and stuff like that. I don't really know too much about the rating systems."

Alicia: "I see the E, I know it's for everyone. When I see the Teen, I know the ten-year-old, he can't have it. Then I see Mature: that's when I say, 'OK, I'm going to read to see exactly what's going on here.' "

Bill: "If they listed what you got points for in the game, that would tell you a lot about the kind of game that it is. I mean, if you were able to get extra points for lighting a prostitute on fire, or a lot of these other things that happen . . ."

John: "I can't play them, so I'm pretty much lost. I could look at them for five minutes and he could show me what he wants to show me. So I try to let him use his best judgment. And he knows what I would let him do and what he can't do."

Almost all the parents we spoke with agreed with the age categories of the ESRB ratings—but for other people's children, not for their own. They tended to let their younger teenagers play M-rated games and their preteen children play T-rated games. A few, however, were adamant about enforcing the age guidelines.

Parent vs. Child

We interviewed Barbara and her thirteen-year-old son, Matt, in separate rooms. Barbara had strong feelings about what was appropriate for her two teenage children.

> Researcher: "Have you ever bought them an M-rated game?"
>
> Barbara: "*No!* Absolutely not. Not even a consideration. They don't even bring it to me. They don't even ask me because they know the answer is no."
>
> Researcher: "What about T-rated games?"
>
> Barbara: "Well, it can't be a violent game. There should be no shooting, no guns. It has to be a racing game or a sports game."
>
> Researcher: "How do you know if they have shooting or guns?"
>
> Barbara: "Most times I look at the box and I read the back of it. Sometimes I'll ask [my kids], 'Is there shooting in it?' And they'll say, 'A little bit.' And I'll say, 'Put it back!' "

Matt confirmed that his mother was strict in her approach to video games. But he told a different story about what happens. His brother and he use an approach that not only has been used for many generations—perhaps even millennia—but that also demonstrates their empathy and interpersonal skills: they manipulate the framework within which their mother makes her decisions. In other words, they set her up.

Matt (seeing the printout of a screenshot from *Grand Theft Auto: Vice City*): "That's Tommy Vercetti. That's the main character right there. He's really cool. . . .

"What I also like about this game is the vehicles and stuff. They're really cool vehicles. My favorite is the motorcycle. I've watched my brother play this game so many times. He's really good at it, and he'd beat, like, all the missions. And he has like three helicopters and stuff, so he can fly around in the helicopters. That's the best. . . ."

Researcher: "Is your brother older?"

Matt: "He's seventeen. He's a senior in high school. . . ." (He looks at several screen shots from other T- and M-rated games and recognizes some of the characters.)

Researcher: "What would your mother say about them?"

Matt: "She would go, well, they're way too violent and they're bloody and gory and stuff. . . ."

He described the strategy he and his brother regularly used when they bought or rented video games with their mother.

Matt: "[We'd select the] bloodiest game you've ever seen in your life, with zombies and ghosts and everything in it, and blood and gore and knives and tortured blood all over and stuff. And then she'd be like, 'You're not getting that!' And then we'd choose something less gory, but still gory, and she'd say, 'Well, that's better. . . .' "

Researcher: "You show her the worse thing, and then you show her the thing you really want?"

Matt: "Yeah. . . ." (Matt then spots another screenshot that he recognizes.) "This one's *Grand Theft Auto 3. GTA!*"

Researcher: "Do you own it?"

Matt: "No, but I've played it, though."

Researcher: "Where do you play it?"

Matt: "My brother—he has friends and the friends sometimes had him borrow some games. So we don't own them, but yes, we play them."

Researcher: "Does your mom know that you play?"

Matt: "No, I don't think she does. . . ."

Researcher: "What do you think she would do?"

Matt: "She'd say, 'What's that game?' And then she'd flip out."

Researcher: "What does 'flipping out' mean for your mom?"

Matt: "All rationality is out the window. . . . Get grounded until you graduate from college. Until you're your own legal guardian—like that kind of grounded."

Do Parents Use Game Ratings?

In chapter 4, we described our survey of seventh- and eighth-grade students in Pennsylvania and South Carolina. We also sent brief mail-back questionnaires to their parents. The parent and child surveys both came with peel-off name labels. We asked that they write their names on the labels to allow matching of parent and child responses; we then removed the labels to ensure that no survey responses could be traced back to individuals. Mail-back surveys tend to have low response rates; we received an impressive 50 percent response from the Pennsylvania school and a more typical 30 percent at the South Carolina school. We were able to match 456 of the 501 parent surveys to a student survey.

Several questions concerned parents' restrictions on game play, such as "My child is allowed to choose the games he/she plays" and "My child is allowed to play a new game without a parent watching or playing it first." Responses were on a five-point scale from "never" to "always."

We also asked parents, "When you decide to buy or rent an electronic game for your child, how often do you pay attention to the following? (What affects your decision to buy the game, or put it back on the shelf?)"

How Parents Decide What Games to Rent or Buy for Their Preteen/Teen Child

	NEVER	RARELY	SOMETIMES	OFTEN	ALWAYS
The drawings or photos on the box	11.7%	7.4%	29.5%	27.7%	23.7%
The writing on the box	10.1	6.4	24.5	28.3	30.7
The game's title	8.1	7.3	22.0	32.3	30.4
The game's rating (E, T or M)	5.3	3.4	10.8	22.5	57.9
How much your child wants that particular game	5.1	9.7	37.2	31.5	16.4
What other parents say about the game	21.6	21.3	32.6	17.8	6.7
A review of the game (from a newspaper, magazine or Web site)	26.2	25.4	27.8	14.2	6.4
How much the game costs	8.6	12.6	34.9	25.0	18.8

We found that the method parents used to make purchase decisions affected how closely they monitored their child's play. Parents who often or always made decisions based on a game's rating were significantly less likely to supervise the game's content. Parents who often/always made decisions based on their son or daughter's level of desire for the game were significantly more likely to supervise the content.

Parents' attention to game ratings was also related to their children's M-rated game play. We found that parents who said they often or always pay attention to game ratings were significantly *more* likely to have a son who plays M-rated games (i.e., had at least one M-rated title among five games he played "a lot in the past six months"). The trend was similar for parents of girls, but there were not enough M-game-playing girls in our sample to get a statistically significant result. (Interestingly, we found that parents with more education—those holding a master's or doctoral degree—were more likely to have children who played M-rated games.)

We're not sure how to interpret these seemingly contradictory findings. Parents may not fully understand the ratings or may over-rely on them to keep children away from violent or sexual content. Or parents may be carefully reviewing individual games and deciding that some M-rated titles are not a problem for their particular child. To better understand these results, we'd need to follow parents through store aisles, observe them as they study game displays and boxes, and ask them to think out loud as they make decisions.

Posturing and Spin

While it has earned plaudits from groups such as the Federal Trade Commission,[20] not everyone is happy with the ESRB rating system. The National Institute on Media and the Family (NIMF), which we quoted at the beginning of this chapter, is one of the most oft-cited critics of the video game industry in general and the current ESRB rating system in particular.

The organization's name is misleading, especially to the general public. Although it sounds similar, it is not affiliated in any way with the National Institutes of Health, the National Institute of Child Health and Human Development or the National Institute of Mental Health, all of which are large and distinguished government research centers. In fact, it would be absurd to describe it as either national or as an institute that's on par with those similar-sounding organizations.

According to a recent (2005) informational tax filing with the Internal Revenue Service, which is a public record, all of the members of its board of directors are from the Minneapolis–Saint Paul metropolitan area. The NIMF, during that year at least, had only one senior employee[21]: David Walsh, PhD, a psychologist, although the IRS filing notes that his wife received an undisclosed amount of money as an independent contractor. Also, the NIMF Web site is disingenuous in describing several independent part-time consultants as "staff,"[22] a description usually reserved for employees.

The NIMF has gotten into trouble for other misleading statements. For example, in its tenth annual MediaWise Video Game Report Card, which gave the ESRB rating system a failing grade, it stated that it would soon hold a "national video game summit" (a phrase as hyperbolic as its use of "National Institute") on video game ratings along with the

National PTA. The PTA bristled at the implication that it supported the report card's findings:

> The 10th Annual MediaWise® Video and Computer Game Report Card, released yesterday by the National Institute on Media and the Family (NIMF), contained erroneous statements about National PTA's position on the Entertainment Software Rating Board's (ESRB) rating system. In fact, National PTA does not endorse NIMF's report. Further, it does not agree with the report's characterization of ESRB and its rating system.[23]

The PTA did not participate in the summit that took place later that year in Minneapolis.

Let's take a look at expanded versions of the two quotes we printed at the beginning of this chapter:

> After years of criticizing the ESRB ratings and calling for improvement and overhaul of the system, we have come to the conclusion that the system itself is beyond repair. The system supposedly put in place to keep killographic [*sic*] games out of the hands of kids seems to often produce the opposite results. . . .
>
> The so-called "hot coffee" scandal does not simply reveal the bad faith of one of the industry's most prominent companies; it has shown once and for all that the present rating system is broken and can't be fixed. . . .
>
> Using data generated by PSVratings, a content-based ratings system measuring actual levels of profanity, sex, and violence, we found that games in 2004 were on average more violent, contained more sexual content and had more profane language when compared to games from the late '90s. . . .
>
> The continual increase in adult content, the failure to use the AO rating and the "hot coffee" scandal of 2005 all point toward the deep flaws in the ESRB rating system.[24]

This is clearly a set of emotional statements. Undoubtedly, they're heartfelt. But do they make sense? In this case, the political spin is dizzying.

The ESRB rating system was not designed to "keep killographic [whatever that means] games out of the hands of kids." It was designed to provide consumers with information about games so that they could make more-informed choices about whether to purchase or rent them. NIMF presents no evidence that the ESRB rating system produces "the opposite results." In fact, it's unclear what that means as well. It implies that having this rating system makes it easier for children to get their hands on violent games.

The "hot coffee" scandal had nothing to do with the ESRB rating system. (As we mentioned earlier, the NIMF's actions were partially responsible for the wide distribution of the materials they were trying to protect children from.) In fact, the content of the disabled minigame within *Grand Theft Auto: San Andreas* was more benign than the titillating media coverage implied. There was no nudity in any of the six animated sex scenes. The poor quality of the animation indicated that the minigame had been abandoned by the programmers before completion and simply programmed around, thereby making it inaccessible to game players who are not hackers. (Independent programmers later made "patches" available that made the scenes more graphic.)

The secretary-general of the Video Standards Council in Great Britain expressed amazement at the reaction in the United States: "I know the scene depicting a sex act caused a great stir in America," said Laurie Hall. "Even Hillary Clinton got involved. But we looked at it and it seemed relatively trivial. Did we change the rating? No, because it was already rated 18 for violence, which is the highest it can go. Would we have raised it if we could? I think not; as I said, that sort of thing is considered mild over here."[25]

We should keep in mind that even if the ESRB game raters had played every part of the game, they would not have come across the "hot coffee" scenes. The incident has nothing to do with the quality or appropriateness of ESRB ratings.

The statement that video games from 2004 were on average more violent, had more sexual content and had more profane language than games from the late 1990s is not meaningful. (It also may be wrong, as we'll see in a few pages.) We don't know what the NIMF means by "average." Are they only measuring newly released games? If a game is available on multiple platforms, is each version counted as an individual game? Are these measures of exposure to profanity, sex and violence weighted by game sales or simply by number of titles? Have they included online games? The list of questions goes on.

We'll get to the ironic story of PSVratings in a moment. By claiming that they use a "content-based ratings system," is the NIMF implying that other rating systems are not content based? How do we know that they're measuring "actual levels of profanity, sex and violence"? A glance at the PSVratings Web site hints at the snake oil quality of their ratings process.

> Data Capture Specialists are rigorously trained to "audit" as opposed to "review" media and identify all instances of Profanity, Sex and Violence without any judgment or interpretation. Not only do they note the occurrence itself, but recognize relationship combinations for as many as 15 different character types (man, woman, teen, child, fantasy figure, role model, etc.), the relationship(s) between the character types, the consequences of the occurrence, the level of graphic detail and whether it is seen, heard or sensed.[26]
>
> Once the data capture process has been completed, every element of the information is mapped to any or all of the applicable rules in the PSVratings database. Data Mappers are extensively trained in the process of locating and identifying the appropriate rule(s) from the in excess of 3,000 rules and 10 million rule combinations. In instances in which a situation is encountered for which there is no rule, a new rule will be created and submitted to the PSVratings Standards Board for approval and rating.[27]

It sounds impressive at first blush, especially with the references to data capture specialists performing an "audit," "extensively trained" data mappers, the absence of "interpretation" and those three thousand rules and ten million rule combinations. It provides the image of dedicated, tireless workers using the latest in computer technology to safeguard our vulnerable children. The problem is that none of this means anything. It's gibberish—the type of double-talk a con artist might use.

Which brings us to the story of PSVratings, a for-profit division of MediaData Corporation. The initials "PSV," according to the company's Web site,[28] stand for "Profanity, Sex and Violence," which were the main categories of the rating systems it developed and promoted for a variety of media. It tried for several years to market its video game rating system as a replacement for the one offered by the ESRB, claiming that it would help parents protect their children from inappropriate content and corrupting influences.

PSVratings shut down in 2006 after the U.S. Securities and Exchange Commission seized the assets of MediaData, charging individuals and companies related to MediaData with participation in multi-million–dollar securities fraud, including money laundering and a Ponzi scheme.[29] This was real-world behavior that would have fit right in with the characters of *Grand Theft Auto*!

Are We Awash in Violent Games?

Many of the parents we spoke with in our focus groups firmly believed three things:

- Most video game players are kids.
- A large proportion of commercially produced games are rated M because of violence or sexual content.
- The problem is growing, with an increasing proportion of games being rated M.

According to Patricia Vance, president of the Entertainment Software Rating Board, none of these statements is true. "The average age of a game player today is thirty-three," she says. Research by the Entertainment Software Association, the national trade association for the video game industry, found that the average age of a video game buyer is forty.[30] That age difference is probably a reflection of purchases by parents and other adults of games for children.

"There's a misperception that the majority of video games are violent or Mature rated," she continues. "The M-rated category represented eight percent of the nearly 1,300 ratings we assigned in 2006. That's down from 12 percent the year before."

John Feil is a video game designer in Seattle and a member of the board of directors of the International Game Developers Association. He concurs that many people misunderstand the principal target audience for the video game industry, which he says is not children, but men age eighteen to twenty-five who have the disposable income to buy games.

When we spoke to him in May 2007, the bestselling video games for the previous week, along with their ratings and content descriptors, had been:

- *Pokémon Diamond* (E, no descriptors)
- *Pokémon Pearl* (E, no descriptors)
- *Wii Sports* (E, mild violence)
- *Guitar Hero II* (T, lyrics)
- *Super Paper Mario* (E, comic mischief, mild cartoon violence)
- *F.E.A.R.* (M, blood and gore, intense violence, strong language)

"Only one of them has realistic blood and violence in it," says Feil, who has a young daughter. "The bestselling games tend to be perfectly OK for children, but not all of the games."

The ESRB responded to its failing grade in the NIMF report card by creating some spin of its own.

NIMF failed to disclose that its own age recommendations for the 36 video games they have reviewed and posted on their Web site are virtually identical to ESRB age recommendations. In fact, in most of the cases where there are differences it is only by a single year, e.g. 17 year old vs. 18 year old, 13 year old vs. 14 year old. In several other cases, ESRB ratings are stricter than those issued by NIMF.[31]

While they're technically correct, this comparison is a tad disingenuous on the part of the ESRB. Since the two organizations used different age categories, it's not surprising that the results would be different. Why is a one-year difference applied by the NIMF called "virtually identical," but that same one-year difference applied by the ESRB is called "stricter"?

What's lost among these age comparisons is the real issue: money. Almost all retailers will sell video games that carry an ESRB rating of M (17+); few will carry one with a rating of AO (18+). That one-year difference can be worth many millions of dollars. The ESRB addresses this in its response to the Video Game Report Card:

> There is no scientific or medical justification from a developmental standpoint to distinguish games that are more suitable for 17 year olds vs. 18 year olds, so this seems an extremely shaky basis on which to declare that ESRB ratings are inaccurate. In truth, this has nothing to do with accuracy of ratings. Knowing that retailers generally will not carry AO games, NIMF's attack on ESRB ratings has nothing to do with whether a rating is accurate and everything to do with the real agenda of NIMF, which is to ban the sale of games it does not like.[32]

In the next chapter, we'll examine what happens when American politicians try to follow the lead of Australia and Germany and ban certain games.

What Parents Want from a Game Rating System

We asked parents in our focus groups what information they'd like to see on the back of a video game box. Most topics—nudity, drugs, blood, swearing—are covered by current ESRB content descriptors. Another concern, realism of violence, is part of the definition of some content descriptors, as explained on the ESRB Web site. Here are some things that more than one parent wanted to see and aren't currently addressed:

- **A summary of the plot.** "I'd like to read a little bit about what happens. . . . I don't mind standing there and reading a paragraph on the back of the package." "A summary of what the content is, what the focus is."
- **Participation in crime or terrorism.** "Like, if they have to go in the bank and come out with X amount of dollars and get away from the cops." "If the

object of the game is to, I don't know, mastermind world terrorism, I might be concerned." Watching other game characters commit a crime was not as much of a concern as "mastering" the crime by doing it oneself. This is reminiscent of the PEGI system's instruction about games that "encourage the games player to think that 'crime pays' or has no negative repercussions," which automatically bumps up the age rating.

- **Sexism and violence against women:** "the misogynistic attitude." When some parents heard the description of *Def Jam Vendetta*, which involves fighting women as well as winning women as trophies, they were quite upset. Some versions of this game are rated T.
- **Violence against human characters.** "My kids play T games, which I'm not too happy about. Particularly the ones that involve killing people. I don't mind if they kill an alien or something like that. But I do have a problem with humans killing humans."
- **Pictures of the most extreme content.** Some parents wanted to see pictures of key content, because "the categories, they're so vague." Pictures would help address hard-to-describe concerns such as "the ways in which women are depicted, because I think women are largely absent from video games . . . and when they do show up, they're doing a 'hoochie mama' thing."
- **Nature of the violence.** "A little more detail to distinguish the violence. Gun violence versus battery and assault. I mean, let's use legal terms." "It's one thing, killing; it's another thing, you know, chopping, decapitating, lighting on fire. . . ."

Tweaking the ESRB System

As of now, content descriptors address levels of gore, but not the nature, goals or targets of violence. In the game *SWAT 4*, avoiding deaths (even of the "bad guys") and getting medical help for the injured gets you the greatest number of points. *SWAT 4* has the same violence-related content descriptors as *Hitman: Blood Money*: Blood and Intense Violence. As you might guess, the latter game requires killing to advance and win. (To be fair, *Hitman: Blood Money* also has descriptors for Partial Nudity, Sexual Themes and Use of Drugs. Both games have descriptors for Strong Language.)

As we saw in chapter 5, context trumps gore when it comes to learning from and possibly imitating media violence.[33] Parents need information that, at a glance, distinguishes *SWAT* from *Hitman*.

Groups such as the American Academy of Pediatrics have proposed the creation of a simplified, content-based rating system that crosses all types of media[34] (similar to the Australian system). A universal system does seem easier for parents to remember. However, the Federal Trade Commission has done a series of reports on marketing violent entertainment to children, including surveys of parents that "reflect positively on the ESRB system."[35] The FTC's 2006 survey found that 87 percent of parents were aware of ESRB ratings (up from 61 percent in 2000) and that 61 percent use them most or all of the time (up from 22% in 2000).

One could also argue that a rating system designed for passive, unidirectional media might not do justice to interactive media. In turn, ESRB-style content descriptors are too complicated for television screens. But the best argument against replacing the ESRB system may be practical. Changing to another system would be a massive, expensive undertaking. Just one example: the new-generation game consoles from Microsoft, Nintendo and Sony all have parental controls (similar to V-chips in televisions) designed to work with the current system.

Replacement systems (such as the one proposed by PSVratings) don't strike us as much of an improvement, if any. No system will ever be able to scrutinize and label all potentially offensive or upsetting content. The more complicated a system becomes, the less likely busy parents are to understand it and to actually use it. Given the constraints, we think the ESRB has done a good job.

A Research-Oriented Rating System

We and other researchers have called for greater consideration of game content in future research on video games. Although we used ESRB ratings in our recent survey research, the ESRB system is designed to meet the needs of parents, which is as it should be. It's unfair to expect the ESRB to meet the needs of academics as well. Those needs include detailed but clear-cut descriptions of key game features that previous studies suggest may be important (such as violence against realistic-looking people vs. violence against nonrealistic aliens or zombies) to see how they may affect the thinking, attitudes or behavior of different types of children.

As part of our research program, we created a new Center for Mental Health and Media rating scale for future research use. (Research associate Dorothy E. Warner, PhD, took the lead on developing and testing the new scale.) We mention the new scale here because some aspects could be incorporated into the current ESRB rating system to improve rating methods and quality, and give more of the information parents have told us that they want in order to make decisions for their children.

The CMHM rating scale includes the following sections that are not directly incorporated or reported by the ESRB:

1. How central is physical violence to the game?
2. What is the social context of the game violence?
3. What are the consequences of being violent in the game?
4. How possible is it for kids to imitate the kind of violence shown in the game? (E.g., do game weapons and their effects "look real," and are ordinary objects or fists used as weapons in the game?)
5. Does the game feature human-like characters with unhealthy or exaggerated body proportions, including men's muscularity and women's breast size?

CHAPTER 8

All Politics Is Local

Common sense should tell us that positively reinforcing sadistic behavior, as these games do, cannot be good for our children. . . . There is no longer a question as to whether exposing children to violent entertainment is a public health risk. The question is: what are we going to do about it? What does it take for the entertainment industry, and its licensees and retailers, to stop exposing children to poison?

—*Senator Sam Brownback, January 25, 2001*[1]

IF WE WERE POLITICIANS, IT WOULD BE VERY TEMPTING to jump on that "stop exposing children to poison" bandwagon. It's the ideal campaign issue. The alleged villain is a group of impersonal corporations (the "entertainment industry"). The supposed victims—young children—are presumed to be peaceable, innocent and vulnerable. Parents worry that they are powerless in the face of overwhelming cultural forces and are looking for someone or something to blame.

Predictably, this particular bandwagon is getting crowded. Some have climbed on with the best of motives and intentions. Others are more cynical, caring less about the data than their image. Who among politicians wouldn't want to be photographed like senators Hillary Clinton and Joe Lieberman standing at a lectern decorated with a "Helping Parents Protect Kids" banner?[2] How could you defend yourself in a political campaign if you didn't rally wholeheartedly and unquestioningly to this noble cause?

But there are problems. As we described earlier, the research data don't support the simplistic claims being made about a causal relationship between violent video games and real-world violence perpetrated by the broad range of teenagers who play them. More important, focusing on such easy but minor targets as violent video games causes parents, social activists and public policy makers to ignore the much more powerful and significant causes of youth violence that have already been well established, including a range of social, behavioral, economic, biological and mental health factors. In other words, the knee-jerk responses distract us from more complex but much more important problems.

That's the real issue. Some antigame activists make the argument that stopping violence in video games is akin to Pascal's wager: it's the smart thing to do because the potential consequences of being wrong (you've mistakenly banned them even though violent video games do no damage) are more than offset by the potential consequences of being right (you've reduced real-world violence because these video games lead to violent behavior among children). But this argument ignores the fact that efforts focused on violent video games remove public attention and government funding from more important and powerful factors that are already well known to lead to violence. In other words, we spend time, money and energy focusing on the wrong things.

We can see this in the tragic shooting on April 16, 2007, at Virginia Polytechnic Institute and State University (Virginia Tech) in Blacksburg. A total of thirty-three students and faculty members were killed, including the gunman, Seung-Hui Cho, who took his own life. Many others were wounded by gunfire. It was the worst mass murder in modern U.S. history. (We'll have more on this in a few pages.)

Please Check Your Swords at the Door

Many cries for legislation to limit the production, distribution or sale of violent video games and other electronic media are based on the notion that things were much better and safer in years gone by. Nostalgia can be a powerful force, but it's not always grounded in fact.

In the 1990s, a host of politicians, pundits and journalists cited supposed national surveys conducted in 1940 and again in any of several more recent years, which listed the top behavior problems teachers dealt with in public schools. The list from 1940 exuded innocence:

1. Talking
2. Chewing gum
3. Running in the halls
4. Making noise
5. Getting out of line
6. Violating the dress code
7. Littering

The recent list was much more ominous:

1. Drugs
2. Alcohol
3. Pregnancy
4. Suicide
5. Rape
6. Robbery

Even a casual glance at the two lists will tell you that they're actually responses to two different questions. The first is about behavioral problems at school. The second is about general problems in society. So contrasting the two is inherently misleading.

Nevertheless, politicians of all stripes and at all levels of government cited these starkly contrasting lists as if they gave insights into profound changes in our culture. Liberal newspaper columnist Carl Rowan mentioned them, as did conservative talk show host Rush Limbaugh. Former secretary of education William Bennett was one of their most frequent disseminators.

There was one other problem: the lists are a fraud. Barry O'Neill, PhD, who was an associate professor of management at Yale University in the mid-1990s, tracked down their history.[3] It is a tale worth telling.

The lists were created by Texas multimillionaire oilman T. Cullen Davis, who is best known for his arrests in 1977 for the double murder of his estranged wife's lover and daughter, and again the next year for allegedly hiring a hit man to kill the judge who was presiding over his ongoing divorce litigation. Davis was acquitted of all charges in both cases.

The legal fees he incurred drove him into bankruptcy. He became an evangelical Christian who devoted his time to lobbying against sex education and the teaching of evolution in the Fort Worth school system.

Davis admitted to O'Neill that he had made the lists up, although there is some evidence that several of the items in the supposed 1940s list may have come from an actual survey at the time. Davis said he developed the second list by reading the newspapers.

Like H. L. Mencken's history of the bathtub, described in chapter 3, these lists of teachers' concerns are still cited as fact despite their thorough debunking. Many of today's politicians lament the growth in violence in schools and in the schoolyard. They compare today's problems to evocative images of the good old days when everything was calm and orderly. Little do they know what things were really like on campus.

Historian Philippe Ariès, who wrote the classic book *Centuries of Childhood: A Social History of Family Life*, vividly described daily life in European schools during the seventeenth century. Keep in mind that a "college" at that time included students of high school and even primary school age, many of whom were preparing for "the robe," a career in the church.

> Schoolchildren used to be armed. The Jesuits' *ratio studiorum* ["plan of studies"] provided for their disarmament on entering the college, weapons being placed in safe custody in return for a receipt, and handed back to the pupil when he went out. In 1680, the disciplinary regulations of the Collège de Bourgogne repeated this rule: "Neither firearms nor swords are to be retained in pupils' rooms and those who possess such weapons must hand them over to the Principal, who will keep them in a place chosen for that purpose. . . ." The youngest children, from the age of five, could already wear a sword, which was not simply for ornament or prestige. . . .[4]

The school behavior problems faced by the church and the government included schoolyard bullying, drinking and dueling, as well as common neighborhood problems such as student thieving and begging. Riots occurred often.

Can Video Games Train Snipers?

Fourteen-year-old Michael Carneal steals a gun from a neighbor's house, brings it to school, and fires eight shots into a student prayer meeting that is breaking up. Prior to stealing the gun, he had never shot a real handgun in his life. The FBI says that the average experienced law enforcement officer, in the average shootout, at an average range of seven yards, hits with approximately one bullet in five. So how many hits did Michael Carneal make? He fired eight shots; he got eight hits, on eight different kids. . . . Nowhere in the annals of law enforcement or military or criminal history can we find an equivalent achievement. And this from a boy on his first try.

How did Michael Carneal acquire this kind of killing ability? Simple: practice. At the tender age of fourteen he had practiced killing literally thousands of people. His simulators were point-and-shoot video games he played for hundreds of hours in video arcades and in the comfort of his own home.[5]

Descriptions like this one by Dave Grossman of the 1997 Paducah, Kentucky, school shooter, are dramatic, even breathless. Whenever such horrible incidents take place, pundits and attorneys are quick to raise the claim that first-person shooter video games can turn a novice into an accurate and deadly marksman with a real weapon. That issue was put forth following Columbine, Virginia Tech, the DC snipers and a host of other shootings. But does it make sense? We tried to find out.

There's no question that George Harris can make you a better marksman. As the director of Sig Sauer Academy in New Hampshire, he designs and teaches a wide range of firearms courses for federal, state and local law enforcement officers as well as for the public. He's run seminars for the firearms instructors at the FBI Academy in Quantico, Virginia, and has been a nationally ranked competitive shooter for many years.

As we drove around his sprawling facility, Harris proudly pointed out the sniper training area used by police departments from throughout New England and the "shoot house" used to train SWAT teams. A group of federal air marshals practiced firing at a gun range next to the classrooms. At another range down the road, a police unit worked on tactics. The reports of their high-powered rifles and large-bore pistols punctuated our conversation.

Harris has devoted his life to studying how people learn to shoot. His eldest son, a former police officer, is now an executive with a major video game publisher. So it shouldn't have come as a surprise that when we asked what seemed to us like a simple question, he gave a thoughtful, complex and nuanced answer.

"Playing some types of video games can help you identify and respond to targets quickly," he said. (His observations are in line with the experimental work of Daphne Bavelier, PhD, which we will describe in the next chapter.)

But what about the traditionally taught components of good marksmanship such as stance, balance, breath control and follow-through? Clearly, those aren't components of video games.

"Those are important for competitive target shooting, but not for combat situations," said Harris. Through the window we could see an air marshal a few dozen yards down range. The instructor had him on his back, shooting targets from unusual positions. It seemed to emphasize Harris's point.

He added that linking video games to the supposedly precise aim of the shooters in school shooting cases misses some critical factors. The first is that hitting a large target, such as a person, is not difficult at all. It takes little more than the ability to point, especially if the victims are not moving quickly and are close by, as was the case at the schools.

"Beginning shooters have a self-preservation response—a flinch—when they fire a gun. But in these school shootings, the victims are so close to the shooter that jerking the trigger really doesn't matter," he added.

As for Lee Malvo, the young DC sniper, Harris said that those shots were also pretty easy for a beginner, especially one who, like Malvo, had practiced with a real rifle. "He had a stable position, a telescopic sight, lots of time to aim, and targets who were standing pretty still," Harris said.

Which leads us back to the claims made by Grossman about Michael Carneal, the fourteen-year-old school shooter in Paducah, Kentucky. First, he's making inappropriate comparisons. Unlike the situations described by the FBI's statistics, Carneal was not involved in a "shootout." He was the only one with a weapon; no one was firing at him. He was also much closer to the other students than seven yards. He simply walked up to them and fired.

Grossman also has his facts wrong. According to a report published by the National Research Council and Institute of Medicine,[6] Carneal did have experience firing guns. "He snuck into a friend's father's garage and stole a .22 pistol and ammunition, the gun he ultimately used in the shooting. He had previously fired guns with this young man and his father."[7] "After school on the Wednesday before Thanksgiving [five days before the school shooting], Carneal went to a friend's house, and they used the pistol for target practice on a rubber ball."[8]

But what about his supposed remarkable accuracy? Picture the scene: It's 7:42 A.M., the start of the school day. Students crowd the lobby of Heath High School. A prayer group has gathered in that lobby for its daily meeting. "Just as the group was finishing its morning prayer, Carneal slowly fired three shots and then five in rapid succession, making an arc around the lobby. He would later say that he was not aiming the weapon but simply firing into the crowd."[9]

So it was not precise marksmanship at all, just bullets shot into a crowd of helpless students.

The Giant Leap

Within hours of the shootings at Virginia Tech, pundits were on the airwaves and the Internet blaming video games for Cho's behavior. (This was reminiscent of the instant but unsupported links between video games and the DC sniper or the Columbine school shooters that we described in chapter 1.) It didn't matter that the police found no video games, consoles or other gaming equipment when they searched his room.[10] Nor did it matter that one of his college roommates told reporters that he'd never seen Cho play video games or take any interest in them; he'd spent most of his time at the computer writing. Despite all of this, the supposed link between Cho's murderous behavior and violent video games was assumed to be there.

It's easy to chalk this up to sloppy tabloid journalism, the relentless pressure on twenty-four-hour news operations to fill time, and the desires of self-appointed experts for publicity. Why else would they ignore the fact that the second-worst school shooting in U.S. history (thirty-one wounded and sixteen killed, including Charles Whitman, the shooter) occurred at the University of Texas at Austin in 1966—well before video games were available? In that case, the likely cause of Whitman's violent behavior was a brain tumor that was discovered during his autopsy.

Focusing on video games distracted many people from the much more powerful factors that seem to have contributed to this tragedy: the failure of the people around Cho (including his family, teachers, school administrators, court officials and fellow students) to respond appropriately and effectively to his profound and obvious mental illness, as well as the easy availability of firearms to Cho, despite his court-mandated psychiatric treatment in 2005—treatment that he apparently never received.*

But the rhetoric on the airwaves, over the Internet and in the newspapers seldom touched in a substantive way on those issues. The shortage of mental health services on campuses and throughout the country was rarely mentioned. Upcoming state and national elections kept gun control off the political table, other than through some repeated but unthinking claims that the incident might have been mostly avoided if only the other students had been armed with their own pistols so that they could have shot Cho earlier. Indeed, a month after the Virginia Tech shootings, a subcommittee of the South Carolina legislature passed a measure that would allow adults to carry concealed firearms on public school campuses, from elementary school through college. (Now *that's* a recipe for dramatically increasing violence on campus!)

In fact, if you wanted to decrease the number of deaths among college students, you wouldn't look at school homicides at all. They're dramatic but extremely rare. Instead, you would focus on preventing suicides. There are approximately three suicides on college campuses *every day*; about 95 percent of those college students who commit suicide are suffering from a mental illness, usually depression.[11] The deaths at Virginia Tech and those few other colleges where school shootings have occurred,

---

*Another unfortunate consequence of this event was the unwarranted association of mental illness with violent behavior. Cho's violent behavior was extremely rare. Most people who suffer from a mental illness are much more likely to be the *victims* of violence than the perpetrators of violence. The vast majority of people who act violently are not mentally ill.

while clearly newsworthy, represent a tiny fraction of the college students who die from preventable causes each year. (Interestingly, the suicide rate among college students is roughly half the suicide rate among people the same age who are not attending college.)[12]

Yet within hours of the shooting, Fox News was interviewing Jack Thompson, an attorney and antigame activist, who blamed the events on Cho's having played *Counter-Strike* in high school. "These are real lives. These are real people that are in the ground now because of this game. I have no doubt about it," said Thompson.[13]

He made similar claims on other broadcasts, using the circular logic that since other school shooters had been "immersed" in violent video games, obviously this school shooting was caused by Cho playing *Counter-Strike*. The problem is that his premise is false, and so is his conclusion.

The next evening, pop psychologist and television host Dr. Phil McGraw was interviewed on CNN's *Larry King Live*. He, too, placed the blame for the Virginia Tech murders on violent video games and other media.

> McGraw: The problem is we are programming these people as a society. You cannot tell me—common sense tells you that if these kids are playing video games, where they're on a mass killing spree in a video game, it's glamorized on the big screen, it's become part of the fiber of our society. You take that and mix it with a psychopath, a sociopath or someone suffering from mental illness and add in a dose of rage, the suggestibility is too high. And we're going to have to start dealing with that. We're going to have to start addressing those issues and recognizing that the mass murders [sic] of tomorrow are the children of today that are being programmed with this massive violence overdose.
>
> King: Well said.[14]

Republican presidential candidate Mitt Romney used more vivid imagery to link video games to this shooting when he addressed Christian conservatives at a graduation speech at Regent University a few weeks later: "Pornography and violence poison our music and movies and TV and video games. The Virginia Tech shooter, like the Columbine shooters before him, had drunk from this cesspool."[15]

Did these claims bear out? No. In fact, the report of the Virginia Tech Review Panel[16] specifically dismissed the purported links between Seung-Hui Cho's use of video games and his extremely violent behavior. In the chapter on Cho's mental health history, video games are mentioned on only three pages.

When he was nine years old, "he was enrolled in a Tae Kwon Do program for awhile, watched TV, and played video games like *Sonic the Hedgehog*. None of the video games were war games or had violent themes." (pg. 32) In college, "Cho's roommate never saw him play video games." (p. 42) During his senior year of college, his roommate "never saw him play a video game, which he thought strange since he and most other students play them." (p. 51)

This is consistent with our research findings that it's highly unusual for a teenage boy not to play video games, including violent video games, because they use these games to build and strengthen social relationships with peers. In fact, his lack of involvement with video games was a marker of his poor social skills and his status as a social outcast.

It doesn't take an event as dramatic as the mass murders at Virginia Tech to bring out social commentators who claim that video games are the path to self-destruction. When the Sony PlayStation 3 gaming console was introduced in November 2006, conservative pundit Bill O'Reilly warned on his radio program of the evils of video game technology. (He apparently didn't appreciate the irony of his using radio, which had been similarly accused by an earlier generation of promoting a host of sins, to spread his message.)

> American society is changing for the worse because of the machines. . . . In the past, to flee the real world people usually chose drugs or alcohol. . . . Now you don't have to do that. Now all you have to do is have enough money to buy a machine. . . .
>
> Basically what you have is a large portion of the population, mostly younger people under the age of 45, who don't deal with reality—ever. So they don't know what day it is; they don't know what temperature it is; they don't know what their neighbor looks

like. They don't know anything . . . because they are constantly diverted by a machine. Now what this does is it takes a person away from reality because they've created their own reality. . . .[17]

That's quite a bleak picture. But does it ring true? Given the popularity of video games, one would think that the number of people—especially men, since they play games the most—who are disoriented and psychotic would have shot up. It has not. Even allowing for hyperbole, such claims are utter nonsense.

Focusing on the Real Issues

Laurence Steinberg, PhD, is one of the world's leading experts on child development. He's the distinguished university professor and Laura H. Carnell professor of psychology at Temple University in Philadelphia. He literally "wrote the book" on adolescence. (His classic textbook *Adolescence* has recently been published in its eighth edition.) He says that focusing violence prevention efforts on such things as video games is a waste of time and money.

"Being exposed to harsh and inconsistent parenting is the most important environmental factor," he says. "The mass media probably rank at the bottom of that list. The one place where there's some empirical evidence is that video games and other media may desensitize kids to witnessing violence. But what about the local evening news?"

He adds that the people who claim that children are taught to become violent may have it backward. "Kids start off in life being aggressive," says Dr. Steinberg. "Fifty percent of all kids' interactions with other kids during the preschool years are aggressive. But most kids show a steady and dramatic decline in aggression over time. The question is what enables some kids to *stop* being aggressive, not to start being aggressive."

Also, people have different abilities to regulate their emotions. Reacting violently to a nonviolent situation can be a function of brain development and wiring. "A lot of studies of violent juvenile offenders find that these kids have neurological or neurobiological deficits," he says.

So what can you do? Dr. Steinberg's practical advice for parents on how to lower the likelihood that your children will act violently in the real world is based, in part, on findings that children are more likely to imitate the behaviors of people with whom they have a close relationship than the behaviors of strangers or of people they see in video games or other media.

- Reduce the *real* aggression in your household that your child is exposed to. Hitting, verbal abuse and other forms of violence at home are strong predictors of children and adolescents acting violently toward others. "That's the single most important thing that parents could do that would make a difference," he says. "We know that exposure to violence in the household, even if the children aren't involved, increases the likelihood of their becoming violent."
- Know whom your child is hanging out with and how they act toward each other. "We know that kids who affiliate with violent, aggressive kids are more likely to be violent, in part because they learn it as a self-defense."
- Don't use corporal punishment on your child; use alternative, nonviolent methods, including shifting your focus to rewarding positive behaviors. "Physical punishment is correlated with aggressive and violent behavior in kids," Steinberg adds.
- Teach your child to literally or figuratively take a breath before responding: "Another important thing is to get kids to insert a little pause before they act," Steinberg says. Violent children often respond immediately or even reflexively to what they perceive as a threat, whereas other children take a moment to evaluate the situation.

Do as I Say, Not as I Do

On October 7, 2005, California governor Arnold Schwarzenegger signed a bill to prohibit the sale or rental of violent video games to minors. This is, of course, the same Arnold Schwarzenegger who made his financial fortune and launched his political career by starring in such violent movies as the *Terminator* series (cyborgs are sent back in time to wipe out human life on the planet), *Collateral Damage* (a man tries to kill the terrorists who killed his family), *End of Days* (an atheist ex-cop tries to kill the devil, who's in New York City looking for a bride so that he can end the world), *Predator* (a team of commandos is hunted by an alien who butchers bodies and makes trophies from their skulls) and countless others of this genre. In fact, Schwarzenegger has recorded voice-overs for two Terminator video games. His years of profiting from media violence specifically aimed at teenage audiences belie his newfound political concerns about exposing children to violent media.

In taking this legislative approach, Schwarzenegger was far from alone. During 2005, for example, legislators in twenty states and the District of Columbia put forth at least one bill attempting to restrict the sale of, rental of or access to video games as a way to protect children from their supposedly harmful effects. California, Michigan and Illinois passed such legislation that year. All these laws have been challenged in the courts. All have been overturned.

Doug Lowenstein, the founding president of the video game industry group the Entertainment Software Association (ESA), says that one issue triggering these laws is a demographic divide between legislators currently in power and the young people who grew up playing video games. Older legislators and public policy makers simply don't understand what video games are all about and react viscerally to the stories they hear and the images they see—stories and images that are not representative of the games children and young adults play the most.

Lowenstein, who left the ESA in 2007, had been intimately involved in the litigation that led courts to overturn those proposed laws. He sees other factors at work in these bills.

At some point it really just does become about politics. The attacks on games are coming in part from people who are completely uninterested in facts and who see it as a political issue they can pop out a press release on that denounces violent games as harmful to our kids' psyches. It's the most cynical kind of politics you can imagine, because when you've had nine federal courts strike down virtually identical statutes over three years, everybody pushing for these bills knows the outcome. Everybody knows that they'll never become law. They're putting the taxpayers of their states through a completely wasteful exercise that will cost them hundreds of thousands of dollars to defend a statute that everybody knows from the beginning is fatally flawed.

There's nothing more cynical than that. This isn't about helping parents. It is purely about trying to score cheap political
points.

While some activists and legislators might be quick to dismiss
Lowenstein's comments because of his close ties to the video game
industry, his statements and his frustration are clearly reflected in several recent court rulings on these bills. In fact, judges have become
increasingly skeptical not only of the claims about potential harm being
made by proponents of such legislation, but also of the motives of the
legislators who support them.

The Illinois legislature's 2005 bill made it a criminal offense to sell or
rent to minors any violent or sexually explicit video game. It unartfully
defined a violent video game as one that includes "depictions of or simulations of human-on-human violence in which the player kills or otherwise causes serious physical harm to another human. 'Serious physical
harm' includes depictions of death, dismemberment, amputation, decap-
itation, maiming, disfigurement, mutilation of body parts, or rape."[18]

It defined sexually explicit video games as "those that the average
person, applying contemporary community standards would find, with
respect to minors, is designed to appeal or pander to the prurient interest and depict or represent in a manner patently offensive with respect
to minors, an actual or simulated sexual act or sexual content, an actual
or simulated normal or perverted sexual act or a lewd exhibition of the
genitals or the post-pubescent female breast."[19] The law also required all
such games to carry a two-inch-by-two-inch sticker with the number
"18" on it.

Soon after Governor Rod Blagojevich signed the bill, the ESA, the
Video Software Dealers Association and the Illinois Retail Merchants
Association filed a suit to enjoin the law from taking effect. Some of the
reasons cited in the lawsuit included the law having a chilling effect on
free speech by forcing retailers to make decisions about whether they
could sell each game (the legislation circumvented the ESRB ratings
system) and the unconstitutional vagueness of the law's description of
both violence and sexual content.

The core of the lawsuit, however, focused on the scientific research that led to the Illinois legislature's actions. Two researchers whose work had been seminal to the bill, Craig Anderson, PhD, of Iowa State University, and William Kronenberger, PhD, of the University of Indiana School of Medicine, testified on its behalf. Anderson described his reviews of the literature and his experiments involving the timing of air horn blasts, which we mentioned in chapter 3. Kronenberger described his use of fMRI imaging (a way of looking at activity within different parts of the brain) on four groups of children who had high or low exposure to media violence and who had or did not have behavioral problems.

Testifying on the quality and usefulness of that research on behalf of the plaintiffs were Jeffrey Goldstein, PhD, of the University of Utrecht in the Netherlands, a social psychologist specializing in video games; Dmitri Williams, PhD, of the University of Illinois, a communications researcher who had studied violent video games; and Howard Nusbaum, PhD, of the University of Chicago, an fMRI researcher.

In his ruling, U.S. District Judge Matthew F. Kennelly excoriated both the legislators who passed the law and the researchers whose work was used to justify it, essentially calling that research junk science.

Neither Dr. Anderson's testimony nor his research establishes a solid causal link between violent video game exposure and aggressive thinking and behavior. As Dr. Goldstein and Dr. Williams noted, researchers in this field have not eliminated the most obvious alternative explanation: aggressive individuals may themselves be attracted to violent video games.

Even if one were to accept the proposition that playing violent video games increases aggressive thoughts or behavior, there is no evidence that this is at all significant. Dr. Anderson provided no evidence supporting the view that playing violent video games has a lasting effect on aggressive thoughts and behavior—in other words, an effect that lingers more than a short time after the player stops playing the game. . . .

Finally, the Court is concerned that the legislative record does not indicate that the Illinois General Assembly considered any of the evidence that showed no relationship or a negative relationship between violent video game play and increases in aggressive thoughts and behavior. The legislative record included none of the articles cited by Dr. Goldstein or Dr. Williams. It included no data whatsoever that was critical of research finding a causal link between violent video game play and aggression. These omissions further undermine defendants' claim that the legislature made "reasonable inferences" from the scientific literature based on "substantial evidence."[20]

Kronenberger had claimed that his fMRI research had demonstrated that exposure to violent media was correlated with behavioral disorders and that those disorders were caused by decreased activity in areas of the brain that are used to regulate violent behaviors. In discussing that research, Judge Kennelly was even more skeptical after Nusbaum pointed out fundamental flaws in both the underlying assumptions and the methodology of that research.

> The Court found Dr. Nusbaum's testimony credible and persuasive, and Dr. Kronenberger's unpersuasive. Consistent with Dr. Nusbaum's testimony, the Court finds that Dr. Kronenberger's studies cannot support the weight he attempts to put on them via his conclusions. The defendants have offered no basis to permit a reasonable conclusion that, as the legislature found, minors who play violent video games are more likely to "experience a reduction of activity in the frontal lobes of the brain which is responsible for controlling behavior."

Judge Kennelly made it clear that he was disappointed by the scientific arguments made by the state to justify the legislation, even resorting to a bit of his own hyperbole.

> Defendants have come nowhere near making the necessary showing in this case. First, they have offered no evidence that the violent content in video games is "directed to inciting or producing imminent lawless action." Rather, the only evidence in the record is that video games are designed for entertainment. And second, the evidence they offered regarding the purported effects

on minors of playing violent video games does not even approach *Brandenburg's* requirement that violent video games are "likely to" produce "imminent" violence. . . .

Next, there is barely any evidence at all, let alone substantial evidence, showing that playing violent video games causes minors to "experience a reduction of activity in the frontal lobes of the brain which is responsible for controlling behavior." Defendants rely heavily on this finding because it is based on research by Dr. Kronenberger that was unavailable when the Seventh Circuit decided *Kendrick* in 2001. This finding, however, is unsupported by scientific evidence.[21]

Judge Kennelly was equally unimpressed by the state's claim that the law was justified because it had a compelling interest in preventing developmental or psychological harm to children. His findings took them to task by giving them a stern lecture on constitutional law.

In this country, the State lacks the authority to ban protected speech on the ground that it affects the listener's or observer's thoughts and attitudes. . . . As Justice Jackson stated over a half-century ago, "[t]he priceless heritage of our society is the unrestricted constitutional right of each member to think as he will. Thought control is a copyright of totalitarianism, and we have no claim to it. It is not the function of our Government to keep the citizen from falling into error; it is the function of the citizen to keep the Government from falling into error." . . . If controlling access to allegedly "dangerous" speech is important in promoting the positive psychological development of children, in our society that role is properly accorded to parents and families, not the State.[22]

Judge Kennelly also ordered the state of Illinois to reimburse the video game industry and retailers' groups $510,528.64 for their legal fees.[23] This is in addition to the cost to the state of its own attorneys and expert witnesses.

Still, it wasn't over. Despite this thorough chastising of the Illinois legislature and the governor by the court, and the fact that the Illinois ruling was consistent with other court opinions in this area, in mid-2007 it was revealed that Governor Blagojevich had spent nearly $1 million in additional attorneys' fees to appeal the ruling.

According to news reports, "The governor raided funds throughout state government to pay for the litigation. Some of the areas money came from included the public health department, the state's welfare agency and even the economic development department."[24] These are, of course, departments whose activities are well known to have a direct and significant effect on real-world violence.

"This Court is Dumbfounded . . ."

Judge Kennelly is not alone in losing patience with the heavy-handed political posturing behind these proposed laws. In 2006, the Louisiana legislature unanimously passed a law that restricted the sale of violent video games. That bill had been drafted by Jack Thompson, the attorney who would later blame Seung-Hui's Cho murderous rampage at Virginia Tech on his allegedly having played the game *Counter-Strike* when he was a teenager.

There are numerous ironies here as well. Louisiana had recently suffered tremendous death and destruction from Hurricane Katrina, made all the worse by the inept government response to that disaster. New Orleans is known for having many of the real-world problems portrayed in such video games as the *Grand Theft Auto* series, including high levels of street and family violence, alcohol and drug abuse, drug importation, gangs, prostitution and corruption. Yet the legislature chose to focus on video games!

The ESA and the Entertainment Merchants Association (EMA) immediately filed for an injunction to block the law from going into effect. U.S. District Judge James J. Brady granted a temporary and then a permanent injunction. The ESA and the EMA then asked the judge to force the State of Louisiana to reimburse them for $91,993.67 in legal fees.

In April 2007, Judge Brady agreed and ruled that the state must send the industry's law firms a check. But he didn't leave it at that. In his decision, he lambasted the state legislature for passing such a bill, questioning their fundamental legal competence and awareness of the U.S.

Constitution, and saying that they'd blatantly wasted everyone's time and money:

> This Court is dumbfounded that the Attorney General and the State are in the position of having to pay taxpayer money as attorney's fees and costs in this lawsuit. The Act which this Court found to be unconstitutional passed through committees in both the State House and Senate, then through the full House and Senate, and to be promptly signed by the Governor. There are lawyers at each stage of this process. Some of the members of these committees are themselves lawyers. Presumably, they have staff members who are attorneys as well. The State House and Senate certainly have staff members who are attorneys. The Governor has additional attorneys—the executive counsel. Prior to the passage of the Act, there were a number of reported cases from a number of jurisdictions which held similar statutes to be unconstitutional (and in which the defendant was ordered to pay attorney's fees). The Court wonders why nobody objected to the enactment of this statute. In this Court's view, the taxpayers deserve more from their elected officials.[25]

You would think that the sponsor of this misguided, poorly crafted and ill-fated bill, State Representative Roy A. Burrell, would hang his head in shame. Many in the press had been highly critical of the bill, seeing it for the political posturing that it was. But the issue is too juicy and the opportunities for grandstanding are too great to ignore.

Soon after the defeat, Burrell decided that it was time for some political spin. He claimed that the judge's ruling was the ill-founded opinion of one man instead of a legal finding that was consistent with every other video game case heard by the courts. He described the wasted taxpayer money as a noble investment in child safety and promoted the impression that the profoundly and rightfully embarrassed Louisiana legislators were, in reality, working tirelessly behind the scenes to protect that state's helpless children from this terrible menace. On May 10, 2007, Burrell wrote an over-the-top op-ed for the Shreveport *Times* in which he used the First Amendment to defend his attack against the First Amendment:

The unsuspected cost of $100,000 to taxpayers for legal fees is but a small price paid to save the life of just one child, given the many killed or maimed, linked to the mind-altering harmful ultra-violent video games. Oftentimes, the fight to protect our constituents and their children against the predatory tactics of the video game industry goes on behind the scenes. The only information the public sees is a negative perception from these greedy individuals who don't mind using the law for continual use of legal corruption of young minds; our desperate attempts to save children and offer the families more parental control and a better quality of life are circumvented. Therefore, we must find ways to place legal restraints on such a "self-regulated" industry while they veil themselves behind First Amendment protection.[26]

And so the political battle, full of sound and fury, continues.

CHAPTER 9

Practical Advice for Parents

I don't know if it's an addiction, but he's just glued to it. I think most parents are concerned about it. It's the same with my daughter with her laptop computer in her room; instead of using the telephone, she's on that, and I can't be watching both of them all the time to see if they're talking to strangers or to see if someone is getting killed in the other room on the PlayStation. It's just nerve wracking!

—*A Massachusetts mother of twins*

ONE OF THE TOUGHEST TASKS FACED BY PARENTS IS MAINtaining our sense of perspective. We see this difficulty most clearly during two periods of our children's development: infancy, when everything is new and we're not sure what to expect, and adolescence, when we're acutely aware of the dangers in their environment and of how teenagers often view those dangers differently than we do.

It's tempting, during those times of stress, to long for the good old days when things were simpler and more carefree. The problem is that those simpler, carefree times are largely figments of our imaginations. Our parents worried about their teenagers (us) coping with the sexual revolution brought about by the birth control pill, among other things. Our grandparents worried about their teenagers (our parents) struggling with World War II and the Korean War. The list goes on, with each generation's concerns supplanted by the next's. Times were never simpler, they were just different.

One of the keys to success as a parent is learning how to work within the context of your child's stage of development. It's more like aikido than boxing; you redirect the child's energy and momentum instead of meeting force with force.

Perhaps the biggest lesson learned from our research is that most parents should not worry about violent or other M-rated video games having a profound effect on their children's behavior or values. Throughout our interviews with young teens who played such games, we were repeatedly impressed by how they had incorporated their parents' fundamental values into their lives. They realized that the video games were play and that, like the crime and horror comic books, gangster films and penny blood novels sold to earlier generations, these games were entertaining but outrageous fantasies.

But our research did reveal patterns of play that might serve as markers of emotional or behavioral problems. This shouldn't come as a surprise, for we see similar markers in *all* types of play, not just video games. To pick up on signs of a problem, you should look beyond the video games for a deterioration of or breakdown in the key elements of your child's life: family relationships, friendships, school achievement, health and emotions.

It's tempting to state that children should not play video games more than X hours per day, but that focuses on the wrong issue. A child who plays video games for three hours per day and who's doing well in school, has strong reciprocal friendships, gets along at home and feels good physically and emotionally is probably doing just fine. A child who plays only two hours per week but whose grades have declined, is feeling sad and withdrawn, no longer wants to spend time with friends and is angry at home is not.

If the video game play seems to have an addictive or compulsive quality to it—playing video games is the only thing that your child wants to do—then it's a sign of a problem. Sometimes, as we'll discuss in a few pages, that's a reflection of normal adolescent brain development and not a deeper pathology. Still, a child in this situation probably needs help to get his life back on track and to learn ways to set limits on his game playing.

Our research found that a significant number of teens play video games primarily as a way of handling emotional problems or stress. Again, this should not be surprising. It's a creative and perhaps an appropriate coping mechanism, especially if it's not the only way a child learns to handle such problems. Noticing when and why she plays can give you insights into other things going on in her life and how well she's handling them. If the stress is ongoing, or your child is routinely depressed, anxious or angry, you should get her help no matter how little she's playing video games.

What Parents Worry About

Our study found that parents had four areas of concern when it came to video games:

❖ Were their kids striking a reasonable balance between video game play and other age-appropriate activities?

❖ What restrictions should they place on video games in their home?

❖ What video game content is appropriate or inappropriate for their children at different ages?

❖ What influence could video games, especially violent games, have on their children's behaviors?

Of these, the most frequently mentioned and usually the first concern voiced by parents was not game content, but time.

> Scott: "He plays a bit too much. We've tried to create more balance in his life. He does get out, but he'd prefer to be sitting there playing that game."

> Joanne: "I have taken the machine away and I have hidden it because he loses all concept of time."

The underlying issue here is not video games per se, but an understanding of normal child development. The children's behaviors are simply not what the parents expect or what they remember themselves doing at that age. Many kids try to indulge their passions by spending a lot of time involved with them. We have fewer concerns about the avid reader or the aspiring basketball player who spends hour after hour with books or on the court because, as parents, we're more comfortable with those activities. But most likely, the underlying motivations and behaviors—wanting to do something a lot and losing track of time—are shared by the gamer, the bookworm and the athlete. It's a matter of biology and development.

That's why we'd be much more worried about a twenty-three-year-old who couldn't tear himself away from playing video games than we would a thirteen-year-old who had the same problem. The adult's brain, specifically his prefrontal cortex, should be sufficiently developed that he behaves differently.

Recently, one mother who had heard about our research approached us and asked if her son's interest in video games was normal. He was twenty-two years old, had dropped out of college, refused to look for a job, had no social life, was living in her basement and spent eighteen hours per day alone playing video games. Clearly, this young man had some major problems. The obsessive video game play was much more likely a symptom than the root cause. We encouraged this woman to seek immediate help for her son. (She was a clinical psychologist, but because the young man was her child she had lost all perspective.)

Hurting or Helping Social Skills

The concerns about access, content and behavioral influence were often woven together. For example, many of the parents we interviewed wondered whether playing video games interfered with their children's development of social skills:

> Jamie: "I'm concerned that this game playing is so autonomous; just the kid and the TV screen. And I wonder, how is this going to affect his social skills?"

> Yvette: "Five or six years from now, will they be able to socialize in a group with people who don't necessarily play these games?"

Yet when we talked to the children, they viewed video game play as largely a social activity, not an isolating one. It did more than provide a topic of conversation; it provided a structure through multiplayer games in which they practiced and improved their verbal communication skills.

Two of the key tasks of adolescence are improving social skills and interpersonal communication. When we give presentations on adolescent development to parents, we often describe how a fourteen-year-old girl who comes home from a school dance will immediately get on the phone or send instant messages to a friend she had seen in person only minutes earlier. The essence of their conversation is predictable: Did you see what I saw? What do you think that means? How do you feel about it? They are trying to determine whether they're paying attention to the right things and if they're interpreting them correctly.

But why didn't they simply do this in person? In this case, technology gives them an advantage. The telephone or the computer offers a combination of intimacy and anonymity that helps them get comfortable more quickly with these complex social and communication skills. The fourteen-year-old may blush when she recalls what a friend did on the dance floor, but if she's at her computer or on the phone her friend can't see her turn crimson. Therefore, she can safely take more social risks.

It's possible that computer games may serve the same purpose, especially for boys. The structure of the games may allow them to test social boundaries and relationships in ways that they might not recover from as easily in face-to-face discourse. They can be more assertive. They can be sneaky or sarcastic. After all, it's only a game.

Supervision of game play was another issue. Our research found that nearly one third of the young teens we surveyed said that they had a computer in their bedroom. Nearly half had a game console in there. The consequences of having such easy access to video game equipment was reflected in the amount of time they spent playing. Those children who had both a computer and a game console in their bedroom were more than twice as likely as other children to spend more than fifteen hours per week playing video games and to play M-rated games.

Shooting Trolls, Shooting People

Concerns about on-screen violence varied considerably among parents but centered on three interconnected issues: the realism, the nature of the targets, and the context or goal of the violence. "They can shoot as many trolls as they want, and it can be pretty bloody without really bothering me that much," said Roy. "But if you had a game where it looks like [they're shooting] real people, that bothers me more. There might be some carryover."

> Yvette: "I'm not concerned about the violence. I'm concerned about the way they *portray* the violence. It's not accidental; it's intentional. You know, they're just out to kill people in some of these games, and I don't think that kids should watch it. I don't think kids should participate in it."

Several parents specifically raised concerns about the stereotyping of women and minorities.

> Jamie: "The way that women are portrayed and the way that people of color are portrayed really bugs me. I don't know how [my son is] interpreting those images."

These clusters of concerns should help guide conversations with your children about your values. Children are likely to brush aside a sweeping statement about all violence being unacceptable. After all, violent behavior is a staple of every medium from fairy tales to religious stories to cartoons. But if you focus on specific concerns and differentiate them from other concerns, you'll encourage your child to think more critically about each game's content. (We'll have more on this below when we examine improving children's media literacy.)

Couch Potatoes?

Parents were also concerned that their children were not getting enough exercise because of their video game play.

> Patti: "When I was a kid, everyone was out in the street playing. . . . Now kids are just lazy, overweight and zombie-like."

> Clara: "My concern is making sure there's a balance with what they do with their spare time. I don't want it to channel into just

one type of play. They think diversification is a video game on this system versus a video game on another system. When I'm there, the balance is well monitored. But I always come home with this suspicion somebody's been playing. I can tell because the control is moved over to it."

Obesity is a significant problem in the United States, especially among children. But it makes no sense to lay the blame on video games. In several generations we have gone from an environment of food scarcity to abundance. At the same time, work is becoming increasingly sedentary and school budget cuts have reduced physical education programs.

For a variety of reasons, a lot of childhood play has shifted from informal pickup games to organized, supervised leagues of youth versions of adult sports. Little League has replaced sandlot pickup baseball games. Community soccer teams start as young as age four. The dropout and nonparticipant rates in such organized sports is high among middle schoolers. They realize that the goal of playing has shifted from having fun to winning. If they're not good at the sport, they have little reason to stay involved, even if they enjoy it.

Some sports, such as skateboarding, appear to be an exception. Participants compete largely against themselves; their primary reward is a sense of mastery. The culture of skateboarding, like the culture of video games, encourages helping people who are new to the sport. That emphasis on growth rather than simply winning may partially explain the popularity of video games as sporting events, especially in countries like South Korea.

Competitive gaming, known in South Korea as E-sports, has millions of young Korean participants, and the country has at least three television networks devoted to gaming (akin to ESPN and Fox Sports in North America). Top professional *StarCraft* players like Lim Yo Hwan are national celebrities on the order of film stars and pop music idols.[1]

Two findings in our research provide hope for parents concerned about kids turning into couch potatoes. Boys we surveyed who played realistic sports games, such as basketball, football and skateboarding, spent significantly more time on exercise than the kids who didn't play those games. It's likely that many of these teenagers were already athletes. They used the video games to improve their skills and understanding of the sports they already enjoyed. In our focus groups, boys told us that they'd see a move on a video game and then go outside and practice it on the court or the street. "Like in basketball," said Antonio, "if you see them do a fancy crossover, whatever, you want to learn how to do the same thing." Jared added, "I think that's how we get better and better, 'cause we actually want to be one of the people in the game."

Sports games also motivated some boys to try new things. "When I was younger, I only had Nintendo, and one of my favorites was the baseball game," said Eric. "And that's how I really got into baseball. I probably wouldn't have been so much into sports right now if I didn't play some of the video games that I have."

Also, games like *Dance Dance Revolution* have become increasingly popular. Because it involves aerobic exercise, some children's weight reduction plans incorporate *Dance Dance Revolution* and similar games into their programs. School physical education programs and even some commercial gyms have begun to use it as well.

> Wendy: "I was complaining for a good long year about physical activity: 'You can't just stay up there!' So he got *Dance Dance Revolution*. He plays that all the time, and that's good—moving, you know."

The Nintendo Wii game system has one of the first of what will surely be a series of game interfaces that allow a player to use his whole body to play video games. In the future, we're likely to see many more games that help us burn calories and stay in shape. They're not a replacement for real-world sports, but they're potentially a nice complement to them.

"I Was Horrified. Horrified!"

"The boys had saved their money; they were eleven and twelve at the time," Claire recalled to the other parents in the room. "And they said,

'Everybody has this *Grand Theft Auto 3*; it's the best.' And I really didn't know about the ratings situation. The guy behind the counter at KB Toys said, 'Oh no, it's not that bad.' So I bought it, and they were playing it and playing it and playing it, and my brother happened to come over. He said, 'Did you see what they're playing? They're lighting people on fire, they're going into the saloon and getting lap dances.'

"I was horrified. Horrified!" she continued. "And it was really my own fault. I should have done some more investigating. I had no idea that the video games were like this. I returned it to KB and made them give me my money back."

The issue of restrictions on game content is complex. Both our focus groups with teenagers and our surveys clearly showed that while parents can generally control the games that are played in their home, they cannot control the games their children play elsewhere. This should not come as a surprise. There's tremendous social pressure on children, especially boys, to try games that push the envelope on a wide range of social and developmental issues, including violence and sex.

> Bobby: "My parents don't really know about my games. If they come upstairs to my room and see it, they'll say, 'Oh, that's nice. That looks like fun,' or something like that."

During our focus groups, we were struck by how often the young teenagers referenced their parents' stated values when describing their game play. They knew which types of content would be unacceptable.

> Jason: "Being around my mom so much has told me which games not to even ask her to play. And those games, I now don't even like. . . . So really, it's like she's given me the image of what to play, what not to play."

When we asked them about letting younger siblings play violent games, they were quite protective. Their concerns were remarkably similar to those held by their parents when it came to the potential for behavioral or attitudinal problems from being exposed to inappropriate content.

Josh: "In M games, there's a lot of swearing, a lot of killing and a lot of things that I don't want my younger brother knowing."

Daryl: "Well, if he was younger than eight, then I wouldn't let him play. At eight, I'd probably let him, but I'd lower down the volume so he wouldn't hear the swears."

Carlos: "In *Grand Theft Auto*, when you're driving around, you could see girls that you could pick up, like hookers. So I think children under thirteen or fourteen should not be buying it."

This tells us that parents' messages are getting through to their children. For the most part, children incorporated those messages into their judgments about playing violent video games. That doesn't mean that they always did what their parents wanted; their behaviors reflected the limits of their development as young adolescents. Indeed, rebellion against such restrictions is part of the "job description" of being an adolescent. But they used their parents' values and concerns as part of their frame of reference when interpreting the violence and sexual content they saw in the games.

Video Game Benefits: Are Girls Missing Out?

Research suggests that on average, boys have an edge over girls in several types of cognitive skills, such as imagining how three-dimensional objects would look from various perspectives and calculating the trajectory of an object (such as a bullet or a football) toward a moving target. This makes it easier for boys to immerse themselves in the shooting, fighting and sports games that require these skills—and may be another reason that boys are more likely than girls to prefer these genres. (Girls tend to have superior skills in other areas, such as remembering colors and object locations, and working with and recalling words.)[2]

Although superior visual-spatial skills may attract boys to action video games, research also suggests that video game play can substantially improve those skills. Daphne Bavelier, PhD, a professor of Brain and Cognitive sciences at the University of Rochester, chanced upon this while studying brain plasticity, the ability of the brain to adjust and improve its functioning by rewiring its connections.

"We noticed that some of our subjects were very good at some of the things we were testing, and they played a lot of video games," said Bavelier, who had been looking at ways to improve people's ability to process complex visual information. She decided to see if certain types of video games helped teach the brain better ways of identifying and analyzing what a person's eyes see.

Earlier studies had shown that it's possible to improve the brain's ability to handle a particular visual task. But that training was very specific; the improved skills did not transfer from one task to another. After having subjects play different types of video games and then testing their brains' abilities to process visual information, she found that some types of games could improve multiple visual skills simultaneously.

"Not every game has the same effect on the brain," she says. "In the case of vision, action video games are good. We suspect that they are good because they require you to monitor your visual environment—you can't know when or where things will happen. It's a very challenging task. You have to distribute your visual attention." She's using these findings to explore whether video games can help the elderly improve their attention and visual processing.

Bavelier adds that these games can also help children with tasks that have little to do with vision. "Video games can help children learn to make decisions, use strategies and anticipate consequences."

Other real-world studies appear to support this link between playing certain video games and visual-spatial ability. A study of thirty-three surgeons (including eighteen women) found that past experience playing video games for at least three hours a week and scoring high in video game skills (based on playing three different games) were related to their ability to perform laparoscopic surgery with greater speed and fewer errors. Game skill accounted for almost one-third of the difference in surgical performance, past experience with games accounted for 10 percent and gender of the surgeon only 2 percent. In other words, while men were more likely to have played games in the past than women, "correction for actual game playtime showed there was no sex difference in skill acquisition."[3]

A study of college students at the University of Toronto[4] confirmed a significant gender difference in spatial abilities between video game players and nonplayers, and between male and female students among the latter group. They then recruited six men and fourteen women who had not played video games during the previous four years and assigned half to play a popular 3-D first-person shooter game with lots of action (*Medal of Honor: Pacific Assault*) and half to play a 3-D puzzle game.

The students' spatial attention and mental rotation skills were tested at the beginning of the study. They then played their assigned game for ten hours, one or two hours at a time over a four-week period. At the post-test, puzzle game players showed no improvement, but the action game players improved substantially; their spatial attention abilities approached those of experienced game players. What's more, the women showed greater improvement than the men. Given these results, the researchers suggest that training with appropriate action video games could potentially lead more women into science or engineering careers.

What Should You Do As a Parent?

The first step is to reframe the often-asked question "How do I protect my child from violent video games?" to "How do I help my child make the most of time spent playing video games?" As we said earlier, it's not boxing, it's aikido. You don't want to meet force with force or to abdicate control. Instead, you want to work with and redirect your child's skills and interests.

Stay involved. The majority of the teenage boys we interviewed said that their parents were ignorant about video games in general and about their own game play in particular. (Before undertaking this research, we counted ourselves among that group.) Our survey found that only 5 percent of boys and 6 percent of girls said that they played video games always or often with a parent, stepparent or foster parent. More than three quarters of the teenagers said that they rarely or never did so.

A good place to begin is by learning some of the terms gamers use. How is a "first-person shooter" such as *Doom* or *Halo* structurally differ-ent from a "third-person shooter" such as *Grand Theft Auto* or *Tomb Raider*? (In the former, you see the game environment as if you are a character enmeshed in it. In the latter, you see the body of the character you're controlling as that character moves through the game environment.) What's an MMORPG? (A Massively Multiplayer Online Role-Playing Game, like *World of Warcraft*, is a game in which many players interact online in a complex virtual world.) What's a cheat code? (These are programming codes used by game testers and players to alter the behavior of a game or its characters, allowing you to skip a level or get unlimited ammunition, or preventing you from being killed.)

Have your children tell you about these game genres and terms. Why do they like some types of games but not others? When and why do they use cheat codes? Get the conversation going.

For many parents, using the game interface can be a barrier, whether it's a computer keyboard or a game console. It's intimidating to see a child fluidly manipulate a joystick or a set of buttons, especially when our own first efforts usually result in our on-screen characters repeatedly walking into virtual walls or crashing cars. Our children rapidly toggle between views of the game's landscape. We see all the data on the screen, but we don't know where to look. Experiences like this leave us feeling as frustrated as toddlers trying unsuccessfully to take their first steps.

Terry: "We actually attempted to teach our mom how to play *ESPN Football* once. Mom turns my controller on, and then she says, 'How do I choose my team?' My brother says, 'Oh, just press the analog stick.' 'But where is the analog stick?' 'There's two of them right there.' 'Which one do I use?' It was hilarious, really."

Trisha shared her sense of incompetence with the other parents in her group. "I know how to turn the PlayStation on, but I don't know how to use the controllers at all."

Michael Jellinek, MD, says that parents' awkwardness and hesitancy with video game controls and their lack of familiarity with the games can be used to their advantage when it comes to strengthening relationships with their children. He's sometimes "prescribed" video games that parents and kids can play together. "I've used golf, football or car racing games," he said. "It changes the dynamic of the parent constantly teaching the child to the child teaching the parent."

At home, Jellinek plays a variety of video games with his children. "We've played *Grand Theft Auto* and a lot of football and racing games. We played *Sniper*; it's a pretty exciting game. I like the technical aspects of it. We've played *U-Boat*. We used to have family contests on *Caterpillar*."

Daphne Bavelier, PhD, has preteen twins who play video games. "They will do fifteen minutes of back-and-forth argumentation about moves, and how this Pokémon would have been better than the other in that situation." For parents who are uncomfortable with game controllers, she suggests looking for games that allow you to talk about strategies and decision making with your child as a way to connect and teach.

Research conducted in the Netherlands found that those parents who played video games themselves had a different perspective on the risks and benefits of those games on their children. "[They] were more optimistic about the positive effects and less worried about the negative effects."[5] They also were more likely to play video games with their children.

Reframe your perspective. As we mentioned in chapter 4, video game play can be a marker for increased risk of certain behaviors. For example, M-gamer girls were three times as likely to say that they'd damaged property just for fun during the previous year than non-M-gamer girls. M-gamer boys were more than twice as likely as non-M-gamer boys to do so.

But there are several important things to keep in mind, even though these differences sound dramatic and perhaps even frightening. First, the category of behavior is broad, as are many categories of delinquent behaviors. There's a big difference between throwing a rock at an abandoned building and setting fire to someone's car, even though both acts would qualify as damaging property.

Second, remember that the actual number of kids who do these things is pretty low. While 15 percent of the M-gamer girls said that they'd damaged property for fun, that also means that 85 percent of the M-gamer girls said that they had not. For almost all of the problem behaviors we measured, the majority—and often the vast majority—of M-gamer kids didn't do those things.

Third, as we've said several times throughout this book, we can talk about relationships or correlations, but not causality. We don't know if playing M-rated games inspires some kids to act that way, if acting that way inspires kids to play M-rated games or if something else is going on.

The best approach, we believe, is to look at violent game play—especially if it constitutes the majority of time spent gaming—as a sign that you should be paying closer attention to a host of potential behavioral issues. Most of the time there won't be any problems. But it's a marker of increased risk.

Focus on media literacy. No matter how many or what restrictions or controls you may place on your children's video game play or their access to the Web, odds are that your child will be exposed to the type of material that concerns you, whether it's violence, sex, radical politics or anything else. Children need the tools and perspective to handle (or ignore) that material.

In fact, focusing exclusively on restricting your children's access can backfire. The "forbidden fruit" can become more attractive. This is not to say that you should not use the parental controls that come with most new game systems, or that you should not set standards for what your children might play at different ages. We encourage both of those things, but they're not enough.

Children, and especially teenagers, need the tools to make informed judgments about media content when you're not around—no matter what, or how inflammatory, that content may be. They also need to understand and to be able to identify likely motives behind the creation and distribution of that material. We touched on this in chapter 6 with respect to advergames and recruitment games. The concept applies just as much to commercial games.

Lessons from a Tram

Parents' approaches to helping their children become media literate should be similar to the other areas in which they help prepare their children to become more independent while staying safe. You usually know your children better than anyone else does. You have a good sense of when a child is ready to walk to school alone or spend the night at a friend's house.

When our son was nine years old, we moved to Basel, Switzerland. To get to his school, he had to take two trams, changing at a downtown stop. (Young children routinely ride trams solo in Basel.) One of us rode with him for the first two weeks, pointing out how the mass transit system worked and what he should look for. After a few days, we let him take the lead. He would point out the stop before the one where he had to transfer. He would identify the tram that would take him past the zoo to where his school was. He pulled the cord to signal the driver to let him off at the closest stop to his school, the one that was by the castle with the moat.

After two weeks, he had the confidence to travel to school alone. More important, we shared that confidence because we'd seen him handle the hustle and bustle of rush hour. When he made his first solo trip he was beaming with pride. (So were we!) By the end of that week, it was old hat. In fact, he soon became more of an expert on the Basel tram system than either of us.

But what if we had not let him do this alone? What if we'd insisted on riding to school with him each day? For some kids, that type of protectiveness is comforting and even necessary for a much longer time. They're not emotionally or intellectually ready to handle the trip alone. Our son probably would have tolerated it for a while. Then it would have become embarrassing and frustrating for him. His normal drive for autonomy would have put us into conflict. He might have gotten angry. He might even have tried to demonstrate his independence by using the tram to go somewhere else by himself.

We see this all the time, occasionally with disastrous results, among children whose parents are overprotective. This can lead to particular problems during the pre-teen and teenage years, when children struggle awkwardly to test and demonstrate their independence. If you're too restrictive, or if you don't acknowledge your child's need to feel and show increasing autonomy, your actions may backfire.

Here are some of the issues that you should be addressing when you're trying to help your children become more media literate. Remember that you should do this through two-way conversations, not by lecturing. In fact, things will probably go better if you listen more than you speak. After all, your goal is to encourage your children to think about these issues.

❖ Who created this message (the video game, magazine ad or TV program)? Why are they sending it? Who owns and profits from it?

❖ What techniques are they using to attract and hold your attention?

❖ What lifestyles, values and points of view are represented in this message? How are they different from your family's? How are they the same? Are they realistic? (It always amazes us how some of the young adults in television programs have low-paying jobs but live in spacious and luxurious homes!)

❖ What is omitted from this message? Why was it left out? Are there other ways to handle this situation?

❖ How might different people interpret this message? Why might they interpret it differently?

This isn't an exhaustive list, of course. Nor should you go through it mechanically. Rather, it should help you structure discussions with your children in ways and at levels that are most appropriate and useful for them and for you.

If you're talking about a violent game, directing that discussion to the lifestyles and values of some of the characters will help your child think about those things from a new perspective. Why might one person resort to violence in a given situation, while another person might not? Is that on-screen person behaving the way people you know do? What do you like or respect about that character? What don't you? (Remember that sometimes kids enjoy game content precisely because it's so unlike real life.)

These conversations shouldn't be ponderous. They should take advantage of children's increasing ability to see the world in all its complexity, in shades of gray instead of just black and white. They might love something in a villain's character and relish the flaws in a hero.

Use the tools available. We were struck in our research by the number of parents who cried out for help but didn't know what help was already available. The ESRB ratings, for all their potential flaws, are a good resource. But there are numerous online tools as well. As long as you keep in mind their respective biases and points of view, they can help you decide whether a particular game is a good match for your child right now.

New video game consoles have parental controls that allow you to restrict both game play and Web browsing. Each console has a slightly different approach to filtering. All of them require that you use a four-digit passcode to bypass the restrictions. (Don't leave the passcode at its default setting, which is usually four zeros. Your kids know the default. And if they're trying to bypass it, they'll probably start with family members' birthdays or your street address, so don't use those, either!)

There are Internet filters you can purchase that screen out Web sites that contain forbidden words. Filtering software is of mixed value; it can over-block and prevent access to innocuous sites, or under-block and allow problematic material to slip through.

Additional software can monitor which Web sites your children visit, allow you to take a look at their e-mail and chat room activity and set time limits on computer use. We have mixed feelings about these tools. For some children, this level of scrutiny may be necessary. For others, it sets a tone of distrust, especially among adolescents. They will simply find another computer in order to access forbidden material or engage in discouraged communication. That's why we believe that helping them develop good judgment and media literacy skills should be at the core of any approach to protecting them.

As you might expect, the Web is filled with information on video games. The game publisher's Web site is a good place to start. The plot synopsis, screenshots and trailers will give you an idea of the tone, graphic realism and other aspects of the game.

Online Resources for Parents

There are quite a few Web sites that offer reviews of games and other useful information. Here are a few places to start:

- **Common Sense Media** (www.commonsensemedia.org) offers reviews of a variety of entertainment media, including games. Their evaluations include information on sexual content, violence, language, message, social behavior, commercialism, drug/alcohol/tobacco use and educational value.

- **The Coalition for Quality Children's Media** (www.kidsfirst.org) is a collaboration between the media industry, educators and child advocacy organizations. In addition to providing film and DVD reviews, it offers an inexpensive course in media literacy for parents and teenagers.
- **The Federal Trade Commission** (FTC) Web site on entertainment ratings, www.ftc.gov/bcp/conline/edcams/ratings/ratings.htm, provides basic information on different media rating systems, offers research reports and explains how to file complaints. Another useful FTC Web site, www.ftc.gov/bcp/conline/edcams/kidzprivacy/, focuses on ways that your children can protect their privacy online.
- **GamerDad** www.gamerdad.com is the Web site of an electronic media journalist whose reviews are aimed at parents who want to share games with their kids or learn about what their kids are playing.
- **Gamerankings.com** (www.gamerankings.com) and **Metacritic.com** (www.metacritic.com) compile reviews from a variety of print publications, Web sites and individual players. They're an efficient way of seeing how different audiences perceive a game.
- **GameSpot** (www.gamespot.com) is a commercial Web site that provides detailed reviews and screenshots of games, as well as information on cheat codes. Its streaming video reviews allow you to see excerpts of the game while listening to a critique, which often focuses on technical issues more than game content. (Some Web site content requires a paid subscription.)
- **GetNetWise** (www.kids.getnetwise.org) is a coalition of industry and advocacy groups. It offers an online safety guide that provides advice tailored to children's ages and likely activities (including chat, e-mail, instant messaging and newsgroups). The site also reviews the technologies available to families to restrict access to Internet content, including tools that block outgoing content or limit time spent online (total time or times of day), monitor children's online activity (such as storing addresses of Web sites visited), filter or block content by Web site address (URL) and review Web pages or keywords.
- **Parental Media Guide** (www.parentalguide.org) is a gateway for accessing the industry-sponsored ratings program Web sites for films, television, music and games.

Focus on the Real Dangers

Probably the most important thing you can do as a parent to protect your children from the consequences of violence is to shift your focus to those issues that are much more likely to result in making children behave violently or having them be the victims of someone else's violence. Despite the urban legends and political grandstanding, violent video games are pretty low on that list.

Violent children and victimized children tend to come from violent and abusive environments. We hear this again and again from child development researchers.

Limit your child's access to real weapons, especially guns. We weren't going to bother mentioning this. After all, it sounds so obvious. But as we were finishing this chapter, a journal article[6] crossed our desks that pointed out some disturbing statistics: in a random survey of nearly four thousand families from across the United States and Canada that brought their children to pediatricians for well-child visits, only one third of those parents who kept guns in their homes stored them safely (i.e., unloaded, in a locked container, and with ammunition stored in a separate locked container).

The most dangerous weapons for children, handguns, were the *least* likely to be stored safely and unloaded. Parents who had preteen children tended to store their guns less safely than those who had toddlers and preschoolers, even though those older children are more likely to gain access to the guns.

Other research has shown that among families with children that have firearms at home, more than 40 percent had at least one unlocked gun.[7] Having guns available in the home is associated with an increased risk of adolescent suicide and accidental injury.[8] The risks of violent video games pale by comparison.

Finally, seek help for your children if you have concerns about changes in their behavior or if other people share their concerns with you. As we've illustrated in some of our stories, there may be nothing wrong; your expectations may simply be off. If that's the case, then you can readjust those expectations and move on.

Since video games are so common, emotionally engaging and social, they may provide one environment in which behavioral and mental health problems come to the fore. They may not be the cause of the problems, but they may be where you notice them.

A cluster of changes in your children's behaviors, performance, attitude and emotions—things like a change in friends, a substantial drop in grades, increased moodiness or emotional sensitivity, a lack of joy or persistent feelings of despair—can be a sign of treatable mental health problems. It may also reflect issues of real-world violence, such as bullying. Yet too many parents who feel quite comfortable bringing their child to a doctor for a benign rash hesitate to seek professional help for emotional and behavioral concerns.

For most kids and most parents, the bottom-line results of our research can be summed up in a single word: relax. While concerns about the effects of violent video games are understandable, they're basically no different from the unfounded concerns previous generations had about the new media of their day. Remember, we're a remarkably resilient species.

Notes

CHAPTER 1: THE BIG FEAR

1. Transcript at www.pbs.org/newshour/bb/entertainment/july-dec03/video_07-07.html (accessed May 9, 2007).
2. American Psychological Association, "Resolution on Violence in Video Games and Interactive Media," August 17, 2005.
3. Liptak, A. "Defense portrays sniper suspect as indoctrinated." *New York Times,* November 21, 2003.
4. Anderson, C. A., and Dill, K. E. "Video games and aggressive thoughts, feelings, and behavior in the laboratory and in life." *Journal of Personality and Social Psychology* 78(4), pp. 772–90.
5. "Modern life 'has turned children into loners.'" www.telegraph.co.uk/news/main.jhtml?xml=/news/2007/05/04/nkids04.xml (accessed on May 5, 2005).
6. Ibid.
7. Cumberbatch, G. "Video violence: Villain or victim? A review of the research evidence concerning media violence and its effects in the real world with additional reference to video games." London: Video Standards Council, 2004, p. 34.
8. *National Television Violence Study 3*. Thousand Oaks, CA: Sage Publications, 1998. The 73 percent figure referred to the percentage of violent scenes during which there was "no regret, remorse or negative sanctions."
9. Miller, S. A. "Malvo team cites role of violent media: Movie, video games seen brainwashing defendant." *Washington Times*, December 9, 2003, p. B-01.
10. Cullen, D. "The depressive and the psychopath: At last we know why the Columbine killers did it." *Slate,* April 20, 2004.
11. Snyder, H. N. *Juvenile Arrests 2004*. Washington, DC: Juvenile Justice Bulletin, U.S. Department of Justice, December 2006.
12. According to the National School Safety Center's report "School Associated Violent Deaths" (www.schoolsafety.us/School-Associated-Violent-Deaths-p-6.html), from 1995 to 2004 there were a total of 282 violent deaths of adults and children while on or near school property, while traveling to or from school or school-related events and in the areas

adjacent to schools. (This broad definition of school violence includes at least sixty-three suicides, as well as several heart attacks suffered by staff, faculty and a police officer, murders of school employees by estranged spouses or lovers, the stabbing death of a nun by a monastery student, accidental shootings by children under the age of seven, and other incidents not usually considered violent youth crime.) During that same period, according to the National Oceanic and Atmospheric Administration, lightning killed 489 people in the United States (www.nws.noaa.gov/om/hazstats.shtml).

13. Snyder, H. N., *Juvenile Arrests 2004*.
14. Vossekuil, B., et al. *The Final Report and Findings of the Safe School Initiative: Implications for the Prevention of School Attacks in the United States*. Washington, DC: United States Secret Service and United States Department of Education, 2002. www.secretservice.gov/ntac_ssi.shtml.
15. DeVoe, J. F., et al. "Indicators of school crime and safety: 2003." Washington, DC: National Center for Education Statistics, Bureau of Justice Statistics, 2003.
16. Grunbaum, J. A., et al. "Youth Risk Behavior Surveillance—United States, 2001." Centers for Disease Control—Surveillance Summaries, 51(SS-4). Atlanta: Centers for Disease Control, 2002.
17. "Save the Children study shows primary school children's ability to make friends deteriorating Britain." www.savethechildren.org.uk/en/41_503.htm (accessed on September 29, 2007).
18. www.esrb.org/about_employment.asp
19. *National Television Violence Study 3*.
20. Haninger, K., and Thompson, K. N. "Content and ratings of Teen-rated video games." *Journal of the American Medical Association* 291(7), February 18, 2004, pp. 856–65.
21. "Jews see a brutal fascist in a computer game addict," January 13, 2006. www.english.pravda.ru/main/18/87/347/16738_Jews.html (accessed on April 10, 2007).
22. "Moscow Synagogue Attacker Charged with Hate Crimes," January 13, 2006. www.newsfromrussia.com/main/2006/01/13/71094.html (accessed on April 10, 2007).
23. Shoja, M. M., et al. "Video game epilepsy in the twentieth century: a review." *Child's Nervous System* 23(3), March 2007, pp. 265–67.
24. Grant No. 2003-JN-FX-0078, awarded by the Office of Juvenile Justice and Delinquency Prevention, Office of Justice Programs, U.S. Department of Justice.
25. Schechter, H. *Savage Pastimes: A Cultural History of Violent Entertainment*. New York: St. Martin's Press, 2005.

CHAPTER 2: DÉJÀ VU ALL OVER AGAIN, AND AGAIN

1. An interesting selection of dime novel covers as well as other details about the entire collection can be found on the Web site run by the Library of Congress: www.loc.gov/exhibits/treasures/tri015.html.
2. Cieply, M. "Government to take a hard look at horror." *New York Times*, March 24, 2007, p. A15.
3. A footpad was a thief who stole from travelers who were on foot.
4. Ritchie, J. *Here and There in London*. London: W. Tweedie, 1859, p. 116.
5. "The early Victorian period had been wracked by very high levels of theft, homicide, violence, and public disorder. Public discussion of crime in the 1840s had frequently assumed that it was widely endemic among the working population, and indeed that the categories of criminal, pauper and labouring poor, if not absolutely identical, were part of an interlocking social continuum. Crime rates began to fall, however, in the 1850s and 1860s, and plummeted after 1870." From Harris, J., *Private Lives, Public Spirit: Britain 1870-1914*. New York: Penguin USA, 1995.
6. Johannsen, A. *The House of Beadle and Adams and Its Dime and Nickel Novels: The Story of a Vanished Literature*. A project of the Northern Illinois University Libraries. www.ulib.niu.edu/badndp/chapt1.html.
7. Petersen, J. R. *The Century of Sex: Playboy's History of the Sexual Revolution, 1900-1999*. New York: Grove Press, 1999.
8. Comstock, A. *Traps for the Young*. New York: Funk & Wagnalls, 1884, p. 5.
9. Ibid., p. 240.
10. For additional details, see the Unitarian Universalist Association Web site: www.uua.org/uuhs/duub/articles/horatioalgerjr.html.
11. Edison Films Catalog, No. 200 (1904).
12. This is widely considered to be the first close-up shot of a person to be used in a dramatic film. Because of the influence of live theater and the bulkiness of early cameras, early films consisted almost entirely of wide shots.
13. "Would close all movies. Kansas educator wants martial law until they are purged." Special to *The New York Times*, September 14, 1921, p. 3.
14. "Arbuckle acquitted in one-minute verdict; one of his films to be released immediately." *New York Times*, April 13, 1922, p. 1.
15. Andress, R. "Film censorship in New York State." Archives of the New York State Education Department. www.archives.nysed.gov/a/research/res_topics_film_censor.shtml.
16. "Movie morals under fire: Reformers demand a national inquiry

because of the Arbuckle and Taylor cases." *New York Times*, February 12, 1922, p. 80.

17. Forman, H. J. *Our Movie Made Children*. New York: Macmillan, 1933, p. 197.

18. Ibid., p. 203.

19. Hall, J. Review of *Our Movie Made Children. American Journal of Public Health*. 23(12), December 1933, pp. 1333–34.

20. Wertham, F. *Seduction of the Innocent*. New York: Rinehart & Co., 1954, pp. 190–91.

21. *Comics Books and Juvenile Delinquency*. Interim report of the committee on the judiciary pursuant to S. Res. 89 and S. Res. 190 (1955-56).

22. Wertham, F., *Seduction of the Innocent*, pp. 192–93.

23. Trelease, J. *The Read-Aloud Handbook*. New York: Penguin, 2006.

24. Wertham, F. *Seduction of the Innocent*, p. 369.

25. *Hearing America: A Century of Music on the Radio* (radio program), American Radio Works. americanradioworks.publicradio.org/features/radio/transcript.html (accessed April 2, 2007).

CHAPTER 3: SCIENCE, NONSENSE AND COMMON SENSE

1. Policy statement of the American Academy of Pediatrics on Media Violence. *Pediatrics* 108:5, November 2001, pp. 1222–26.

2. www.ncac.org/media/related/20011205~USA~Letter_to_AAP_Concerning_Media_Violence_Statements.cfm (accessed May 9, 2007). This is a letter to the American Academy of Pediatrics signed by eleven scholars and media researchers.

3. Anderson, C.A., and Bushman, B. "Effects of violent video games on aggressive behavior, aggressive cognition, aggressive affect, physiological arousal, and prosocial behavior: A meta-analytic review of the scientific literature." *Psychological Science* 12(5), 2001, pp. 353–59.

4. Goldstein, J. "Effects of electronic games on children." Testimony submitted to a hearing held by the U.S. Senate Committee on Commerce, Science, and Transportation, "The Impact of Interactive Violence on Children," March 21, 2000. Available at senategov/comm/commerce/general/hearings/0321gol.pdf.

5. Grossman, D., and DeGaetano, G. *Stop Teaching Our Kids to Kill : A Call to Action Against TV, Movie and Video Game Violence*. New York: Crown, 1999.

6. Griffiths, M. "Video games and health" (editorial). *British Medical Journal* 331, 2005, pp. 122–23.

7. Gonzalez, L. "When two tribes go to war: A history of video game con-

troversy." *GameSpot*, March 2004. Available at www.gamespot.com/features/6090892/index.html.

8. Snyder, H. N. *Juvenile Arrests 2004*. Juvenile Justice Bulletin, U.S. Department of Justice, Washington, DC, December 2006.

9. Snyder, H. N., and Sickmund, M. *Juvenile Offenders and Victims: 2006 National Report*. Washington, DC: U.S. Department of Justice, Office of Justice Programs, Office of Juvenile Justice and Delinquency Prevention, 2006.

10. U.S. Census Bureau. "Annual demographic survey, March supplement, POV01, age and sex of all people, family members and unrelated individuals iterated by income-to-poverty ratio and race." Revised July 14, 2004.

11. Buka, S.; Stichick, T.; Birdthistle, I.; and Earls, F. "Youth exposure to violence: Prevalence, risks and consequences." *American Journal of Orthopsychiatry*, July 2001, 298–310.

12. Office of Juvenile Justice and Delinquency Prevention. *1999 National Report Series: Challenging the Myths*. Juvenile Justice Bulletin, U.S. Department of Justice, Washington, DC, February 2000.

13. Bushman, B., and Anderson, C. A. "Media violence and the American public: Scientific facts versus media misinformation." *American Psychologist*, June/July 2001, pp. 477–89

14. Browne, K. D., and Hamilton-Giachritsis, C. "The influence of violent media on children and adolescents: A public-health approach." *Lancet* 365, February 19, 2005, pp. 702–710.

15. Kirsh, S. J. "The effects of violent video games on adolescents: The overlooked influence of development." *Aggression and Violent Behavior* 8(4), July 2003, pp. 377–89

16. Jenkins, H. "Reality bytes: Eight myths about video games debunked." An essay written for the Web site of the PBS program *The Video Game Revolution*, produced in 2004 by KCTS/Seattle. www.pbs.org/kcts/videogamerevolution/impact/myths.html (accessed on May 10, 2007).

17. Anderson, C. A., and Bushman, B. "External validity of 'trivial' experiments: The case of laboratory aggression." *Review of General Psychology* 1, March 1997, pp. 19–41.

18. Milgram, S. "Behavioral study of obedience." *Journal of Abnormal and Social Psychology* 67, October 1963, pp. 371–78.

19. National Public Radio. "Remembering Tuskegee." July 25, 2002. You can read and listen to the story at www.npr.org/programs/morning/features/2002/jul/tuskegee/index.html.

20. Thompson, K., and Haninger, K. "Violence in E-rated video games." *Journal of the American Medical Association* 286(5), August 1, 2001, pp. 591–98.

21. Griffiths, M., "Video games and health."
22. Johnson, J.; Cohen, P.; Smailes, E.; Kasen, S.; and Brook, J. "Television viewing and aggressive behavior during adolescence and adulthood." *Science* 295, March 29, 2002, pp. 2468–71.
23. Huesmann, L. R.; Moise-Titus, J; Podolski, C. L.; and Eron, L. "Longitudinal relations between children's exposure to TV violence and their aggressive and violent behavior in young adulthood: 1977–1992." *Developmental Psychology* 39(2), March 2003, pp. 201–21.
24. Anderson, C. A., and Dill, K. E. "Video games and aggressive thoughts, feelings and behavior in the laboratory and in life." *Journal of Personality and Social Psychology* 78, June 2000, pp. 772–90.
25. www.medical-dictionary.thefreedictionary.com/Aggression+(psychology)
26. Bandura, A.; Ross, D.; and Ross, S. A. "Imitation of film-mediated aggressive models." *Journal of Abnormal and Social Psychology* 66, January 1963, pp. 3–11.
27. Anderson, C. A., and Dill, K., "Video games and agressive thoughts."
28. *Youth Violence: A Report of the Surgeon General.* Washington, DC: U.S. Department of Health and Human Services, 2001.
29. Unsworth, G.; Devilly, G. J.; and Ward, T. "The effect of playing violent videogames on adolescents: Should parents be quaking in their boots?" *Psychology, Crime & Law.* 13(4), June 2007, pp. 383–94.
30. Anderson, C. A. "An update on the effects of playing violent video games." *Journal of Adolescence* 27, February 2004, pp. 113–22.
31. Mencken, H. L. *The Bathtub Hoax and other Blasts & Bravos from the Chicago Tribune.* New York: Octagon Books, 1985, p. 10.
32. Ibid., p. 11.
33. Wartella, E.; Olivarez, A.; and Jennings, N. "Children and television violence in the United States." In Carlsson, U., and von Feilitzen, C. (eds.), *Children and Media Violence: Yearbook from the UNESCO International Clearinghouse on Children and Violence on the Screen.* Goteborg, Sweden: Nordicom, Goteborg University, 1998, p. 57.
34. Sherry, J. L. "The effects of violent video games on aggression: A meta-analysis." *Human Communication Research* 27, July 2001, pp. 409–31.
35. Anderson, C. A., and Bushman, B. "Effects of violent video games on aggressive behavior, aggressive cognition, aggressive affect, physiological arousal, and prosocial behavior: A meta-analytic review of the scientific literature." *Psychological Science* 12(5), September 2001, pp. 353–59.
36. Colwell, J., and Payne, J. "Negative correlates of computer game play in adolescents." *British Journal of Psychology* 91, August 2000, pp. 295–310.
37. Gliner, J.; Morgan, G.; and Harmon, R. "Meta-analysis: Formulation

and interpretation." *Journal of the American Academy of Child and Ado-lescent Psychiatry,* November 2003, pp. 1376–79.

38. Goldstein, J. "Effects of electronic games on children." Testimony submitted to a hearing held by the U.S. Senate Committee on Commerce, Science, and Transportation, "The Impact of Interactive Violence on Children," March 21, 2000. Available at www.senate.gov/comm/commerce/general/hearings/0321gol.pdf.

39. Ferguson, C. J. "Evidence for publication bias in video game violence effects literature: A meta-analytic review." *Aggressive and Violent Behavior* 2007 12(4), July/August 2007, pp. 470–82.

40. Bushman, B. J.; Ridge, R. D.; Das, E.; Key, C. W.; and Busath, G. L. "When God sanctions killing: Effect of scriptural violence on aggression." *Psychological Science* 3, March 2007, pp. 204–07.

41. Ibid.

CHAPTER 4: GRAND THEFT CHILDHOOD?

1. O'Toole, M. E. *The School Shooter: A Threat Assessment Perspective.* Critical Incident Response Group, National Center for the Analysis of Violent Crime, FBI Academy; Quantico, VA, 2000. www.fbi.gov/publications/school/school2.pdf.

2. Ibid., pp. 2-3.

3. Solberg, M. E., and Olweus, D. "Prevalence estimation of school bullying with the Olweus Bully/Victim Questionnaire." *Aggressive Behavior* 29, June 2003, pp. 239–68.

4. Leffert, N.; Benson, P. L.; Scales, P. C.; Sharma, A.; Drake, D.; and Blyth, D. A. "Developmental assets: Measurement and prediction of risk behaviors among adolescents." *Applied Developmental Science* 2(4), 1998, pp. 209–30.

5. Brener, N. D.; Kann, L.; McManus, T.; et al. "Reliability of the 1999 Youth Risk Behavior Survey Questionnaire." *Journal of Adolescent Health* 31, October 2002, pp. 336–42.

6. Dahlberg, L. L.; Toal, S. B.; and Behrens, C. B., eds. *Measuring Violence-Related Attitudes, Beliefs and Behaviors Among Youths: A Compendium of Assessment Tools.* Atlanta, GA: National Center for Injury Prevention and Control, Centers for Disease Control and Prevention, 1998.

7. Roberts, D. F.; Foehr, U. G.; and Rideout, V. *Generation M: Media in the Lives of 8–18 Year-Olds.* Menlo Park, CA: Kaiser Family Foundation, 2005.

8. Ibid.

9. Snyder, H. N. *Juvenile Arrests 2004.* Juvenile Justice Bulletin, Office of Juvenile Justice and Delinquency Prevention, U.S. Department of Justice, December 2006.

10. DeVoe, J. F; Peter, K.; Noonan, M.; Snyder, T. D.; and Baum, K. *Indicators of School Crime and Safety: 2006* (NCES 2007-003/NCJ 214262). U.S. Departments of Education and Justice. Washington, DC: U.S. Government Printing Office, December 2006.

11. Nansel, T. R.; Craig, W.; Overpeck, M. D.; et al. "Cross-national consistency in the relationship between bullying behaviors and psychosocial adjustment." *Archives of Pediatrics and Adolescent Medicine* 158, August 2004, pp. 730–36.

12. Solberg M. E., and Olweus, D., "Prevalence estimation of school bullying."

13. Thomas, A.; Chess, S.; and Birch, H. G. *Temperament and Behavior Disorders in Children.* New York: New York University Press, 1968.

14. Kirsh, S. J. "The effects of violent video games on adolescents: The overlooked influence of development." *Aggression and Violent Behavior* 8(4), 2003, pp. 377–89.

15. Unsworth, G.; Devilly, G. J.; and Ward, T. "The effect of playing violent videogames on adolescents: Should parents be quaking in their boots?"

16. Brookmeyer, K. A.; Fanti, K. A.; and Henrich, C. C. "Schools, parents, and youth violence: A multilevel, ecological analysis." *Journal of Clinical Child and Adolescent Psychology* 35(4), 2006, pp. 504–514

17. Steinberg, L. "Youth violence: Do parents and families make a difference?" *National Institute of Justice Journal*, April 2000, pp. 31–38.

18. Funk, J. "Children's exposure to violent video games and desensitization to violence." *Child and Adolescent Psychiatric Clinics of North America*, July 2005, pp. 387–404.

19. Funk, J. B.; Baldacci, H. B.; Pasold, T.; and Baumgardner, J. "Violence exposure in real life, video games, television, movies and the Internet: Is there desensitization?" *Journal of Adolescence* 27, February 2004, pp. 23–39.

20. Dawley, H. "Kids get news from weird places. Not. In fact, local TV is the leading source." *Media Life,* August 16, 2006. See also van der Molen, JHW, "Violence and suffering in television news: Toward a broader conception of harmful television content for children." *Pediatrics* 113, June 2004, pp. 1771–75.

21. Soulliere, D. "Prime-time murder: Presentations of murder on popular television justice programs." *Journal of Criminal Justice and Popular Culture* 10(1), 2003, pp. 12–38.

22. van der Molen, "Violence and suffering in television news."

23. Fremont, W. P.; Pataki, C.; and Beresin, E. V. "The impact of terrorism on children and adolescents: Terror in the skies, terror on television." *Child and Adolescent Psychiatric Clinics of North America* 14, July 2005, pp. 429–51.

24. Savage, J. "Does viewing violent media really cause criminal violence? A methodological review." *Aggression and Violent Behavior* 10, November/December 2004, pp. 99–128.

CHAPTER 5: WHY KIDS PLAY VIOLENT GAMES

1. Hoffner, C. A., and Levine, K. J. "Enjoyment of mediated fright and violence: A meta-analysis." *Media Psychology* 7(2), 2005, pp. 207–37.
2. Zuckerman, M.; Eysenck, S.; and Eysenck, H. J. "Sensation seeking in England and America: Cross cultural, age, and sex comparisons." *Journal of Consulting and Clinical Psychology* 46, February 1978, pp. 139–49.
3. Marti, C. A.; Kelly, T. H.; Rayens, M. K.; et al. "Sensation seeking, puberty, and nicotine, alcohol and marijuana use in adolescence." *Journal of the American Academy of Child and Adolescent Psychiatry* 41, December 2002, pp. 1495–1502.
4. Malliet, S. "An exploration of adolescents' perceptions of videogame realism." *Learning, Media and Technology* 31(4), 2006, pp. 377–94.
5. Ibid.
6. Schneider, E. F.; Lang, A.; Shin, M.; and Bradley, S. D. "Death with a story: How story impacts emotional, motivational and physiological responses to first-person shooter video games." *Human Communication Research* 30, July 2004, pp. 361–75.
7. Orenstein, C. *Little Red Riding Hood Uncloaked: Sex, Morality and the Evolution of a Fairy Tale.* New York: Basic Books, 2003, p. 54.
8. Ibid., p. 66.
9. Smith, S. L.; Wilson, B. J.; Kunkel, D.; et al. "Violence in television programming overall: University of California, Santa Barbara study." In Federman, J (ed.), *National Television Violence Study 3.* Thousand Oaks, CA: Sage, 1998.
10. Federman, *National Television Violence Study 3,* p. 48.
11. Yee, N. "Motivations of play in online games." *CyberPsychology and Behavior,* 9, December 2006, pp. 772–75.
12. Funk, J. B.; Chan, M.; Brouwer, J.; and Curtiss, K. "A biopsychosocial analysis of the video game-playing experience of children and adults in the United States." *SIMILE: Studies in Media and Information Literacy Education* 6, August 2006.
13. Jansz, J. "The emotional appeal of violent video games for adolescent males." *Communication Theory* 15, August 2005, pp. 219–41.
14. Cragg, A., et al. *Video Games: Research to Improve Understanding of What Players Enjoy About Video Games, and to Explain Their Preferences for Particular Games.* London: British Board of Film Classification, 2007, p. 31.

15. Ibid.
16. Yee, "Motivations of play in online games."
17. Goldstein, "Effects of electronic games on children," p. 273.
18. Pellegrini, A. D. "Perceptions and functions of play and real fighting in early adolescence." *Child Development* 74, October 2003, pp. 1522–33.
19. Ibid.
20. Mitchell, K. J.; Finkelhor, D.; and Wolak, J. "The Internet and family and acquaintance sexual abuse." *Child Maltreatment* 10, February 2005, pp. 49–60.
21. Chan, P. A., and Rabinowitz, T. "A cross-sectional analysis of video games and attention deficit hyperactivity disorder symptoms in adolescents." *Annals of General Psychiatry,* October 24, 2006. Available at www.annals-general-psychiatry.com/content/5/1/16.
22. Gardner, W.; Murphy, M.; Childs, G.; et al. "The PSC-17: A brief pediatric symptom checklist with psychological problem subscales." *Ambulatory Child Health* 5, March 1999, pp. 225–36.
23. Tartaro, A., and Cassell, J. "Authorable virtual peers for autism spectrum disorders." Proceedings of the Workshop on Language-Enabled Educational Technology at the seventeenth European Conference on Artificial Intelligence (ECAI06), August 28–31, 2006, Riva del Garda, Italy.
24. Funk, et al. "A biopsychosocial analysis," p. 3.
25. Houghton, S.; Milner, N.; West, J.; et al. "Motor control and sequencing of boys with Attention-Deficit/Hyperactivity Disorder (ADHD) during computer game play." *British Journal of Educational Technology* 35, January 2004, pp. 21–34.
26. Gardner et al. "The PSC-17."

CHAPTER 6: SEX, HATE, GAME ADDICTION AND OTHER WORRIES

1. www.resistance.com/ethniccleansing/catalog.htm (accessed April 3, 2007).
2. Escobar-Chaves, S. L., et al. "Impact of the media on adolescent sexual attitudes and behaviors." *Pediatrics* 116:1, July 2005, pp. 303–26.
3. Collins, R. L.; Elliott, M. N.; Berry, S. H.; et al. "Watching sex on television predicts adolescent initiation of sexual behavior." *Pediatrics* 114, September 2004, pp. e280–89.
4. Martino, S. C.; Collins, R. L.; Elliott, M. N.; et al. "Exposure to degrading vs. nondegrading music lyrics and sexual behavior among youth." *Pediatrics* 118, August 2006, pp. e430–41.
5. www.bkgamer.com/SneakKing.aspx (accessed on April 4, 2007).

6. www.bkgamer.com/Signup.aspx (accessed on April 4, 2007).

7. www.bkgamer.com/Rules.aspx (accessed on April 4, 2007).

8. www.ftc.gov/ogc/coppa1.htm (accessed on April 4, 2007).

9. www.darfurisdying.com/aboutgame.html (accessed on April 4, 2007).

10. Ibid.

11. Ibid.

12. Jansz, J, and Martis, RG. "The Lara phenomenon: Powerful female characters in video games." *Sex Roles* 56, February 2007, pp. 141–48.

13. www.drug-pusher.net (accessed on April 15, 2007).

14. www.nsm88.com/articles/computer%20games.html (accessed on April 10, 2007).

15. www.vae.americasarmy.com/ (accessed on April 12, 2007).

16. www.htgn.net/ (accessed on April 12, 2007).

17. www.underash.net/emessage.htm (accessed on April 12, 2007).

18. www.afkarmedia.com/en/index.htm (accessed on April 13, 2007).

19. www.underash.net/en_download.htm (accessed on April 12, 2007).

20. Patrizio, A. "Did game play role in suicide?" *Wired* online, April 23, 2002, www.wired.com/print/gaming/gamingreviews/news/2002/04/51490 (accessed on April 14, 2007).

CHAPTER 7: I'M FROM THE VIDEO GAME INDUSTRY AND I'M HERE TO HELP

1. www.mediafamily.org/research/report_vgrc_2005.shtml (accessed May 12, 2007).

2. www.esrb.org/about/news/downloads/nimf_fail.pdf (accessed May 12, 2007).

3. New York State Senate press release. "Senate passes legislation to crack down on video game violence," May 21, 2007. www.senate.state.ny.us/pressreleases.nsf/public_bruno?openform.

4. "Virtual school shootings: Interviewing two of the most hated game creators alive." Destructoid.com, May 18, 2007. www.destructoid.com/virtual-school-shootings-interviewing-two-of-the-most-hated-game-creators-alive-31610.phtml.

5. www.esrb.org/ratings/ratings_guide.jsp (accessed May 14, 2007).

6. Boliek, B. "Senators fight hidden sex in 'Grand Theft Auto.'" *Hollywood Reporter*, July 15, 2005.

7. Brathwaite, B. "Hot Coffee's effects on the mod scene." Gamasutra.com, October 27, 2006. www.gamasutra.com/features/20061027/brathwaite_01.shtml (accessed May 31, 2007).

8. www.pegi.info/en/

9. Hyman, P. "Rated and willing: Where game rating boards differ." Gama
sutra.com, December 15, 2005. www.gamasutra.com/features/20051215/
hyman_01.shtml.

10. www.kotaku.com/gaming/esrb/japan-gets-new-game-ratings-177219.php
(accessed May 30, 2007).

11. Films have two additional categories: R18+ (Restricted—can only be
seen by people eighteen and older) and X18+ (Pornographic—can only
be seen by people eighteen and older).

12. Office of Film and Literature Classification: *Guidelines for the Classifica-
tion of Films and Computer Games*. 2005. Commonwealth of Australia
Law, Legislative Instrument F2005L01286. www.comlaw.gov.au/
ComLaw/Legislation/LegislativeInstrument1.nsf/0/A3B39BA36F22D
FE5CA25700D0029AEE4?OpenDocument

13. Ibid., p. 13.

14. Australian Federal Register of Legislative Instruments F2005L01284.

15. Hyman, P., "Rated and willing."

16. Vastag, B. "Does video game violence sow aggression?" *Journal of the
American Medical Association* 291(15), April 21, 2004, pp. 1822–24.

17. www.esrb.org/ratings/ratings_guide.jsp (accessed May 18, 2007).

18. Ibid.

19. *National Television Violence Study*. Thousand Oaks, CA: Sage Publications, 1998, p. 46.

20. Federal Trade Commission. "Marketing violent entertainment to children: A fifth follow-up review of industry practices in the motion picture, music recording and electronic game industries." Report to
Congress, April 2007, p. 27.

21. The IRS only requires nonprofit organizations to list the names and
salaries of its five highest-paid nonofficer employees who receive more
than $50,000 per year. In addition to Walsh's salary, the filing lists only
$58,909 in total additional salaries for the institute during that year,
which gives insight into its size.

22. www.mediafamily.org/about/index.shtml (accessed on May 12, 2007).

23. National PTA statement on Video Game Report Card. www.pta.org/ne_
press_release_detail_1133460190390.html (accessed May 12, 2007).

24. www.mediafamily.org/research/report_vgrc_2005.shtml (accessed May
12, 2007).

25. Hyman, P. "Rated and willing."

26. www.familymediaguide.com/aboutfmg/psv_process/page2.html (accessed
May 17, 2007).

27. www.familymediaguide.com/aboutfmg/psv_process/page3.html (accessed
May 17, 2007).

28. www.psvratings.com (accessed May 13, 2007).

29. U.S. Securities and Exchange Commission, Litigation Release No. 19744/June 28, 2006, *SEC v. Frank J. Russo, FJR Corporation, Russo Associates Limited Partnership, Eliot Partners, and Relief Defendant Veritasiti Corporation d/b/a MediaData Corporation* (United States District Court for the District of Massachusetts, C.A. No. 06-10984-MEL); "SEC Freezes Assets of California Corporation That Received Proceeds of Fraudulent Investment Scheme": www.sec.gov/litigation/litreleases/2006/lr19744.htm (accessed May 13, 2007); Securities and Exchange Commission, *Plaintiff v. Frank J. Russo, FJR Corporation, Russo Associates Limited Partnership and Eliot Partners, Defendants.* U.S. District Court, District of Massachusetts. Filed June 6, 2006.

30. www.theesa.com/facts/top_10_facts.php (accessed May 17, 2007).

31. Comments on MediaWise Video Game Report Card 2005. www.esrb.org/about/news/downloads/nimf_fail.pdf (accessed May 12, 2007).

32. Ibid.

33. Federman, J. (ed.). *National Television Violence Study 3.* Thousand Oaks, CA: Sage, 1998.

34. American Academy of Pediatrics Committee on Public Education. "Media violence." *Pediatrics* 108(5), November 2001, pp. 1222–26.

35. Federal Trade Commission, "Marketing violent entertainment to children."

CHAPTER 8: ALL POLITICS IS LOCAL

1. "Brownback Unveils 5th Annual Video Game Report Card." Press release dated January 25, 2001. www.brownback.senate.gov/pressapp/record.cfm?id=175747 (accessed May 2, 2007).

2. "Senators Clinton, Lieberman and Bayh Introduce Federal Legislation to Protect Children from Inappropriate Video Games." Press release dated December 16, 2005. www.lieberman.senate.gov/newsroom/release.cfm?id=249933 (accessed May 3, 2007).

3. O'Neill, B. "How 'facts' are created: The invention of the School Discipline Lists." *The School Administrator* 51(11), December 1994, pp. 8–11.

4. Ariès, P. *Centuries of Childhood: A Social History of Family Life.* (Translated from the French by Robert Baldick.) New York: Vintage Books, p. 315.

5. Grossman, G., and DeGaetano, G. *Stop Teaching Our Kids to Kill: A Call to Action Against TV, Movie and Video Game Violence.* New York: Crown, 1999, p. 4.

6. Harding, D.; Mahta, J.; and Newman, K. "No exit: Mental illness, marginality, and school violence in West Paducah, Kentucky." In National Research Council and Institute of Medicine, *Deadly Lessons: Under-*

standing Lethal School Violence. Washington, DC: The National Academies Press, 2003, pp. 132–62.

7. Ibid., p. 140.

8. Ibid.

9. Ibid., pp. 141–42.

10. www.i.a.cnn.net/cnn/2007/images/04/17/warrant.pdf (accessed on May 6, 2007).

11. American Foundation for Suicide Prevention. www.afsp.org/index.cfm?fuseaction=home.viewPage&page_id=052618D2-02D2-04B4-00EDA31CFC336B63 (accessed May 4, 2007).

12. Ellen, E. F. "Suicide prevention on campus." *Psychiatric Times* 29:10, October 2002.

13. Benedett, W. "Were video games to blame for the massacre? Pundits rushed to judge industry, gamers in the wake of shooting." Msnbc.msn.com (April 20, 2007), www.msnbc.msn.com/id/18220228/ (accessed May 4, 2007).

14. www.transcripts.cnn.com/TRANSCRIPTS/0704/16/lkl.01.html (accessed on May 4, 2007).

15. Bacon P. "Romney reaches to the Christian right." *Washington Post,* May 6, 2007, pp. A4.

16. *Mass Shootings at Virginia Tech April 16, 2007: Report of the Virginia Tech Review Panel.* www.governor.virginia.gov/TempContent/techPanel Report.cfm (accessed August, 2007).

17. www.gamepolitics.com/2006/11/18/bill-oreilly-slams-playstation-3-launch-gamers-ipods-tech-not-in-that-order/ (accessed May 6, 2007).

18. *Entertainment Software Association; Video Software Dealers Association; and Illinois Retail Merchants Association, plaintiffs v. Rod Blagojevich, in his official capacity as Governor of the State of Illinois; Lisa Madigan, in her official capacity as Attorney General of the State of Illinois; and Richard A. Devine, in his official capacity as State's Attorney of Cook County, defendants.* Case No. 05 C 4265.

19. Ibid.

20. Ibid.

21. Ibid. "Brandenburg" refers to *Brandenburg v. Ohio*, 395 U.S. 444 91969.

22. Ibid.

23. Beydler, J. "The price of political pandering: $510,528.64." Qconline.com, August 17, 2006. www.qconline.com/archives/qco/display.php?id=301745 (accessed May 25, 2007).

24. Stelte, M. "Blagojevich's quest to ban violent video games cost nearly $1M." Qconline.com, May 25, 2007. www.qconline.com/archives/qco/display.php?id=339802 (accessed May 25, 2007).

25. *Entertainment Software Association and Entertainment Merchants Association, plaintiffs v. Charles C. Foti and Doug Moreau.* Ruling on Plaintiffs' Motion for Attorney's Fees and Costs. Case No. 06-431-JJB-CN.
26. Burrell, R. A. "Violent video games affect children's behavior." Shreveport *Times*, May 10, 2007. Conversations section, p. 2.

CHAPTER 9: PRACTICAL ADVICE FOR PARENTS

1. Scheisel, S. "To the glee of South Korean fans, a game's sequel is announced." *New York Times*, May 21, 2007.
2. Sherry, J. L. "Flow and media enjoyment." *Communication Theory* 14, November 2004, pp. 328–47.
3. Rosser, J. C.; Lynch, P. J.; Cuddihy, L.; Gentile, D. A.; Klonsky, J.; and Merrell, R. "The impact of video games on training surgeons in the 21st century." *Archives of Surgery* 142, February 2007, pp. 181–86.
4. Feng, J.; Spence, I.; and Pratt, J. "Playing an action video game reduces gender differences in spatial cognition." *Psychological Science* 18(10), October 2007, pp. 850–55.
5. Nikken, P., and Jansz, J. "Parental mediation of children's videogame playing: A comparison of the reports by parents and children." *Learning, Media and Technology* 31:2, June 2006, pp. 181–202.
6. DuRant, R. H., et al. "Firearm ownership and storage pattern among families with children who receive well-child care in pediatric offices." *Pediatrics* 119:6 June 2007, pp. 1271–79.
7. Schuster, M. A., et al. "Firearm storage patterns in U.S. homes with children." *American Journal of Public Health* 90, April 2000, pp. 588–94.
8. Krug, E. G.; Dahlberg, L. L.; and Powell, K. E. "Childhood homicide, suicide, and firearm deaths: an international comparison." *World Health Statistics Quarterly* 49, December 1996, pp. 230–35; Zavoski, R. W., et al. "A population-based study of severe firearm injury among children and youth." *Pediatrics* 96, August 1995, pp. 278–82.

If you're interested in reading some of the academic publications based on this study, here are a few examples:

Kutner, L. A., Olson, C. K., Warner, D. E., and Hertzog, S. M. "Parents' and sons' perspectives on video game play: A Qualitative study." *Journal of Adolescent Research,* 23(1), 2008, pp. 76–96.
Olson, C. K. "Media violence research and youth violence data: Why do they conflict?" *Adolescent Psychiatry,* 28(2), 2004, pp. 144–150.

Olson. C. K., Kutner, L. A., and Beresin, E. V. "Children and video games: How much do we know?" *Psychiatric Times* 24(12), 2007, pp. 41–45.

Olson, C. K., Kutner, L. A., Warner, D. E., Almerigi, J. B., Baer, L., Nicholi, A. M. II, and Beresin, E. V. "Factors correlated with violent video game use by adolescent boys and girls." *Journal of Adolescent Health, 41,* 2007, pp. 77–83.

Olson, C. K., Kutner, L. A., and Warner, D. E. "The role of violent video game content in adolescent development: Boys' perspectives." *Journal of Adolescent Research, 23*(1), 2008, pp. 55–75.

Villani, V. S., Olson, C. K., and Jellinek, M. S. "Media literacy for clinicians and parents." *Child and Adolescent Psychiatric Clinics of North America, 14*(3), 2005, pp. 523–553.

Index

About the Authors

Lawrence Kutner, Ph.D. and Cheryl Olson, M.P.H, Sc.D. are cofounders and directors of the Harvard Medical School Center for Mental Health and Media. Both are on the psychiatry faculty at Harvard Medical School and Massachusetts General Hospital in Boston.

Dr. Kutner is the author of five books about child psychology and wrote the award-winning weekly *New York Times* "Parent & Child" column from 1987 to 1994. He wrote for *Parents* magazine for eight years and spent several years as a columnist and contributing editor at *Parenting* and *Baby Talk* magazines.

Cheryl Olson was the principal investigator for the first federally funded, large-scale research project to take an in-depth look at the effects of electronic games on teenagers and preteens. She is an accomplished author, ghostwriter and editor, and worked as a columnist for *Parents* magazine for six years. She has served as a health behavior consultant at a number of nonprofits and corporations and is an award-winning video producer, writer and director.

CPSIA information can be obtained at www.ICGtesting.com
Printed in the USA
LVOW122011140313

324332LV00001B/212/P

9 781451 631708